*Jill Raggett*

PENGUIN BOOKS

# PLANTS FROM THE PAST

Dr David Stuart trained as a botanist, but after various academic jobs has devoted himself to gardening and writing about gardens. Previous books include *Georgian Gardens*, *The Kitchen Garden* and, his most recent, *The Garden Triumphant* which is published in Viking. He is garden columnist for the *Scotsman* and writes regularly for magazines and other newspapers. He has restored several period gardens of his own and has designed a number of other private gardens.

James Sutherland, after various jobs, Drama School and a stint in theatre-in-education, decided to devote himself to gardening. He now travels the country looking for old plants to add to his extensive collection.

Together they run a nursery called 'Plants from the Past' based in a sequence of seventeenth- and eighteenth-century walled gardens overlooking the sea at Belhaven in East Lothian.

D1579335

A bouquet of florists' flowers from the title-page of Gerard's *Herball*
of 1633

DAVID STUART

AND JAMES SUTHERLAND

# *Plants from the Past*

OLD FLOWERS FOR NEW GARDENS

PENGUIN BOOKS

PENGUIN BOOKS

Published by the Penguin Group
27 Wrights Lane, London w8 5TZ, England
Viking Penguin Inc., 40 West 23rd Street, New York, New York 10010, USA
Penguin Books Australia Ltd, Ringwood, Victoria, Australia
Penguin Books Canada Ltd, 2801 John Street, Markham, Ontario, Canada L3R 1B4
Penguin Books (NZ) Ltd, 182–190 Wairau Road, Auckland 10, New Zealand

Penguin Books Ltd, Registered Offices: Harmondsworth, Middlesex, England

First published by Viking 1987
Published in Penguin Books 1989
1 3 5 7 9 10 8 6 4 2

Filmset in 11/13pt Bembo
Printed and bound in Great Britain by
Butler & Tanner Ltd, Frome and London

# Contents

# List of Colour Plates

ACKNOWLEDGEMENTS

Grateful acknowledgement is made to the following for permission to reproduce
illustrations in the text:

The British Library, 36
Charlton Park, 10
Christie's, 20
The London Museum, 52
The Tate Gallery, 25
The Usher Art Gallery, Lincoln,
Miss Bostock Collection, 59

Illustrations on pp. 34, 38, 39, 40, 44, 54, 75, 113, 156, 166, 229, and 234 were
photographed by Ken Grant.
The colour photographs were all taken by the authors.

# Introduction

E ven the most modern garden can be full of history. As soon as it is planted, it can contain flowers domesticated by the earliest civilizations of Mesopotamia, or plants once food crops of the Incas long before Columbus discovered the Americas. Any gardener can grow plants bred and loved by the artisans of eighteenth-century England, admired by the princes of Renaissance Italy, or collected in the Himalayas for Victorian millionaires.

Hundreds of plant genera which play important roles in the garden scene have long and fascinating histories. The gorgeous antiques of the garden are every bit as important as are more obvious antiques like furnishings, paintings, even houses, and they are just as much part of our past. Yet many are in danger of extinction.

Garden plants can conveniently be separated into two categories: the longer-lasting 'hardware' plants (the trees and shrubs), and the more ephemeral 'software' plants (the herbaceous flowers, bulbs, annuals and so on). This book is mainly about the 'software', the flowers, of past centuries.

We have concentrated on flowers for several reasons. These are the plants we ourselves grow and know most about. They don't in general have such long lifespans, and they will not survive long-term neglect. While trees will continue to grow quite happily amidst derelict gardens, and shrub roses can be found in gardens that have reverted completely to the wild, the small plants usually survive only if someone, somewhere, is caring for them. This sometimes happens through mental inertia (it is less bother to the gardener to leave it where it is than to decide to throw it out), sometimes for reasons of sentiment (a peony or primula, for instance, being handed down through generations of gardeners). Sometimes there is a sharp-eyed and nostalgic plantsman or plantswoman around in the nick of time to rescue a plant perhaps he or she alone sees is of value. Lastly, we have concentrated on flowers because they are very subject to the vagaries of fashion, and therefore they often tell us much about changing gardening taste.

If you have never thought of plants as being real antiques, we hope that this book will show you the often astonishing beauty of plants grown in earlier ages, and will help interested gardeners to recognize

Formal orchard, terraced kitchen garden, and unpretentious parterre in a painting by Thomas Robbins, of Charlton Park; mid eighteenth century

a plant likely to be an old survival worthy of preservation. It takes only a short while for even the loveliest plant to disappear entirely (many fine cultivars bred even in our own century have already done so), and in the course of the book we have mentioned many sad losses. There are, though, hosts of survivors left, which can still be grown and enjoyed today. If you think our enthusiasm is justified, then perhaps you will grow these plants too and ensure their further survival. Then, in the centuries ahead, it will still be possible to put together a reasonable copy of a Gertrude Jekyll border, a piece of

Victorian bedding, a perfectly organized eighteenth-century kitchen garden, a seventeenth-century parterre or an entire medieval garden.

When does a plant become a 'plant from the past'? The answer to that, we think, is as soon as gardeners forget where they have planted it, as soon as the label has rotted away, as soon as gardeners turn to something more fashionable. This has happened so often that it leaves a vast field from which we have had to choose; we wanted to produce a book which was both manageable in size, and intelligible to the relative newcomer to gardening.

Our first aim has been that the reader, European or American, should be able, if he or she so chooses, to put together a small garden of any period from the plants that we have included. There are plants, therefore, from all periods, and for a wide range of soils and positions. We have been deliberately undogmatic (not to say idiosyncratic) about our choices, and though most plants are hardy perennials (the backbone of the border after the trees and shrubs), there are also hardy and half-hardy annuals, biennials, some small shrubs, some bulbs and a few half-hardy perennials. Our eye has always been on what past gardeners thought were essential garden plants.

They are all plants which are still good and useful in the garden today and most should be reasonably easily obtainable to anyone willing to put in a little work (though we could not help mentioning a few rarities). We've included all the old 'florists'' genera (see Chapter 1), for their changing fortunes are an education in themselves as regards the evolution of gardening taste and fashion. We can, we realize, be criticized endlessly for our exclusions (we do it ourselves). However, in the end, it seemed better to have a more detailed description of the few than too slight descriptions of the many.

The arguments for conserving anything, whether a rusty and forgotten hand tool, an ancient piece of furniture, or a lovely old building, are exactly the same, and don't need to be rehearsed here. Suffice it to say that only if we save features from the past will we get a full picture of how our ancestors thought and felt. Only then will we be touched by a real sense of history and feel our identity with and closeness to the sixteenth-century lady who pins a fritillary or a bunch of Plymouth strawberries to her sleeve, or the eighteenth-century gentleman who treasures a double auricula.

Though most readers, we imagine, will want simply to grow some of the plants and be (we hope) fascinated by their histories, we envisage some more ambitious souls who may want to plant a complete period garden of their own. Unfortunately, we have not been able to include detailed garden designs for each design epoch, though we have included a few contemporary illustrations (we had to stop somewhere). We do, though, give you a small book list if you want to follow up some of the possibilities. We also provide you with descriptions of many lovely plants, with information on how they

A group of fritillaries from
Parkinson's *Paradisus*, 1629

were used in different periods, and a list of trees and shrubs for different ages, to enable you to complete the garden picture.

Many of the plants described in these pages will not be stocked in the usual garden centre. This is a pity, but do remember that it is not in the least difficult to approach some of the suppliers, mostly plant nurseries in the old sense, that are listed on p. 244; most will send plants through the post. Some of these businesses are small concerns which, often against difficult odds, provide a bulwark against the extinction of all sorts of lovely plants. Be patient with them; their profit margins are often small and their work extremely hard. Try at least to include a stamp when writing for a catalogue.

One final warning: this book is not and could not be a how-to gardening book (it would be ten times the length). Indeed, few of the plants we discuss are at all difficult to grow. They would not have survived if they had been. However, they do need some attention from time to time. Use this book in conjunction with a good how-to book and a good gardening dictionary. Don't, however, be too intimidated by rules. Experiment and have fun; that's how you'll really learn.

# 1 Plants from the Past

Looked at from a historical perspective, almost every garden flower takes on a new and exciting interest. Even such apparently simple flowers as the primula and the pink can be seen evolving over the centuries into innumerable varieties, each climbing or falling in social esteem as changes in society, or simply of garden fashion, wash over it. Many plants are irrevocably linked with some old style of garden, perhaps of centuries ago, or associated with some famous gardener.

Nostalgia for old flowers has been widespread for several centuries, but naturally the earliest gardeners of all had no such problem. All their plants were simply taken from the wild and were hardly likely to give rise to any untoward emotion. In any case, most early garden plants seem to have been entirely utilitarian, and were generally edible or useful in some other important way. Curiously, in the gardens of northern Europe it is remarkable how long this state of affairs survived. Even in late medieval times, some of the books of hours, psalters and so on show garden flowers, many of them not at all different from the wild species growing in the fields only just beyond the garden walls. Of course, some of the flowers illustrated in these ancient books had a symbolic function on the page, and there may have been plenty of others that had no symbolic meaning and so were never painted.

However simple the flowers of medieval northern Europe, it is important to remember that other and far, far older and more sophisticated gardening civilizations had already developed substantial numbers of once wild species into an elaborate structure of garden varieties. These reached northern Europe sometimes in trickles (as they did from the Middle East, probably since Roman times – and then again in some quantity during the Crusades), sometimes in great waves (as they did from the Americas almost as soon as that continent had been discovered). The way in which they arrived depended on various sorts of economic or political contact, plants being brought to northern European gardens by merchants, ambassadors or soldiers.

Greece and Rome, on whose foundations so much of European culture is based, seem to have contributed only a small legacy of

The lovely double primrose
from Gerard's *Herball* of 1633

flowers (though their contribution to the kitchen garden was very much more important). However, further east, in the late medieval period Turkish and Persian gardeners were beginning to develop various native bulb species. Further east still, the ancient cultures of China and Japan had elaborated upon peonies, chrysanthemums, various citrus species and much else; gardeners in those countries were already growing large numbers of beautiful garden forms. In the new world, the golden nations of the Americas were busily selecting food crops like dahlias, maizes, sunflowers and solanums.

Consequently, our present-day nostalgia for, say, the flowers of

Elizabethan England (or Jacobean Scotland of the same date) is actually rather parochial both in terms of time and geography. However, for the purposes of this book, we expect few gardeners to want an ancient Aztec or even Persian garden, so we have – mostly – deliberately kept the plant stories a little provincial.

The stories can be told only in so far as sources for them exist. By the time that the first really useful European garden books began to appear, in the 1500s, some sophisticated flowers from other cultures had already arrived in Europe. The first oriental tulips and hyacinths were already causing a great stir in northern European gardens; sunflowers, marvels of Peru, tomatoes (called 'love apples') and runner beans were already quite familiar as decorative plants to even simple gardeners. Marvellous though sixteenth-century books are, with illustrations and verbal descriptions of considerable accuracy, they appeared virtually out of the blue. There are almost no equally useful earlier sources. What garden books and herbals there are rarely give sufficiently precise descriptions to allow the flowers and plants that they describe to be identified. Those earlier sources that do show real flowers, often perfectly observed, are both rare and widely scattered. Thus you will find that many of the flowers in these pages have histories which lead directly back to what we might call this medieval frontier, but which can be followed no further.

This is an enormous pity, for when we join the story of many garden flowers in the sixteenth century, a whole culture is already well under way and full of excitement, and many of its well-known flowers (plenty of which we still grow) already have a long and distinguished past.

Indeed, many groups of still-familiar plants, which are based on the wild species of European woodlands and meadows, had already begun their expansion into clusters of identifiable garden varieties. They were being avidly bred by named individuals, like the charming-sounding 'Mistress Tuggy' or 'my good friend Vincent Sion', both of whom must have been busy sowing seed or collecting interesting plants on the Continent in the sixteenth century.

The process by which this expansion happens has always been the same, and happens fastest when two or three factors combine. The most important one is the bringing together in gardens of a large number of related species. One famous and fairly well-documented instance of this happened in London in the early nineteenth century, when a collection of *Viola* species was grown mixed up in one bed in one particular garden. This suddenly gave rise to vast numbers of hybrids which caught gardeners' imaginations, and which went on to become pansies, violas, violettas and so on. Something of the same sort, though absolutely undocumented, had probably happened for pinks and carnations, for tulips, for auriculas, for colchicums, perhaps even for irises, but it happened beyond the medieval frontier, and so the date and the identity of the species involved remain in doubt. Often even the location remains hazy.

Of course, such creative explosions need, as well as the plants, gardeners who are excited by the results, who are prepared to care for the seedlings, and look amongst the progeny for flowers that they find interesting. Some plant genera produce such an abundance of good variants that they begin to fascinate a particular sort of gardener, the gardener who finds a myriad variations on one theme more exciting than an infinite variety of themes.

These gardeners are happy taking vast pains with only a few genera, and they must have existed as soon as gardening began. They were obviously a well-identified type by the late sixteenth century; in the seventeenth century they became known as 'florists', and the plants they grew (and grow, for such gardeners and such plants still exist), were known as 'florists' flowers'. The term is used often in the following pages, and it is important to distinguish this sort of florist from the florist of modern usage: a person who sells flowers.

Amongst all florists' flowers, whether in fifteenth-century Constantinople or nineteenth-century Manchester, once variety production is well under way and the diversity of the seedlings becomes colossal, new factors, as well as the sheer excitement of the new types, come into play. Fashion is the most important of these. Fashion, whether in houses, furniture, clothes or flowers, is constantly on the move; in the case of flowers, for instance, the sort of auricula that everyone admired in 1600 was laughed at by 1650 and thrown on the rubbish heap in 1655. Consequently, the sort of auricula popular between, say, 1600 and 1650 is absolutely particular to that period of time and no other. This happens at all periods and for all florists' flowers. In Europe, classical florists' flowers have included groups like tulips, hyacinths, anemones, ranunculuses, pinks, carnations and auriculas. More recently, similar passions have been aroused by gladioli, begonias and saintpaulias. Varieties that survive the first major 'throw-out' period become what we've called *period indicators.* Sadly, in many cases, the change in fashion has been so abrupt and so absolute that none of the outmoded varieties has survived. Thus amongst the flowers of Chapter 4 there seem to be no really old varieties of auricula, no named laced polyanthus (although hundreds existed in the 1850s), no 'button-flowered' hyacinth of the eighteenth century, and so on.

However, in many cases the loss of varieties of florists' flowers is not always quite complete. Often one or two plants remain; either they've lost their names but not their lives, or sometimes stray seedlings survive. Perhaps a long sequence of gardeners have taken pity on and kept growing them, whether from love, nostalgia or inertia. So it remains possible for the present-day period gardener to use plants which are truly 'period indicators'.

Many of the 'period indicator' plants described in Chapter 4 belong to the florists' genera. While some of these groups, like tulips or carnations, started life as upper-class flowers (the grandest varieties were generally extremely expensive), many then moved quite rapidly down the social scale. This sort of flower was soon grown either by the 'simple country-women' referred to so disdainfully by the priggish John Rea (see p. 240) or by the owners or tenants of small pieces of ground. It was amongst such people, as well as urban tradesmen and artisans (and their wives), that the florists' societies began to appear – a few in the early eighteenth century, but many by its end. They continued to be set up all through the Victorian period, and hundreds exist today (many devoted to modern florists' flowers like the saintpaulia).

Such societies originally devoted themselves to the development of particular genera, at first notably to the pink, the auricula, the hyacinth, the ranunculus and the tulip, and, later on, the geranium, pansy and so on. There was a powerful competitive base to each society, with new plants regularly put on show for judgement. This, such is human nature, necessitated rules for what constituted the perfect flower. Rules became widely standardized, certainly by the 1790s when Maddock published his rather dull *Florists Directory*. It was a widely held belief, when that book was published, that there were 'absolute' canons of taste. Once the correct rules were discovered, it was believed, they would have exactly the same validity as most laws of physics, chemistry and geometry. Consequently, 'the rules' had an enormously strong influence on what sort of flowers were grown, and which ones declined into oblivion.

The old florists' societies (two ancient ones remain in existence today, at York and Paisley), were often interested in several genera, but when Victorian plant breeders began work on some of the genera central to gardens of that period (like violas and pelargoniums), societies specializing in a single genus began to emerge. The most important ones published annual lists of the plant varieties that had won most prizes, thus not only promoting sales of the plants so honoured (and also countrywide uniformity), but also immediate oblivion for less 'correct', if no less lovely, ones. 'Rules' provided such a straitjacket for many plant groups that the flowers actually sank out of sight, weighed down by the mass of regulations.

The gardens of South Stoneham House, Swathling, by S. Buck, in the mid eighteenth century: elegant lawns and espalier fruit trees

Garden plants, however much admired by florists or other sorts of plant collector, need also to be seen in the context of the gardens in which they have found themselves. Most recent interest in 'period' gardens has revolved around garden design, generally of the gardens of the wealthy and the famous. In some ways this is entirely understandable. Until towards the end of the nineteenth century only the gardens of the great and famous were illustrated in paintings, prints or photographs, or were surveyed or described in memoirs, or had famous designers. Consequently, at least for that class of garden, so much is known that, should it be necessary, it is possible to make a reasonable pastiche of a period design. It isn't, alas, possible to do the same thing for more humble gardens; these are scarcely documented before the early nineteenth century. On the whole, few people interested in period gardens are particularly alarmed. Nor are many particularly alarmed about plants; for them, gardens are just designs, with some bits of planting 'hardware'. However, they are more than this; they are flowers too. With the wrong plants, perhaps dahlias in an eighteenth-century garden, or with lush delphiniums in a Tudor one, the results will look, even (we hope) to art historians, decidedly 'wrong' in all sorts of ways, but particularly in terms of

The suburban garden of Turner's Twickenham house,
Sandycombe Lodge, showing a 'picturesque' planting of 1819; from a sketch
by William Havell

colour, scale and texture. 'Look' in the garden is every bit as important as inside the house.

Ideas about authenticity in relation to house restoration, outside and inside, are far in advance of those in gardening, and are far more widely disseminated. While the owners of period houses, cottages or town flats may spend happy months agonizing over colours, fabrics, furnishings, window frames and the rest, many run out of ideas, or rather of information, when they look at the garden and end up planting ericas and groundcover plants. Yet it is still perfectly possible to find flowers that will match almost any house and its interiors for period, and provide just as much colour, perfume and interest as any garden-centre plant is able to do (we think rather more). However, these old plants are still being lost because little attention has been paid to their interesting and often illustrious pasts.

There is one other aspect that governs, in a very major way, what a garden actually looks like. Gardens evolve stylistically, as is now exceptionally well documented, and these changes demand parallel ones not only in the plants they contain, but also in the ways that they are put together. Gardens are used in different ways too, at different periods, and this is often an important part of the aesthetic change. Both Elizabethan and Victorian gardens contained parterres (formal and often complicated beds, frequently edged with clipped box, and filled with flowers) which might be expected to look rather similar. In fact, the results looked totally different. One of the reasons for this was that each age wanted something different from their gardens; the Elizabethans, though adoring 'show', also liked looking at the individual flowers and at their smallest details. And they liked to juxtapose quite different plants, perhaps as a way of showing the infinite variety of nature. They would have shuddered at the Victorian parterre, whose plants were stripped of their individuality and became merely the means of providing a mass of the colour needed for a bed. The Victorian parterre existed purely for its show (and grand ones were very showy indeed), and its value as a status symbol. They did not exist to display the wonderful diversity of nature.

Consequently, plants which had been popular in Elizabethan and Stuart parterres, and had survived even in eighteenth-century flower gardens, were of no use to the Victorian gardener. They exploited new plants like verbena, calceolaria, pelargoniums and the rest. As all these groups gave rise to many new varieties, the old plants began to vanish in huge numbers. Ironically, once fashion began to turn away from the gaudy parterre and its half-hardy denizens (from the 1880s onwards), the plants that had made them possible began themselves to disappear. Now, a great deal of what was once a prosperous garden flora is extinct. The same thing will eventually happen to ericas, dwarf conifers, hostas, day lilies – the plants now most in fashion – which, in a few decades, no one will want to look at.

# 2 Conservation

Plants from the past fall into two main categories. On the one
hand are the plants of all types, whether bulbs, trees, shrubs or
herbaceous flowers, which have been brought into the garden
and then scarcely altered. Even if fashion turns against them and every
gardener throws them out, they are still in no danger of absolute
extinction unless something quite nasty has also happened to their
wild habitat.

The other category consists of those plants which have been
hybridized in all sorts of exciting ways in the gardeners' hands. Once
'good taste' turns its fastidious face away, perhaps from whole groups
of garden varieties, and they are all thrown out of the garden, then
they can be lost for ever. This has already happened to thousands
upon thousands of different varieties.

Some garden plants occupy a rather intermediate position; the
species to which they belong are often rather variable, and gardeners,
over the centuries, have selected for their gardens plants with larger
or prettier flowers, unusually spotted leaves, and so on. Sometimes
the children of these plants are themselves variable, and so the process
of selection can continue, often over many years, or even over centuries. This is almost certainly what happened to, say, the ancient varieties
of the common columbine (*Aquilegia vulgaris*). Even plants at the very
first stage of this selection process are at risk. Charming examples
like the jack-in-the-green primrose (p. 201), or the extraordinary
Plymouth strawberry (p. 136) have been found in the wild by some
beady-eyed gardener, and taken home. In the past, when the garden
flora was quite small, such amusing and naturally occurring oddities,

sports of nature, had exceptional value. Now, when the garden flora is enormously rich, many are being forgotten.

Looking at almost any old garden book, whether Elizabethan or Victorian, will make you realize the enormous scale of the losses. It is perhaps not surprising to discover that only one or two of the hundred

John Parkinson, a portrait;
from Parkinson's *Paradisus*, 1629

or so late Tudor pinks and carnations survive, or that all the Jacobean auriculas seem to have vanished. After all, several centuries have elapsed since they were fashionable. However, of the hundreds of Victorian and Edwardian asters, carnations, irises, verbenas, once in every garden, only a handful remain. Scarcely a dozen or so varieties of the last of the Victorian florists' tulips, out of the multitudes once in existence, survive. They dropped out of commerce in 1957 when Barrs, the noted bulb firm, ceased to stock them, and are now supported in perhaps only a hundred gardens. Although planting schemes of late Victorian gardens, or of gardens of the early twentieth century, survive in considerable numbers, none can be re-created with any very high degree of accuracy because the varieties used no longer exist. Even Gertrude Jekyll's famous flower borders, photographed early in this century, and with surviving planting plans, cannot be reconstructed in their entirety because many of the varieties she used can no longer be found.

Real interest in the conservation of old garden plants and old gardens probably dates only from the late nineteenth century, though sadness for the loss of old-fashioned flowers is itself much older. Even an early-seventeenth-century gardener like John Parkinson regretted the loss of the flowers he remembered from his youth, and fondly imagined that they might still be retrieved from old gardens in remote parts of the kingdom. Philip Miller, in the following century, felt the same loss, and by the end of Queen Victoria's reign almost every garden magazine printed letters and articles bemoaning vanished flowers. None the less, however strong and however vocal these feelings, seventeenth-century gardeners still allowed plants that they were bored with to disappear, as did Georgian gardeners and almost all Victorian gardeners. None of them saw that what made them smile (as some of us now do at hybrid tea roses, violently coloured gladioli, or bath-cap begonias) would a century later feed the nostalgia of gardeners as yet unborn.

When serious interest in plants from the past began, in the 1860s and 1870s, there seemed to be no doubt as to where they might be found – in old cottage gardens. There were various reasons for this, though the most important was that many cottagers were so poor that they naturally tended to grow garden plants handed down by previous generations of cottagers, or grow ones thrown out of more prosperous gardens which were keeping up with fashion. The gardens of the poor thus served as a buffer between unfashionable plants and extinction. Another important reason was the fact that the interest in old-fashioned flowers had also become inextricably linked to a sentimental fantasy of cottage life.

Of course, the wealthy had been having fantasies about this since the late eighteenth century. Many had even built themselves charming 'cottages ornées', the gardens of which had always been filled with all

Arbours around a parterre of irregular beds; many flowers from gardens like this survive. Detail from a portrait of William Style; British school, seventeenth century

the smartest plants from the grand nurseries of London and Paris.

By 1847, the cottage fantasy was widespread enough to appear in print, allowing people like Edward Jesse to write, complete with fake archaic spelling:

> But it is in his garden that he enjoys one of the most innocent delights of human life. There the sweetbriar and the honeysuckle mingle together in pleasing confusion – the gaudy hollyoake and golden sunflower tower above the more humble rose and sky-blue iris. Nor are the pink and carnation neglected, or the modest lilly of the valley with its delicious perfume . . .

Ten years later, this sentimental feeling for cottagers and their gardens had embraced grander gardens too. Shirley Hibberd, writing in his *Garden Favourites* (1857), gives a perfectly simple and straight-forward account of modern genera like chrysanthemum and pelargonium, but is encouraged by old ones like pinks, carnations and the rest to indulge in sweet thoughts of old gardens

in their original quaintness, with their noble trees and mossy lawns, their trim hedges, bowling greens, and luxuriant borders planted with old perennials, where not a single modern bedding plant is to be seen, but where gaiety and fragrance assert the claims of our truly national flowers, and call up many dear remembrances

and where the visitor could 'but turn to the border, and there see the evidence of our ancestors' love of flowers; see how they gloried in their sweet-smelling dainties . . .' and so on.

In the next decade, not only were gardeners beginning to yearn for old gardens and plants from the past, but all sorts of people were looking hard and quite seriously at old buildings, especially those which were domestic in scale and vernacular in style, and becoming concerned at the mounting scale of the losses. Debate about how best to conserve what remained of the past soon began.

The conservation ideal began to take root and, by the 1870s, gardeners like the Revd Harpur Crewe began to look out for surviving period flowers in a systematic way. They came up with all sorts of interesting things, some still in our gardens (like the lovely double yellow wallflower, probably of the sixteenth century, now called 'Harpur Crewe'), some apparently lost once more. Famous gardeners like Gertrude Jekyll and William Robinson also explored cottage gardens and made some interesting finds.

Rather surprisingly, for all the passion expressed in print, nothing much actually happened in gardens themselves, and period restorations and re-creations were hardly attempted. Very few contemporary gardeners could forgo, and who can blame them, the excitements of all the tremendous late-nineteenth-century developments in many herbaceous genera. Consequently, the gardens of period houses of the time were all lovely to look at but not in the least true to period.

It wasn't really until the 1950s that the garden history (and garden conservation) movement really took off. Even then it was mostly concerned with garden style, considered either in an 'art historical' or an architectural way. It did, and still does, very much concentrate on overall design, or the history of particular gardens or garden designers and owners. It pays astonishingly little attention, considering their importance in all gardens, to either garden plants or the flower garden.

Worse, modern commercial pressure makes sure that the range of plants commonly available to the public gets rapidly smaller and smaller, and attitudes evolve to match. There is nowadays so much emphasis on the 'all-round plant', one which is virtually built of plastic, that soon almost every garden will look identical because of the restricted garden flora available.

However, things may be changing. With the recent formation of the National Council for the Conservation of Plants and Gardens, at least some genera of herbaceous plants are beginning to get the attention they need. Even so, representation is still patchy, and some of the 'national collections' consist only of plant varieties which are still in commercial circulation and so are relatively safe (at the moment) from extinction. The excellent Hardy Plant Society supports many interesting plants that would long ago have disappeared. Nevertheless, not every gardener is keen on joining societies and there is still plenty that the individual can do.

Certainly, looking for forgotten garden plants is an interesting business. In a way, it is a new frontier. While there must still be wonderful and unknown plants in China, northern India, farthest South America, all awaiting discovery and fame, the vast floods of new introductions from those countries are certainly now over, except for a slight trickle of obscure rarities to satisfy the vanity of gardeners who refuse to grow anything that anyone else has. So if the geographical frontiers are becoming exhausted, an absolutely new and uncharted one is all around us: the past.

There are various strategies if you feel like doing some of the new sort of plant hunting. The most important one of these is, not surprisingly, to know what you are looking for. You are very much more likely to know if something is interesting if you are already familiar with the variations in the group you are pursuing and, more particularly, if you know something of the group's history. We hope that this book will give you at least a slight outline of both these factors for the genera that we have managed to include. For genera that we have not covered, the book list on p. 242 will give you a starting place for your researches. Another important strategy is to give full rein to greed (most gardeners find this fairly easy). If you hear of an interesting plant, do something about it at once. It is astonishing how many people grow plants that were cuttings from their grandparents' garden, and whose grandparents themselves had taken it from some even older one. We have lost several perhaps important things by saying that we would take cuttings, or dig up the bulbs, at the right time. When the right time has come, natural or unnatural disasters turn out to have got to the plant first.

It also helps to know where to look. Here, we can be of little help. In our experience, the old hope of finding a forgotten cottage with a garden brimful of forgotten plants is nowadays a fantasy. Both cottages and their owners are modernized and prosperous, with gardens to match. More profitable hunting grounds are amongst the Victorian suburbs of industrial cities, especially in front gardens which still have tiled paths and pretty moulded edgings to the flowerbeds. Better still are the gardens of a newly disadvantaged class, who can no longer employ three gardeners, whose peach houses have collapsed, and where the walled garden is beginning to return to the wild. There you can perhaps still find edgings of double hepaticas, the last few double lilies, or possibly an old striped carnation. And you might also find green-gumbooted 'new cottagers' looking for old plants to add to their new cottage garden.

Once you have something nice in view, though, it is important to retain some degree of scepticism. If some charming old gaffer, or even a friend with a sense of humour, tells you that that plant has been growing on that wall since at least 1724 and, even more exciting, that some years ago someone had found an old label tied to it with string (eighteenth-century too), beware. Quite apart from leg-pulling, there are all sorts of problems. Was it the right label? Does the plant increase by cuttings, or is the plant in the wall a self-sown seedling? And so on . . .

There are also problems, as with all 'antiques', of what to do about 'reproductions'. Amongst plants, some 'fakes' are more natural than others. Some variants of wild species probably occur quite often; so although Jacobean gardeners liked double catchflies or some other oddity, it doesn't mean that if you find the same plant somewhere, it is an actual descendant of a plant from some ancient garden. It could have originated from the natural wild species only last year. This does not make it any less pretty; and if the Jacobeans liked it enough to take it into their gardens, then it is, to some extent, truly Jacobean.

More difficult to assess are deliberate fakes, where a gardener has found, or bred, a seedling that looks tolerably close to some period form, and the plant has somehow obtained a suitably historic provenance. This certainly happens, particularly in popular genera with a strong romantic appeal (pinks are especially prone to spurious age).

However, once you have a piece of what you hope is an old plant growing in your garden, preferably without a suspect provenance, it is worth trying to identify it. This can be frustrating, particularly if your plant belongs to one of the florists' groups. If it does, you are unlikely to find its name, for these were generally so numerous, and the differences between the varieties so slight, that to search is fruitless. You may, though, find that it is possible to give it an approximate date, once you have an idea of the history of the species to which it belongs and of its varieties.

It can also be difficult finding names for varieties in non-florists' groups. In any case, the plant you have may just be a chance, though attractive, seedling which has never been given a name. If you think that it is a variety, first find out if there is a national collection. If there is, you may be able to check your plant against other surviving varieties. If there isn't, try and find old garden catalogues. Many plants come from local nurseries, and they might be able to help. Catalogues from vanished nurseries often find their way into the 'local history' section of nearby public libraries, so have a look there too. Best of all, though, is to make a collection of varieties yourself; you'll find endless problems of naming almost as soon as you start, but you will eventually become such an expert that you might end up with a 'national collection' of your own.

# 3 *Putting It Together*

We hope that, in Chapter 4, you will find some nice histories for the plants you already grow, and will be encouraged to fill your garden with plants loved by gardeners of previous centuries. Of course, the genera we have included (important though they all are) are only a part of the whole story.

Gardens aren't made only with these sorts of plants; shrubs, trees and climbers are all necessary, as are some at least of the myriad sorts of rose, or of exotic plants for tubs, pots, glasshouse and porch. In this chapter you can find brief lists of suitable plants in each of these categories. We have divided them into 'period' groups so that you can, if you want to, create a fully 'period' garden in a fairly simple way.

Of course, if a period garden is what you want, you need to know something about period design, and how to combine the various plants together inside it. In this chapter, we have included a few contemporary illustrations to show what the gardens of each of the centuries looked like, though garden design is constantly evolving, and a glimpse every hundred years or so is not entirely sufficient to gauge every stage of the changes. However, this book is primarily about plants, and we hope that if you want, or need, to be a purist in garden design, you will use some of the sources we suggest to get more definitive help. We have tried to include some information on how plants were actually combined in period gardens, as this affects the overall look to an enormous degree. In the early centuries with which we deal this poses considerable difficulties. It is astonishing how many old garden books tell the reader all about the plants of a particular date, but absolutely nothing about the manner of planting. Even careful reading of some of the most important books that exist can leave the reader confused. For us, the most frustrating has been John Reid's *The Scots Gardiner* of 1683, for we had hoped to use it to create a garden of just that date, but we cannot quite get the hang of his suggestions for combining roses, flowers and herbs, in spite of the many pages he devotes to the topic.

However, many of the plants of the past are so lovely that gardeners who have no intention of making a period garden will want to grow them. 'Purism' can be something of a straitjacket, particularly in early gardens. To do, say, a medieval garden well can be immensely satisfying and very great fun; when, that is, the gardener is not secretly hankering after something 'impure', like one really big clump of pink delphiniums, or a patch of white oriental poppies, when all that ought to be planted is yet more of the late medieval daisy 'Alba Plena' (the cure, for a medievalist, is to plant a huge clump of either *Lychnis chalcedonica* (p. 175), *Lilium candidum* (p. 169), or even of *Saponaria officinalis* (p. 215). The non-purist can happily combine plants from all periods in the currently popular cottage-garden manner, and for such happy people, we include a short section on the best way of achieving an attractive combination of planting and design.

We hope that the following short section on each period will give you some idea of the look that you will need to achieve. The lists of plants for each period are, of course, cumulative, though plants that have remained important over many centuries appear in each list to which they are relevant.

## LATE MEDIEVAL GARDENS

The image you need to create if you want a late medieval garden is of a small, enclosed, strongly scented space, with wooden arbours, trellises and railings (which the medievals called 'carpenters' work'), and with raised beds of roses, herbs and lilies, turfed seats and flower-studded grass.

Medieval gardens of almost every size were most often square or rectangular in plan, and the areas were generally subdivided again into smaller square sections by cross-paths (gravelled or sanded). There might be a central well or fountain or, failing that, a central tree, which might perhaps be planted on a raised mound. This tree was quite commonly a bay (*Laurus nobilis*), symbol of constancy, and a popular evergreen. The garden in one of Chaucer's poems has both; a well 'that stood under a laurer always green'.

Flower-studded lawns, or 'flowery medes', were very common. All of the low-growing plants on the lists we append below would be suitable for this, especially the daisy, the sweet violet, periwinkles, the primrose, the cowslip and wild strawberries. Medieval tapestries often show the plants as if the grass in which they were growing was

A medieval garden with an outer paling, a stout
gate, and a flower worth sniffing

kept short while they themselves were allowed their freedom. The grass must have been rather ill-treated, as accounts for re-turfing gardens are common.

Beds for growing herbs and scented flowers were raised a foot or so above the general level of the garden, the sides retained by boards. Against the garden walls were often raised earthen banks, low enough to sit upon, and retained also by planks, bricks, or the wattles of hazel seen in contemporary illustrations. The tops were turfed, with the grass enriched with small flowers, including camomile and thyme. They may sound damp and uncomfortable, but we constructed

1. A white clematis-flowered aquilegia, photographed in David Bromley's Shropshire garden

▷ 3.  A double florists' auricula; modern

▽ 2.  A tawny colour of auricula, popular in the late
     sixteenth century

4.  The late–Victorian double primula 'Marie Crousse', one of the few easily grown sorts

such a bank and find it a great pleasure (though not after rain; perhaps medieval textiles were so thick that they did not notice the damp). The turf seats might be around the entire perimeter of the garden or just in suitable corners. Sometimes they were made around the central tree or fountain. If against the wall, the masonry behind was occasionally decorated with pruned fruit trees, or with roses. Some grand medieval gardens also had a mount, a raised earthwork high enough to give either a good view of the garden or of the outside world. It was

A medieval garden, gated,
but with a simple wattle fence

either placed in the middle of the garden, or to one side, against a wall.

There seems to have been, at least in the sort of gardens then illustrated, a huge amount of woodwork, now alas rather expensive to replicate. Gardens not grand enough to warrant masonry boundaries were often enclosed in a stockade of pointed beams, lesser ones still commonly having a ditch and palisaded or hedged bank behind. Inside, fences and trellises were entwined with the eglantine (*Rosa rubiginosa*, with apple-scented leaves and vigorous growth). Arbours, often made out of a large-scale basketwork of poles, were wreathed with climbing plants, especially vines in warmer parts of the country, or with pruned apple trees in cooler ones. Some arbours followed the inside of the garden to make a delicious green cloister, others simply shaded a turf seat, where the occupant could sniff the jasmine, roses and honeysuckles, or pick the fruit.

Groups of herb and flower beds were surrounded by yet more joinery, often low trellises two to three feet high, with top rails and fancily carved posts. Simple gardens had the same sort of thing, but made out of woven reeds or withies.

Raised beds of flowers, pear trees, and a bench of pots
in a humble medieval garden

As to the flowers, the general colour effect would seem to have been of greenery spangled with touches of brilliance. As far as we know, there is no source that gives much indication of how plants were actually put together. Such as there are suggest that flowers were planted as 'scatters' of mixed flowers, rather than the selfconscious 'drifts' of modern planting. Also, in view of garden conservatism, we feel that the sixteenth and seventeenth centuries' aversion to seeing two plants of the same type growing next to one another may well descend from medieval taste.

We mention many medieval garden plants in the following chapter, but when you make a selection, think about medieval plumbing. All strongly scented plants were highly valued (many had medicinal properties too), so the garden must smell strongly, as well as have some colour. If you want roses, remember that there were very few: the white *Rosa alba*, the red *R. gallica* and *R. gallica* 'Officinalis' (both lovely), or the dog rose (*R. canina*). Some European gardens had a many-petalled scarlet rose, perhaps the damask (*R. damascena*). We have mentioned the eglantine above, but try also the wild *R. arvensis*,

An orchard in quincunx plan,
from Parkinson's *Paradisus*, 1629; the
outer hedge is of roses, currants,
and gooseberries

which can be used as a climber. Whatever roses lacked in variety, they made up for in popularity. There do seem to have been medieval rose gardens.

Along the paths that enclose the garden grow plenty of sage, artemisia, hyssop, camomile, lavender, the native catmint (*Nepeta cataria*, if you can find it), rosemary, rue and thyme. In pots, grow as many sorts of basil as you can find, vast quantities of the white lily (*Lilium candidum*) and scarlet and white carnations.

Orchards, for those who could afford them, were very common,

Light trelliswork and raised beds in a late medieval illustration to the
*Roman de la Rose*

though for less prosperous people, as today, fruit trees would simply be grown as part of the garden. Orchards were enclosed by a wall or a ditch and consisted of plantings of apples or pears, with sometimes vines trained along the walls. They contained cider apples, such as 'bitter-sweets', or 'Pearmains' and other eating apples such as the costard apple. Various sorts of pippin became popular in the fifteenth century. The favoured pear was the 'Warden', which was baked. Other common sorts of fruit were hazelnuts and filberts, and occasionally walnuts, cherries and medlars. Peaches and quinces were only planted by the very rich, and plums do not seem to have been generally grown, perhaps because the wildlings were readily available outside the garden. There are some mentions of mulberries in the fourteenth and fifteenth centuries, though the introduction date is usually given as the sixteenth century. Perhaps they were rare.

Finally, two quotations from Chaucer, to give some further verbal impression of what late medieval gardens were like:

> The yard was large, and railed all the alleys,
> And shadowed with blossomy boughs green,
> And benched new, and sanded all the ways,
> In which she walketh arm and arm between.
> (Troilus and Criseyde)

> Full gay was all the ground, and quaint,
> And powdered, as men had it paint,
> With many a fresh and sundry flower
> That casten up full good savour.
> (Chaucer's translation of the<br>Roman de la Rose)

Important medieval flowers include: *Acanthus*, *Achillea*, single hollyhocks (see *Alcea*), *Aquilegia*, marigolds (see *Calendula*), single wallflowers (see *Cheiranthus*), lily of the valley (see *Convallaria*), foxgloves (see *Digitalis*), *Eryngium maritimum*, meadowsweet (see *Filipendula*), *Helleborus*, *Iris germanica* and *I. pseudacorus*, the single *Lychnis chalcedonica*, the single red *Paeonia officinalis* and the lovely *P. mascula*, the wild and the opium poppy (see *Papaver*), Greek valerian (*Polemonium caeruleum*), the common plantain (see *Plantago*), Solomon's seal (see *Polygonatum*), the single *Saponaria officinalis*, tansy (see *Tanacetum*) and *Verbascum*.

Shrubs and trees include: *Berberis vulgaris*, the native green-flowered spurge laurel (*Daphne laureola*), *Cytisus scoparius*, box, bay, elder, tamarisk, the sorb (*Sorbus domestica*), all basic fruit species, the native oaks and willows, ash, chestnut, walnut, juniper and yew.

Good climbers to use, apart from honeysuckle and vines, include the hop and the jasmine.

This engraving from Sweert's *Florilegium* of 1612 shows a trellis and carved wood cloister around beds of spring flowers

## SIXTEENTH-CENTURY GARDENS

Many of the elements of earlier times were retained; gardens were still square and regularly divided enclosures, with raised beds, railings, trelliswork and arbours, but all the wooden architecture took on (at least for the rich and sophisticated) a Renaissance gloss and formality. The lovely flowery mede became old-fashioned, and vanished. It was replaced by the beginnings of an obsession that was to last for almost two hundred years: the knot garden. Knots were intricate patterns of low hedging, laid out within the enclosed garden, elaborations of the raised bed once used for flowers and herbs. The most popular plants for this were lavender, thyme, hyssop, carefully pruned rosemary, thrift, santolina and, rather rarely at this period, box. Naturally, the spaces within the strands of the knot could be planted, but because the complexity of the hedging had to be seen if it was to 'register', the planting was only of low-growing things. It even seems to have been common to replace flowers altogether, and fill the interstices with coloured earths or sand.

Grandly formal trelliswork,
teamed with raised beds and
classical architecture, in a
late-sixteenth-century garden

Knots could be either closed or open; 'closed' knots were patterns of hedging so interwoven that there were no paths into the centre, while 'open' ones were simpler, having the area merely divided into sections, so that paths could lead between them. Schemes were often very complex. One of Cardinal Wolsey's secretaries wrote that his garden had 'The knots so enknotted it cannot be exprest.' Beds were either in geometric shapes, or 'free form' (one illustration shows them in the shapes of various fruits). Many gardens were simply 'quartered', the four knots (perhaps surrounding a tank of water or an arbour) usually of different designs.

Naturally, gardens with such complex plans looked better from a height than they did from ground level. Mounts therefore began to assume greater importance as places to show off the cost and complexity of one's garden. Many were big enough to need paths spiralling up to a summerhouse or arbour at the apex. The word 'mount' could,

A tiny garden with box-edged beds, topiary, and trellis tunnels;
early seventeenth century

however, also apply to any raised area – perhaps a long terrace with summerhouses at each end.

It was still common for gardens to have green cloister walks around the periphery, or even between the knots, if they were sufficiently grand to warrant it. Aristocratic gardens had the trelliswork got up into elaborate classical designs, though no doubt rustic gardens kept to the simplicity of earlier times.

Orchards and kitchen gardens were still attractive places in which to meander. Most examples seem to have been hedged with a tangle

of wild fruit trees like rowan, gean, filbert, medlar, service tree, hawthorn and elder, all tied together with honeysuckle, wild clematis and
bryony. Grand examples were protected with ditch or moat, grander
ones still with a wall. Trees were planted as a quincunx (see p. 35).

The sixteenth century witnessed a quite spectacular increase in the
range of garden plants that were available. Not only were American
plants beginning to appear all over Europe, but exciting things were
coming in from Turkey and Persia. Good flowers that we have not
yet described include most of the important bulbs, especially daffodils
(see *Narcissus*), fritillaries, grape hyacinths (see *Muscari*), scillas and
hyacinths: other spring flowers like anemones, *Ranunculus* and pasque
flowers (see *Pulsatilla*); summer-flowering plants like the many sorts of
*Campanula*, various sorts of *Dianthus*, *Aster*, European *Chrysanthemum*,
*Digitalis*, *Lychnis* and so on. However, there is so much to try – *Adonis*,
*Amaranthus*, the delightful double form of *Cardamine pratensis*, double
daisies (see *Bellis*), *Catananche* (or cupidone), double wallflowers (see
*Cheiranthus*), *Dictamnus*, *Epimedium*, *Euphorbia*, *Geranium*, *Helianthus*,
day lilies (see *Hemerocallis*), *Hepatica*, *Hesperis matronalis*, dozens of
new lilies, mallows (see *Malva*), and *Mirabilis*. Even the now humble
nasturtium (see *Tropaeolum*) was new, as were auriculas (see *Primula*),
*Tagetes*, *Thalictrum*, *Veratrum* and so on. Sixteenth-century gardeners
must have lived in a fever of excitements.

Good trees and shrubs include the two cistuses, *C. ladanifer* and
*C. salvifolius*, *Daphne mezereum*, the charming stickadove (*Lavandula
stoechas*), *Phlomis fruticosus*, *Syringa vulgaris*, the guelder rose (*Viburnum
opulus*), the underrated cornelian cherry (*Cornus mas*), the spindle tree
(*Euonymus europaeus*), privet, myrtle, black mulberry, the oriental
plane, aspen and white poplar, peaches and nectarines, *Quercus ilex*,
the now fashionable white willow (*Salix alba*, though not, alas, in its
currently grand variety 'Argentea'), and several elms.

Climbers remained rather few; passion flowers were new, the 'poets'
ivy' became popular, and by late in the century there were several
sorts of clematis, including *Clematis flammula*, *C. cirrhosa*, and *C.
viticella*. The perfoliate honeysuckle (*Lonicera caprifolium*) was often
seen in cottage gardens.

Roses now included the summer and autumn damasks, *Rosa damascena* and *R.* × *bifera*, the York and Lancaster (*R. damascena* 'Versicolor'), *R. foetida* and the quite gorgeous *R. foetida* 'Bicolor' (often
now called 'Austrian Copper'). The lovely climbing *R. moschata*,
grown earlier in the rest of Europe, had by now reached Britain.

Plants for pots: the scented though poisonous *Datura stramonium* was popular, as was oleander, aloe (perhaps *Aloe africana*), orange, lemon, olive (a lovely pot plant, with sheaves of tiny yellowish flowers in late spring), and the pomegranate (almost hardy in all but the most exposed gardens).

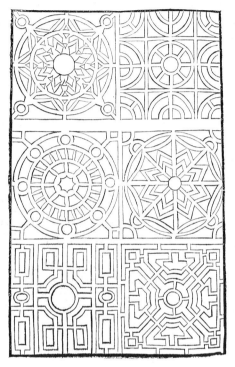

Ideas for knot gardens from Parkinson's
*Paradisus*, 1629

## SEVENTEENTH-CENTURY GARDENS

Seventeenth-century gardens were becoming more diverse. Perhaps by today's visual and gardening standards, some of the effects they produced would have looked a trifle odd, but if you want an authentic garden of the period, they are well worth trying. The apparent oddity is especially true of the arrangement of flowers in flowerbeds and parterres. For the first time in this section of the book, there is clear documentary evidence to go on; a few planting schemes

appear in contemporary garden books, and even in paintings of
the period. Some of the most detailed information we have comes,
surprisingly, from eighteenth- and nineteenth-century florists (see
pp. 149 and 157). Inside the main planting area (just as in the bulb
beds), it was bad form to have two identical plants next to one another.
If the bed was devoted to one species, say of anemones, then different
colour forms were used. More usually, beds seem to have been what
the Victorians called, rather disapprovingly, 'promiscuous' (perhaps
that is why they preferred their carpet bedding). A promiscuous bed
was one in which all sorts of species were mixed together, with taller

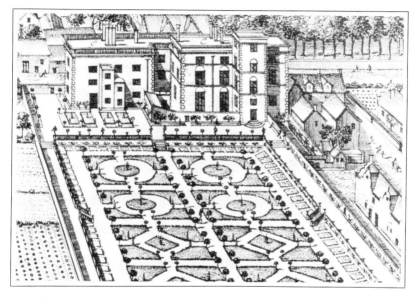

Late-seventeenth-century flowerbeds at Pierrepont House, Nottingham

plants like hollyhocks at the back, grading down quite regularly to
the low plants at the front of the border. The plants were kept quite
tidy. They were also well spaced and planted with perfect regularity,
so that plenty of nice bare earth showed between them.

We have not come across any suggestion that flower colour schemes
were used in any conscious way to unify plantings, but if you want
some help with seventeenth-century colours, it is worth looking at
portraits or fabrics and furnishings of that period to get a feel for the
sorts of combinations that were in use.

Only in the grandest gardens was any sort of spring and summer bedding carried out. In humbler ones, except perhaps for a small tulip or hyacinth bed, the planting seems to have been fairly permanent, with the informality of natural plant growth being offset by topiary obelisks, globes, neat hedges, standard bays, pots of carnations, and perhaps some statuary or a sundial. The knot had broadened out to become the larger-scale and more free-flowing parterre, with elaborate cut-out patterns, which were much more generously planted.

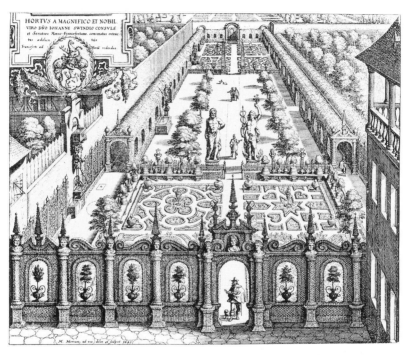

Knot gardens, lawns, trees in quincunx, espaliers, and lots of potted plants in a garden of 1641

In the beds of the parterre, the flowers seem still to have been kept fairly low, to allow the formal elements to register, though taller flowers were often planted in the centre of each section (see p. 189). The long borders commonly had their edges defined by low-growing plants, often clipped box, santolina or hyssop in earlier gardens, with thymes or pinks being used in later ones.

Walls were often covered with roughly espaliered fruit trees. The precise fans and cordons of modern garden manuals are all mid-nineteenth-century inventions; old fruit trees were simply tied up to nails driven into the brick or masonry. Gateways and entrances were decorated by roses, jasmines and honeysuckles.

If your garden is large enough to need an orchard, free-standing fruit trees were planted in a 'quincunx'. These (whatever their plural is) existed in two forms. The simplest had trees planted at the notional corners of a square, usually between fifteen and twenty-five feet apart.

Design for an elegant labyrinth from *The Theory and Practice of Gardening*;
late seventeenth century
(the English translation by John James did not appear until 1712)

Thus a group of trees comprised a number of squares, and so gave rows of trees running north/south and east/west. The other sort was essentially similar, except that a fifth tree was in the centre of each square; this gave a rather more complex picture when the plantation was viewed from the outside. Orchards were usually bounded by some sort of enclosure, whether moat and palisade in the grandest examples or, more usually, a hedge of hawthorn or of mixed native trees and bushes and the more simple hedgerow fruits. Inner paths were further marked out, sometimes with gooseberry or common berberis (*Berberis vulgaris* is the only one to use) as hedges. The trees themselves had an underplanting of grass, commonly enriched with sweet violets, wild strawberries, spring bulbs and even an occasional rose bush (try using *Rosa alba* 'Maxima'). Seventeenth-century orchards could have their paths centred on a statue or an urn, or even a small summerhouse.

The trees themselves should be half or full standards, preferably on a rootstock that will allow them to grow tall. A number of old fruit varieties survive in commerce, some going back to at least the sixteenth century (see p. 242 for sources of more information). Try to use period fruit if you can; many are absolutely delicious, and often surprisingly different from those commonly available now.

Larger gardens might have had a wilderness. Little research has been done on how they were planted, and contemporary illustrations are not a great deal of help. Except in the largest gardens of all, it was a place for bushes and the smaller trees. Some of the coarser perennials we note in the text were also used. Until the late seventeenth century, walks through the wilderness, sometimes set up as a labyrinth, were usually straight (and remained so in Scotland until at least the 1750s). Later on, they became serpentine. The walks were of grass, often edged with flowers or small flowering bushes, even, by the late seventeenth century, perennial candytuft (see p. 159). The general effect seems to have been of wildness and enclosure; a contrast with the sophistication and openness of the parterre. For detailed designs, we suggest sources on p. 242.

Fairly humble gardens, though still perfectly formal in plan, often had rectangular beds of herbs, vegetables, bush fruit and flowers, all held together by old-fashioned clipped hedges of box or santolina, with a ball or obelisk topiary at each corner. Gardens were often centred on a tank of water or a simple sundial. Seats seem often to have been of turf or camomile, though no doubt wood or metal seats existed. Some were certainly covered by arbours, planted up with roses, trained apples (they must have been lovely in spring and autumn), vines ('Wrotham Pinot' is a good seventeenth-century variety still with us) or, quite commonly, scarlet runner beans (the pods were not eaten at this date).

Grander gardens had, against the entrance front, simple grass parterres, or even bowling greens against the house front, with perhaps figs or peaches nailed to the front courtyard walls. Full-scale avenues were planted with wild tree species, though smaller country houses sometimes had groups of geans or fruiting cherries. Double-flowered geans were especially popular in Scotland, and are gorgeous.

Important plants for the period include: *Alcea*, *Amaranthus*, *Anemone*, many sorts of *Aquilegia*, a few *Aster* species, auriculas (see

*Primula*), double sorts of *Cheiranthus*, *Convolvulus*, old sorts of *Delphinium*, *Campanula*, *Crocus*, *Dianthus* (in large quantities and many varieties), *Dictamnus*, *Hepatica*, hyacinths, lilies, irises, *Lobelia cardinalis* and *L. syphilitica*, *Lychnis*, a few old sorts of lupin, *Matthiola*, many sorts of *Ranunculus* and *Thalictrum*, *Tradescantia*, tulips (almost *the* seventeenth-century genus), and double and single sweet violets.

These should be associated with 'clipt greens' – topiary of yew, bay, box, holly, pyracantha (*P. coccinea*, sometimes left unpruned against walls for winter colour), *Viburnum tinus*, and phillyrea (*P. latifolia* and *P. angustifolia*, two lovely evergreens rarely seen today).

Tubs and large terracotta pots can be used to mark the corners of

A so-called English parterre, from *The Theory and Practice of Gardening*; late seventeenth century

walks, or the intervals along straight ones. They were always used for slightly tender plants, even if they had to be kept in cellars or outhouses during the winter (we keep some of ours in the woodshed). Try growing oranges (Sevilles have the sweetest-smelling flowers), lemons, myrtles (including double-flowered and variegated sorts), oleanders (red- and white-flowered varieties, often trained as standards), yuccas and agaves. Smaller pots can hold carnations (see *Dianthus*), Marvels of Peru (see *Mirabilis* – look for striped-flowered ones), or double or dwarf pomegranates.

Fruit trees should include quinces ('Portugal' is a seventeenth-century variety, and tastes and smells wonderful), bullaces, mulberries, medlars, filberts, damsons and greengages ('Reine Claude' is of the right date), as well as peaches and nectarines (we have not discovered any authentic varieties), apples of course ('Ribston Pippin', 'Non-pareil' and 'Golden Pippin', though there are plenty of others of the right period still to be found), pears ('Jargonelle', 'Catillac' and 'Bergamotte' are all small-fruited but quite delicious), cherries ('May-duke', 'Kentish', 'Morello' and especially 'Noble' which was introduced by John Tradescant the Elder).

Roses were extensively grown, and the range was widened to include *Rosa cinnamonea*, *R. francofurtana*, the lovely striped *R. gallica* 'Versicolor' (often called 'Rosa Mundi'), the yellow *R. hemisphaerica*, double-flowered *R. moschata*, and the very first American rose, *R. virginiana*.

Shrubs include the lovely amelanchiers (*A. canadensis* is especially good), two new cistuses (*C. monspeliensis* and *C. populifolius*), the amusing creeping *Cornus stolonifera*, *Euonymus americanus*, *Hibiscus syriacus* (actually grown since the previous century, but now popular), the Rose of Sharon (*Hypericum calycinum*), the cherry laurel and Portuguese laurel (*Prunus laurocerasus* and *P. lusitanica*), two spiraeas (*S. hypericifolia* and *S. salicifolia*), the marvellous Persian lilac (*Syringa × persica*), and the still-popular *Yucca filamentosa*.

Trees can include the horse chestnut, cedar of Lebanon, the Scotch laburnum (*Laburnum alpinum*), the beautiful sweet gum (*Liquidambar styraciflua*), the sumach (now *Cotinus coggygria*), as well as *Rhus glabra* and *R. typhina*, and, late in the century, the tulip tree (*Liriodendron tulipifera*), the first of the magnolias (*M. virginiana*) and the scarlet oak (*Quercus coccinea*).

Climbers include the trumpet vine (*Campsis radicans*), as well as the equally glamorous trumpet honeysuckle (*Lonicera sempervirens*), both best against a warm wall, the true Virginia creeper (*Parthenocissus quinquefolia*), and two rarely seen but attractive vines, *Vitis riparia*, and the fox grape, *V. labrusca*.

In America, layout and treatment were broadly similar. The garden flora seems to have been rather restricted, though the sources of information are so slight that it is difficult to be certain. Important flowers include soapwort, camomile, *Iris germanica*, honesty (said to be the first introduction), santolina, the white lily (in America by 1630), musk mallows, single hollyhocks, marigolds, catmint, *Papaver somniferum*, rue, sage, clary, stocks, pinks and carnations, tansy, wallflowers and sweet violets. Other species from Europe are noted in the plant entries; there were, of course, many lovely native plants that

5. A double blue form of *Campanula persicifolia*, first grown in the late seventeenth century

6. A lovely 'cup-and-saucer' form of *Campanula persicifolia*

A double white form of *Campanula persicifolia*, also seventeenth century

8. 'Columbine', an English florists' tulip of about 1850

9. A Dutch tulip, 'Kaiserskroon'; 1750, or perhaps earlier

may well have been in use. European fruit species seem to have been the main bushes and trees, though some of the native nuts were in use at least late in the century. There seem to have been relatively few roses. Early reports suggest that red or white singles had been brought from Europe, and that dog roses and eglantines were common. William Penn took a number of varieties home to America late in the century, but they do not seem to have become common. Dr William Blackstone (sometimes spelt Blaxton), one of America's earliest gardeners, apparently grew *R. spinosissima* in his Boston garden.

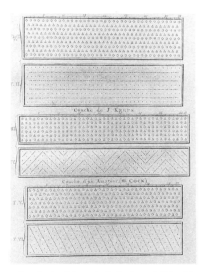

Designs for florists' hyacinth beds published by George
Voorhelm in 1766

# EIGHTEENTH-CENTURY GARDENS

Once the 'landscape garden' movement began to grip Britain in the 1730s (and Europe a decade or two later), gardening was never quite the same. Status was no longer created by elaborate flowerbeds filled with the choice and the rare, by cut-work parterres or by perfectly trimmed topiaries, hedges and *allées*. It was created by broad lawns, groves of entirely natural trees, and mist-girt lakes, all suitably scattered with temples, bridges and towers. Colourful flowers were suppressed, or hidden away inside the walled garden or some discreet clearing in the woodland; they were not allowed to detract from the classical purity of the view.

In the newly sited flower garden, the formal parterre and its associated borders began to dissolve. The beds that replaced them looked alarmingly like today's island beds. Unlike those, they were not mostly filled with ericas and dwarf conifers, but had edges of trimmed or naturally trim plants, and a filling of mixed flowers. Some flowerbeds were designed to be living bouquets, and seem to have been quite densely planted, though the others retained the older system.

A flowing guilloche parterre design from W. Thomson's
*Handy-Book of the Flower Garden*, 1887

However, 'informal' beds of this type seem to have been common only in the most advanced and also rather grand gardens; most kept to straight borders of grass with long flowerbeds filled in the conventional manner, and small gardens nowadays are probably best treated like this. Even late into the century, urban gardens are shown with square or oval lawns, or even with a simple grass parterre (perhaps four rectangles of grass with paths between) and a flower border around the outside of the whole arrangement. The garden could be enlivened with large tubs of citrus trees or oleanders; perhaps even with a classical urn or some statuary.

Florists' gardens still had rectangular beds of hyacinths and tulips, ranks of anemones, and wooden stagings for dozens of pots of auriculas. Flowerbeds often had awnings put over them when their precious contents were in flower, so that the season of show wasn't shortened by rain or too much sun.

In fairly large establishments, the landscape movement would certainly show itself, if in some rather reduced way. If you feel that your garden needs something in the full Georgian mode, turn to the book list on p. 242.

Fruit trees for the grander household were either to be found on the kitchen garden walls, or planted in the kitchen garden 'slips' (a grassed area surrounding the walled garden). Some writers suggest an informal clumping of fruit trees, though most gardens seem to have stuck to a more sensible and regular arrangement. In lesser households, fruit trees might be espaliered to the house walls, or to frameworks dividing the vegetables from the flowers. Soft fruit bushes were often used for hedging inside the garden (gooseberries were common, partly because their prickly branches were good for drying clothes on). A few standard fruit trees would look nice on the lawn, and give somewhere shady to sit on hot afternoons.

In a century that saw such major changes in gardening fashion, it is difficult to assess how fast and to what social level the fashion carried. The parterre, even in simplified forms, and the wilderness seem to have vanished from at least some provincial gardens by the 1760s, as almost everyone tried to have the necessary clumps of trees, lakes, bridges, temples and the rest, even if it was all crammed into a single acre. Perfectly formal gardens survived in remote areas for far longer, and certainly many existed in the north and in Scotland well into the following century. Real cottage gardens seem hardly to be documented, though the 'cottage ornée' became popular towards the end of the century for those rich enough and with a Rousseau-esque turn of mind.

Popular eighteenth-century flowers include: most of the *Anemone* types we mention, aster (especially *Aster novae-angliae*), cornflowers (see *Centaurea*), crocuses, *Dianthus* (especially all the florists' sorts), erythroniums, fritillaries, perennial sunflowers (see *Helianthus*), helichrysums, double *Hesperis matronalis* (use the singles if you can't find the double), hyacinths, *Iberis*, *Oenothera*, many sorts of poppy (especially *Papaver rhoeas* and *P. somniferum*), *Primula* (auriculas and laced polyanthus are both essential), *Ranunculus asiaticus*, mignonette (*Reseda*), scabious, and nasturtiums (*Tropaeolum*).

Good roses for this period not yet mentioned include the gorgeous cabbage rose, *Rosa centifolia*, its small-flowered variant 'Rose de Meaux', the moss rose (*R. centifolia* 'Muscosa'), the wonderful 'Maiden's Blush', and the apple rose (*R. pomifera*).

Good bushes include: *Buddleia globosa*, *Chaenomeles speciosa* (late in the century), the marvellous wintersweet (*Chimonanthus praecox*), the two popular dogwoods (*Cornus alba* and *C. florida*), *Daphne collina* and *D. pontica*, the witch hazel (*Hamamelis virginiana*), *Hydrangea arborescens*, several kalmias (including *K. angustifolia* and *K. latifolia*), the stunning *Magnolia grandiflora*, *Rhododendron ponticum* (now such a scourge in eighteenth-century parks) and *R. maximum*, and a relative of the dreaded snowberry (*Symphoricarpos orbicularis*). Trees include several *Celtis* species, the delightfully elegant snowdrop tree (*Halesia*

Town garden formality of the mid eighteenth century; formality lasted in the park until the 1820s. Detail of a painting by George Lambert, 'St James's Park from the Terrace of No. 10 Downing Street'

*carolina*), the Lombardy poplar (*Populus nigra* 'Italica'), and the ubiquitous weeping willow (*Salix babylonica*).

Climbers should include the Dutchman's pipe (*Aristolochia macrophylla*), *Clematis alpina* (late in the century), *C. florida* and *Lonicera* × *americana*.

Plants for pots: camellias (*Camellia japonica*), canna lilies, brunfelsias, the lemon verbena (*Lippia citriodora*), frangipani, gloriosa lilies, *Plumbago capensis*, and various daturas.

In America, the formal garden, redolent of the seventeenth century, seems to have survived for much longer. Many Americans were ordering their garden plants directly from London, Paris and Amsterdam, but the losses in transit were always heavy and the garden flora 'improved' only rather slowly. Ironically, in the last decades of the century, many Europeans were frantically collecting American plants so that they could stay in fashion. This does not seem to have swayed American gardeners from their desire to have the latest auriculas, tulips and carnations from Europe.

Good flowers for American gardens include: double hollyhocks, helichrysums, China asters, white foxgloves, orange and yellow crown imperials, red martagons, *Narcissus telamoneus*, double tulips, tuberose, *Nerine sarniensis*, double white rocket (however did this survive the trip?), polyanthuses, China pinks, blue and white *Scilla peruviana*, double *Ranunculus ficaria*, aconites, cyclamen, *Lilium bulbiferum*, and tomatoes (these had been sent from Europe, though they originally came from South America).

Bushes like rosemary (the gilded sort had reached America, but not survived), and lavender were treated as tender, and even box was killed in harsh winters. Continuing attempts were made to increase the number of roses, but these seem to have failed. Only *Rosa alba* and *R. rubiginosa* seem to have been common, but some of the native species were beginning to appear in gardens.

# NINETEENTH-CENTURY GARDENS

So much happened to gardening in this century that it is difficult to condense. Gardens were seen again as explicitly contrived works of art, and heavily formal geometric layouts became the ruling passion for all classes of garden. By the mid nineteenth century, the characteristic grand garden was a French or Italianate parterre, with fountains, flowerbeds, terraces, sculpture and evergreen planting. Small gardens were just as heavily formal, crammed with as many elements of grand gardens as they could hold. Bedding schemes, perhaps the dominant planting mode of the whole century, began around the late 1820s, the beds shaped like crescents, stars, or the clubs, hearts, spades and diamonds of playing cards. The most popular of all, because it was thought to be the most pure geometric shape, was the circle. Some flower gardens consisted of tight jumbles of circular beds, though these cannot have looked especially inviting.

Regency flowerbeds, from Maria Jackson's *Florists Manual*

High Victorian gardens resorted to dense planting, though in numerous variations. We cannot deal fully with them here, but the main types were ribbon bedding, often used in long borders, plain bedding and carpet bedding. The first of these consisted of long stripes of colour, as in a ribbon, or fancy linear patterns (scrolls, guilloche or the ancient Greek key-pattern were especially popular). The main area was kept low, with plants either being trimmed or pegged to the ground as they grew, while a background was made using roses on trellis, or dahlias and hollyhocks. The parterre, or the more usual cut-out beds, were filled in the same manner, with stripes of colour surrounding a central ground (this ground itself was sometimes a mix of two or more contrasting species, surrounding a single 'dot' plant, perhaps a cordyline or a canna lily).

Plain bedding was rather earlier than the fancy sort, though it remained popular in humbler gardens. It was quite often carried out with hardy annuals, sometimes a mix of two species to give a more interesting look.

Carpet bedding is a phrase now used for all sorts of bedding, but in the nineteenth century, it was only used for quite specialized schemes using foliage plants. All sorts of plants were used, from echeverias and sempervivums to fancy grasses and pelargoniums, but whatever went into it, the flowers were always suppressed. The colours of the leaves provided the very subtlest schemes, entirely comparable to the oriental carpets on which the designs were often based. Not only could owners pride themselves on their superior taste, but the design was weatherproof, whereas the often garish schemes carried out in verbenas and calceolarias could be wrecked for weeks by an untimely storm.

In the nineteenth century, the old 'wilderness' once again reappeared, this time as the shrubbery. This was used in a rather functional way, often to screen the kitchen quarters from the garden or, in smaller gardens, to act as the external boundary itself. We are still left with the remains of these shrubberies, and almost every gardener will know what they look like. However, early and mid Victorian ones often looked completely unnatural; shrubs were widely spaced, and the whole bed often had a narrow outer band of brightly coloured bedding plants. The earth between the shrubs was carefully dug over every few months. Late Victorian shrubberies looked somewhat more natural, with the earth veiled with ivy, periwinkles or lungworts.

A sea-change began to come over gardens in the last quarter of the century. Hardy herbaceous plants, rather neglected in gardens in the later eighteenth century, and disregarded for much of the nineteenth, began to come back into prominence. This was certainly due in part to a quite strong reaction against the bedding vogue, starting in the 1850s and taken up with passion by William Robinson. Bedding schemes, however, didn't disappear quickly; in many gardens they co-existed with herbaceous borders, which themselves became grander and more accomplished as nurserymen and gardeners devoted their energies to the breeding and improvement of herbaceous flowers. By

A high Victorian parterre, designed in the mid 1850s and neatly bedded out,
at Stoke Erith, Hereford

late in the century, in grand establishments, there were often gravel walks with borders on each side fifteen feet deep and several hundred feet long; examples of ostentation just as extreme as those of earlier bedding schemes.

New influences were also felt in design, as a strongly historicist movement got under way. There were 'Dutch' gardens, with an emphasis on topiary, and 'Queen Anne' gardens complete with standard rose bushes and old-fashioned flowers. Architects like Thomas Mawson designed enormous and expensively detailed formal gardens, with wonderful pergolas, pools, elaborately paved terraces and clipped hedges.

The work of Edwin Lutyens and Gertrude Jekyll combined the best of both architecture and planting. Though most of their schemes were for wealthy garden owners, many of the principles can be adapted for more restricted circumstances. The layout should be formal, with small spaces centred perhaps on a tank of water, a sunken pool, or an attractive sundial. Paths need to be of carefully laid brick, tile, or cut stone (or a judicious combination of all these). Changes in level need to be accomplished by terraces, perhaps with drystone walls to retain the soil, linked by generously scaled flights of steps. Both steps, pool edges and wall heads need to be decorated with terracotta pots, filled with pelargoniums, maiden's wreath (*Francoa ramosa*), and white lilies or hostas. Planting must be carefully thought out in terms of foliage and colour. For the first time, gardens may have a colour theme; try schemes predominantly grey, white, lilac, gold or green.

Good Regency and Victorian flowers are legion, but every selection must include some of the following; agapanthuses, hollyhocks, *Amaranthus*, *Anemone hupehensis*, antirrhinums, *Aster*, calceolarias, campanulas (especially *Campanula lactiflora* and *C. pyramidalis*), chrysanthemums, dahlias, some sorts of *Delphinium*, *Dianthus*, the most attractive sort of *Dicentra*, *Galanthus*, hyacinths, irises, *Kniphofia*, *Lathyrus*, lilies, lobelias, various sorts of *Narcissus*, peonies (especially *Paeonia lactiflora* hybrids), poppies (especially the oriental sort), *Pelargonium*, penstemons and petunias, *Salvia* (the tender species), tulips, verbenas and, most important of all, pansies and violas.

Rose breeding really began in the early nineteenth century, and soon there were hundreds of gorgeous new hybrids. Consequently, the garden devoted to roses (once called a 'rosary' or a 'rosarium') is almost a late Georgian invention, and one that is still immensely popular. Regency and Victorian rose beds could be of almost any shape, though a group of wedge-shaped beds making a circle was always popular. The roses were all of types that did not need pruning in the way that modern ones do, so the final effect was rather attractive. Some of the varieties with floppy stems were grown in circular beds edged with wirework, and had their stems pinned to the ground so that they made a sort of bouquet of flowers.

There are innumerable roses from this period, including many of the loveliest. The ones we like best include: 'Belle de Crécy', 'Madame Legras de St Germain', 'Madame Plantier', 'Comte de Chambord',

'La Ville de Bruxelles', 'Madame Hardy', 'Fantin Latour', 'Tour de Malakoff', 'William Lobb', 'Boule de Neige', 'Madame Isaac Pereire', 'Madame Pierre Oger', 'Madame Alfred Carrière' and so on; there are dozens of equally fine ones to choose from. Look, too, for some of the 'Scotch' roses.

Vast numbers of attractive shrubs were introduced during the period, and soon became widely grown, including species of *Abelia*, *Arundinaria* and other handsome bamboos, *Aucuba*, azaleas (try the Ghent hybrids), *Buddleia*, camellias in all colours, though still in conservatories or camellia houses (try *C. reticulata* 'Captain Rawes'), ceanothuses from the western states of America, cotoneaster, escallonias, forsythias, fuchsias, hebes, all sorts of hydrangeas, jasmines (including the winter-flowering sort), magnolias, olearias, Osmanthus, many hybrids of *Philadelphus*, pieris, many beautiful hybrid sorts of lilac, rhododendrons in abundance, ribes, skimmias, spiraeas, viburnums.

Trees include many sorts of *Abies*, many maples, the famous monkey puzzle (*Araucaria araucana*), *Cedrus atlantica* and *C. deodara*, the infamous Lawson cypress, many sorts of juniper, spruce and larch, and various oriental species of *Prunus*.

Amongst the climbers, try *Actinidia kolomikta*, *Akebia quinata*, many sorts of *Clematis* (and most especially the Jackman hybrids, as well as *C. montana* and *C. tangutica*), many sorts of ivy, *Hydrangea petiolaris*, *Lonicera japonica*, the prodigious Russian vine (*Polygonum baldschuanicum*), the lovely *Vitis vinifera* 'Brandt', and most of the wistarias.

# THE COTTAGE GARDEN

The present-day image of the cottage garden is of somewhere wonderfully romantic and untidy, packed with old roses, antirrhinums, scented pinks and carnations, all grown since time immemorial. It seems to embrace quite a range of garden types. Some gardens claim to be cottage gardens, but have wonderful statues, flights of steps, balustrades and urns; others just have rusty chicken coops, tin cans as pots, and few flowers other than nasturtiums.

We intend to use the phrase to denote gardens that can be an attractive synthesis of any of the features of old gardens, and that can comfortably contain plants of all ages. For readers who do not want a 'purist' period garden, the cottage-garden idea, even if a sort of fantasy, offers a charming way to combine any of the plants we describe.

Gardens of the sort we have in mind are usually small, have simple layouts, with straight paths and planting outlines, but still manage to have sheltered corners for seats and pots, and arches for roses and other climbers. Large ones might just have a small orchard, planted up in a rather seventeenth-century way with roses, violets and strawberries.

If there is no room for an orchard, then the cottage garden should still use fruit species whenever it can; after all, nothing can be more

A real cottage garden, chaotic and tiny, painted by Peter de Wint
at Aldbury in 1847

beautiful than an apple, pear, plum, quince or medlar in full flower, whether free-standing or roughly espaliered to a wall. The fruit themselves, until you or the birds get them, are as good to look at as to eat. Medlars, mulberries and cherries have wonderful autumn leaves as well. In situations where conventional fruit trees are not suitable, use unconventional ones, like the cornelian cherry (*Cornus mas*), the sorb or wild service (*Sorbus aucuparia*), one of the filberts, or even the native bird cherry. Or try using the absolutely marvellous double-flowered wild cherry, popular in the seventeenth century.

The cottage garden, marvellous from late spring to autumn, is rather quiet in winter. Some gardeners try to fill them with exotic winter-flowering plants, or unusual evergreens. However, if your garden needs structural evergreens for winter form, is there anything nicer than bay, holly, yew and ivy?

Seats are essential, and anything that stands outside all year can form an important element in the garden's design. Seats give a sense of invitation to a small and enclosed garden, and a good centre point to a border. Stick, if possible, to old-fashioned materials, especially wood.

Apart from the cucumber-frame,
there is little in this cottage garden painted by J. Varley
in the early nineteenth century

Paths need to be at least three feet wide, and be made of good materials too. Bricks set on edge in a 'weave' pattern are excellent and do not need to be cut. Gravel is also good, and much better than crushed stone. (Bind gravel with one third part of earth; this stops it feeling like a shingle beach when walked on.) Stone flags are fine in rather grand gardens, and look wonderful in front of tumbling borders of flowers. Artificial stone ones can be quite attractive. Cement blocks are cheap and serviceable, but rarely look good.

Boundary hedges in cottage gardens look excellent in hawthorn,

holly or lonicera. Yew and beech are splendid, but are usually associated with grander establishments.

For lesser hedges, especially those bordering flower or vegetable
plots, lavender, rosemary and sage are all perfect. Box, once very
common, is tough, very effective, and easily grown from small
cuttings. There are several very handsome 'gilded' sorts. Hyssop makes
lovely informal hedges, and bees love the flowers.

For really low edgings, especially in the vegetable patch, parsley,
chives, alpine strawberries, silver or gold variegated thymes, and
marjoram are all splendid. Small flowers were once also used for
edgings; try using the many sorts of daisy, auricula and primula, and
even, if you can find enough, hepaticas.

Topiary is most effective when carried out in yew or box. The
simpler the form, the better it is. A peacock on a ball is about the
maximum of elaboration. Battleships, giraffes and elephants are best
left for others. If you don't want to wait for years before it is finished,
build a strong wirework frame in the shape you want, cover the
surface with wire netting, and grow ivy up it.

Herbs can be grown everywhere. While it is worth keeping those
that still have a use in the kitchen in a place of their own, many which
have lost their use can be grown in the general borders. The list
includes the lemon-scented balm (see *Melissa officinalis*), all the various
colours of bergamot (see *Monarda didyma*), southernwood (see *Artemisia*), curry plant (see *Helichrysum*) and golden feverfew (see *Tanacetum*). All the more pungent mints, especially the eau-de-Cologne
mint, look marvellous in big pots, and the plant will not then invade
your borders. We lodge them next to seats as well as the kitchen door.
The striped ginger mint looks by far the most handsome.

For warmer corners, or for pots, look out for lemon-scented
verbena (*Lippia citriodora*), the marvellous pineapple sage (see *Salvia*),
or the pungent tufted lavender (*Lavandula stoechas*).

However, it is the herbaceous plants that are the great strength of
the cottage garden. Grow them beneath fruit trees, or behind lavender
hedges at the side of paths. Modern planting 'good taste' likes drifts
of plants, rather than clearly isolated individuals, so aim for luxuriance.
Try to sort out which colours you like best, and stick to a reasonably
limited range. Remember that a 'blaze of colour' is only what garden
magazines tell gardeners that they need. It can be fun to look at for a
few minutes, but it is much easier actually to live with soft colours
that suit the cottage-garden style and integrate well with stone or

brick walls, tiles or thatch. It is often useful to keep plants with brilliant flowers (like those exciting shocking pink petunias or scarlet geraniums) in pots. They can then be moved around when you get tired of them.

For roses and shrubs, annuals and bulbs, almost anything from the preceding lists are fine in simple gardens. Few of them are in the least hard to get hold of, and almost all are perfectly easy to grow.

So, good luck; whatever sort of garden you have, or whatever you plan, and whatever old flowers you manage to find, we hope that you get as much pleasure from them all as we have from ours.

# 4 The Plants

In this chapter we have listed flowers by the Latin genus name. While we realize that this may annoy some gardeners, we felt, after much thought, that it was by far the simplest thing to do. Alas, there are problems with some of the Latin names too, but we have tried to use the most recent, and probably most correct, one. However, where botanists are in dispute (as they often are), we have chosen the name that we prefer (often the traditional one). Within each genus, we have listed the component species in whichever way seemed most useful both to you and ourselves. Again, we have tried to use the most correct modern name where possible. In quite a number of genera, particularly ones important in the garden, there is considerable confusion and argument about how many species actually exist, and of those that do, how they relate to one another. This becomes particularly difficult when garden plants are hybrids between two or more species. We have tried to make the situation as clear as possible, though some botanically minded readers may feel that we have over-simplified in places. To them we apologize. To deal rigorously with many of the genera we have covered would need a whole book for each genus. Perhaps one day we may have the opportunity to do just that; meanwhile let us get on with the plants we have . . .

One further point: we didn't feel that it was necessary to give the historical source for all our information, but we have used a number of gardeners' names quite frequently in the text. It seemed rather dull to have to give the dates for each time he or she was mentioned, so we give a brief biography (with dates), for all the most important writers on p. 239. We hope that you will soon remember that Gerard was a sixteenth-century author, Robinson a nineteenth-century one, and so on.

# ACANTHUS

Bear's breeches

Two species of this large and handsome genus are grown in gardens, both for their handsome foliage and for their rather grand spikes of hooded greeny-purple flowers. *A. mollis* seems always to have been the most popular, probably because it once had medicinal uses, though the other species (*A. spinosus*) had the nicer common name (Gerard called it the 'wilde or prickly Beares Breeches'), and rather more dramatic foliage.

Both sorts are native to Italy and Greece, and the leaves of *A. mollis* are said to be the source for the curling foliage at the top of Corinthian columns. Dioscorides says that *A. mollis* at least was grown in Roman gardens. It survived the fall of the empire and was still a garden plant when mentioned by Neckham in *De Naturis Rerum*, written in about 1200. Both species were still widely grown in European gardens by the mid 1500s, though Gerard wondered, a few decades later, if his readers might 'somewhat marvaile to see mee curious to plant Thistles in my garden . . .'

The plants do not seem to have been popular in the seventeenth century and, even in 1754, Philip Miller thought them only worthy of collectors' gardens – in spite of the widespread concern for Corinthian architecture. He even warned gardeners against their propensity for swamping, however tastefully, any plants growing nearby – a warning worth remembering today.

William Robinson extolled their virtues in several of his books, most notably in *The Wild Garden* of 1870; they can still be found in wild gardens, but also in rather grand herbaceous borders. However, don't be frightened of them; they can look marvellous in tiny formal gardens (especially in towns), but obviously look finest of all in front of a Georgian house with at least two Corinthian columns or pilasters.

# ACHILLEA

Sneezewort, nosebleed, yarrow, pellitory

Only two sorts were of much importance in the garden before the nineteenth century. These, both native to much of Europe, seem to have been cultivated at least since medieval times, probably as medicinal plants, though purely decorative ones existed by the mid sixteenth century.

### A. ptarmica

Most of Europe. Certainly in gardens by 1500, and probably long before. A double form was grown by Gerard (a few years later Parkinson said it was very rare). It obviously got over that problem, for Rea liked it excessively in 1665, and said that it was common. Today, things are better and there are several double sorts, with 'The Pearl' being perhaps the nicest. There are not enormous differences between them, so probably all will look authentic for any post-Elizabethan garden.

### A. millefolium

Europe. In gardens by 1400. The yarrow can be found wild in several shades of pink and reddish purple, as well as the more common white. Gerard grew one 'of an excellent faire red or crimson colour', as well as a double red form. He does not say if any of these were used to staunch wounds as they were in medieval England. A modern pink form like 'Cerise Queen' makes a good Elizabethan equivalent. The double form seems to have vanished.

### A. filipendulina

Caucasus. 1803. This is the most popular achillea today, with flat discs of rather murky yellow flowers. 'Gold Plate' is especially common, and is a modern selection.

# ACONITUM

Monkshood, monk's cowl, wolfsbane, helmet flower

A genus of beautiful and dangerous flowers, treated by all gardeners with respect. Some sorts have been used to poison arrows, to kill wolves or human rivals, even (in the minutest quantities) as medicine. One species (*A. anthora*) was supposed to act as an antidote to all the others, though oddly it never seems to have been popular in gardens, while many of the others are. All the species are very variable, and botanists find them confusing.

### *A. napellus*

Western and central Europe. In European gardens at least since medieval times; in American gardens since the seventeenth century. This
is the 'Blew Wolfsbaine or Monks Coule' described in Turner's *The
Names of Herbes* of 1548. It can be seen in innumerable illuminated
manuscripts and must have been a widely grown garden plant. Parkinson wrote 'yet beware they come not neere your tongue or lippes,
lest they tell you to your cost, they are not so good as they seeme to
be'. However poisonous, pink and white sorts were popular in the
seventeenth century (rare now), as was the blue and white striped sort
introduced from the Alps in the sixteenth century.

Typical forms of *A. napellus* have single stems of flowers. One
variant, with a branched pyramid of flowers, can still be found and
was a popular cut flower in the eighteenth century. All forms of this
species were popular American garden flowers by 1890.

### *A. septentrionale*

Europe and Russia. In gardens since medieval times. This is the yellow-
flowered wolfsbane (often found under the name *A. lycoctonum* or *A.
vulparia*), and though not especially spectacular in the garden, it seems
always to have had a following. It was especially popular in Victorian
herbaceous borders and flower vases. In the latter, it was often combined with the striped leaves of gardeners' garters (the grass *Phalaris
arundinacea*) and the droopy white plumes of *Aruncus sylvester*. We
find it works well with golden sage, euphorbias, and silvery pink old
roses. Plant catalogues list many named forms. Most of these are
modern, if not absolutely new, crosses between various species.

Many aconitums make sturdy and pestproof garden plants, teaming
excellently with ferns and hostas. Many are happy in quite deep shade
and very damp conditions. Don't plant any (even *A. anthora*, if you
ever find it) where small children might try it as a salad.

## ADONIS

Pheasant's eye, Adonis flower

A genus with several attractive species, with three Europeans (two
annual, and the other perennial), popular in gardens at least since the

sixteenth century. *A. annua*, red flowers having a dark red spot at the base of each petal, has been an occasional garden plant since the late 1500s. Commoner and more attractive is *A. flammea* (sometimes called *A. aestivalis*) which will give you a scattering of glossy blood red flowers on a mass of feathery green. The plant is from southern Europe, but was widely naturalized even in the sixteenth century; Gerard wrote that it 'groweth wild in the West parts of England amongst their corne'.

He thought that the yellow perennial species (much larger flowered, and much earlier in the season than the red-flowered ones) was a stranger in England. However it had become a common garden flower by the seventeenth century, and remained very popular well into the succeeding one. It is called *A. vernalis*, and is still worth having, especially by a path, or somewhere where its rather modest charm can be appreciated. All three species were common in American gardens in the nineteenth century.

The most showy garden adonis is the Japanese and Manchurian *A. amurensis*, which can be found in all sorts of gold and greeny-yellow doubles. It is not suitable, however, for any garden earlier than 1895.

# AGAPANTHUS

### Blue African lily

Really one of the classic plants for tubs or very large pots, especially if standing where the sheaves of strap-like leaves can make their full effect. The species are all South African. The flowers vary from deep evening blue to milky white, but do not despise the intermediate shades. Even the most mid-blue sorts are a valuable colour to have in August and September. Most sorts have flower stems that like to grow towards the sun, and so they sprawl away from nearby walls or shade. Give plants plenty of room.

Many of the easily obtainable hybrids are of very recent breeding, often lovely, and mostly tolerant of winter outdoors. The species first introduced has a long history. *A. africanus* was brought from the Cape about 1629, and is not hardy; it makes a handsome and evergreen plant, best in the conservatory during the winter.

A species more usually available is *A. campanulatus*, and is the one so often seen in photographs of late Victorian or Edwardian terraces.

Some strains of the plant are winter hardy in the south of England, though tough Scottish winters don't suit any of them.

### *A. praecox*

The commonest of all is *A. praecox* (still often called *A. umbellatus*); it is so vigorous that it has naturalized in the Scilly Isles. It exists in many forms, including a good white one. As it was introduced in the early nineteenth century, it is suitable for Regency gardens as well as later ones. In mild gardens, it can be planted in the open border (it looks good with silvery artemisias and old pinks, backed by the greyish pink foliage of musk roses). In harsh ones, keep it in tubs. Don't crowd young plants with other things 'for a bit of contrast'. Let them grow on by themselves until the roots have filled the pot, and the plants will then present you with thirty or forty star-bursts of flowers.

# AJUGA

## Bugle

Native. Now popular because of the vogue for even the most thug-like of groundcover plants. Even when Gerard was writing in the late sixteenth century, two forms were grown in the garden; the normal blue-flowered sort with green leaves (never in today's gardens), and a charming white-flowered one still worth growing. Plants were probably kept in the herb garden; they were in American ones too, from the seventeenth century.

A pink-flowered form was in cultivation by the same date (possibly another species, *A. genevensis*).

The white-flowered sort reappears in late Georgian flower gardens, but the now-popular red-leaved forms (sometimes with exotic variegations), all seem to be modern. Even the ordinary variegated sort, much nicer, does not seem to have been grown before 1900.

# ALCEA

## Hollyhock, holyoke, jagged mallow

The hollyhocks, sometimes called 'Althaea', tall and gorgeous, have a mysterious past. They have been in cultivation in both Europe and

Asia for so long that they have lost any connection with any known wild species. They exist only as garden plants. Even the name is mysterious, appearing more or less in its present form in the early middle ages.

The hollyhock is usually thought to be *A. rosea*, though some of its variants like the 'Antwerp hollyhock' with yellow flowers and large lobed leaves (a plant grown by Gerard, and nowadays often listed as *A. ficifolia*) may be hybrids with other species.

Of the more usual hollyhocks, Gerard grew singles in white, red and deep purple, and doubles in purple and scarlet; these were all in America by the seventeenth century. By the 1670s, in Europe, the colour range included various shades of pink. Early the next century, hollyhock seed was being imported from China, and some of the plants from that source produced much-admired striped flowers. Double-flowered sorts were popular in American gardens by the same date.

Hollyhocks, because of their height, seem never to have been grown in the parterre or flower garden, but were used either in the long borders flanking the walls enclosing it, or in the 'wilderness' area of seventeenth- and early-eighteenth-century gardens. Sometimes they were even grown amongst and behind the trees in the avenue to give late summer colour. Avenues were windy places, and gardeners even then complained of the need to keep the plants well staked.

The great age of the hollyhock really began in early Victorian Britain, by which time the flower garden had become re-established as the only true form of gardening. The hollyhock was taken up as a florists' flower, with lavish prizes (and, presumably, sales), for the best new varieties. Famous breeders appeared, like William May in Yorkshire in the 1840s, and Mr Chater (the most famous of all) in the 1880s. A mid-nineteenth-century way of planting hollyhocks is to use mixed colours at the back of a bed, with dahlias (see p. 114) in front to disguise the hollyhocks' ugly shins. By the 1860s the hollyhock was also widely cultivated all over America, and was thought of as an ancient cottage-garden plant.

Difficulties began to arise in the late nineteenth century, when rust disease began to decimate whole nurseries: it can still destroy plants in modern gardens.

Modern strains include various short-growing sorts which do not need staking, but which also do not have the stately romance of the traditional types. As with most florists' flowers, almost none of the vast numbers of named varieties now exist, although a number of seed strains from the firm of Chater can still be found – and are immensely attractive. If you need some for a Georgian garden, or an even earlier one, keep to suitable colours. Look round nearby gardens, and if you see something nice, beg a few seeds at the end of the summer. Plants are easy to grow.

If you want seed of some true species, either grow the attractive pink-flowered native marshmallow, *A. officinalis* (an important medieval garden plant but also much used in the eighteenth century, planted in the shrubbery, for late summer colour), or the interesting *A. cannabina*. John Parkinson liked that, and so may you.

## ALCHEMILLA

Lady's mantle

The common native plant (*A. vulgaris*) was called 'Our Ladies Mantel' by 1548, and was used by the druggist. The charming European *A. alpina*, with its deep green leaves trimly (even primly) edged with silvery hairs was only thought suitable for botanists' gardens.

Both these species are very much worth growing, but the lady's mantle nowadays so popular in 'cottage' gardens is *A. mollis*. This large and splendid thing, hard to have too much of until you find that you have nothing else, was introduced from Turkey in 1874, and so shouldn't be in any earlier garden. The enthusiasts' *A. erythropoda* (the small leaves have reddish stems) is more recent still, introduced from the Carpathians in the 1900s.

For early gardens, do try to find the wild *A. vulgaris*; it is much neater than the usual one, will seed itself around just as prettily and, even when you have too much, it will at least be authentic.

## ALLIUM

This is one of those genera with such a range of species that some provide essential plants for the kitchen and others, nowadays at least, are almost equally essential for the flower garden. Only a few sorts have ever made much attempt to appear in both places at once, and then only in the seventeenth century.

Several of the decorative types multiply with such freedom that gardeners have been rather wary of them for many centuries. Less rampant sorts, particularly the currently fashionable *A. christophii* and *A. giganteum*, essential in country gardens determined to show the best taste, are late-nineteenth-century Asian introductions now really achieving their first flush of popularity. Also fashionable are a number of smaller species; the marvellous *A. cernuum*, with flower-heads like little rocket explosions (from N. America about 1800), *A. caeruleum* (from Siberia and Turkestan in 1830) and *A. karataviense* (from the same places about forty years later).

If you have a mid- or late-eighteenth-century garden, you could grow the native *A. triquetrum* (in gardens by 1750), but look for the gorgeous *A. narcissiflorum*, perhaps the most elegant of all the smaller onions. It was in cultivation, at least by the discerning, in the 1780s.

## A. moly

Europe. At least since the sixteenth century. Although Gerard grew sixteen sorts of onion or moly, the 'golden garlicke' is the most decorative, with rather brassy yellow flowers and attractive seed-heads (best cut before the seed is shed). Eighteenth-century gardeners were rather lukewarm about it, perhaps because they were too busy to stop the seed reaching the soil. We are too, but in the right place it does not really matter having the hundreds of seedlings.

## A. cepa

Central Asia. Probably one of the earliest garden crops. There are innumerable sorts of onion, and two of them found themselves in the flower garden in the seventeenth century; gardeners of that age were fascinated by oddities and curiosities. The tree onion is certainly quite odd, with its vastly inflated flower stems topped by a cluster of small onions without a single flower. It retired once more to the kitchen garden in the eighteenth century, where it has only recently gone out of use. The tiny onion clusters were sold for pickling at Covent Garden as late as the 1870s. Seventeenth-century gardeners also grew an onion with corkscrew leaves, but that seems to have vanished.

ALOPECURUS, see *Grasses*.

# AMARANTHUS

A genus of annual species, many of which are great fun. They were important in sixteenth- and seventeenth-century gardens, and then once again in some of the showier Victorian ones.

Most are from the tropical world, particularly the Americas, and all like warmth and heavy feeding. Several were grown four to five feet high in the nineteenth century by adding one fifth fresh horse manure to the compost, and then watering them every day with pigeon dung water!

## A. caudatus
Love-lies-bleeding

South America. Still such a popular garden plant that it is a delight to discover that Gerard and Parkinson called it the 'Great Purple Flower-Gentle'. John Rea said that 'country women' called it by its present common name in 1665. It was grown in the parterre, but also in pots to decorate paths and steps, a use for which it is still very effective. There were three forms: purple, purple and green, and white; the first and last are still available, and very handsome indeed.

## A. gangeticus var. tricolor
Joseph's coat, coloured-leaf amaranth

It is quite as old as love-lies-bleeding, and vastly appealed to the rather harsh colour sense of Elizabethan and early Stuart gardeners. Plants must have been grown on hot beds, probably with some protection from the weather. Miller notes in the eighteenth century, and correctly at least for our garden, that plants do not put on much growth once they have been planted out of doors in a British summer, but since in his time gardeners managed to grow them six feet high before being bedded out, this cannot have made too much difference. It is difficult to imagine an eighteenth-century patron, sharpening the purity of his or her taste, admiring such a plant. The types sold today are very much the same as those of the sixteenth century. All were popular in American gardens by 1709.

The floramour is now in the genus *Celosia*. Again, present-day sorts scarcely differ from sixteenth- or seventeenth-century ones, and so it would be perfectly easy, if hard on the eye, to carry out a popular seventeenth-century summer bedding scheme of African marigolds

(*Tagetes*, see p. 219), and celosias which 'make a gallant shew in a garden'. Indeed. Celosias were popular American plants in the early eighteenth century.

The original 'amaranthus' of the ancient world is probably the charming annual (often still grown as an everlasting) called *Gomphrena*. It was popular in seventeenth-century wreaths, mixed with helichrysums and sea lavenders.

AMBERBOA, see *Centaurea*.

# ANEMONE

So many species of anemone have interested gardeners for so many centuries, that quite a few provide good period indicators, while others, always popular, provide none. Only two or three have been taken up by the florists: *A. pavonina* (often still called *A. hortensis* and, broadly speaking, comprising the St Bavo anemones) and *A. coronaria* (equally broadly, the de Caen anemones). However, the species have been selected for the garden, including *A. nemorosa* (the windflowers), *A. ranunculoides*, and *A. blanda*. From the Orient come all the 'Japanese anemones' so popular in Victorian and Edwardian gardens, the white and blue *A. rivularis* and many others.

## FLORISTS' FORMS

### *A. pavonina*

Star, broad-leaved, hard-leaved, St Bavo anemones

Southern Europe and Asia Minor. In gardens at least since the sixteenth century, and in oriental ones probably much earlier. In the wild, the flowers are scarlet, pink or purple. The plants were vastly popular throughout the seventeenth and eighteenth centuries, and even in the early years of the nineteenth century new sorts were still appearing (one firm listed seventy-five sorts in 1820). They were certainly far more popular than the de Caen types and, curiously, single and semi-double sorts were as much admired as the fully double ones. Parkinson grew thirty sorts, with a colour range including greenish orange, dark scarlet, lead red, purple, and all those colours striped with white. Later in the seventeenth century, following the familiar historical pattern for development in markings, forms with concentric markings were

A page of anemones from Parkinson's *Paradisus*, 1629

admired. There were also some gorgeous flowers with broad petals enclosing a mass of coloured filaments or petaloides, often in contrasting colours. These were the anemones that gave rise to the phrase 'anemone flowered' when applied to peonies, dahlias and so on.

Flanders seems to have been a centre of breeding for new varieties. Many reached London via the Walloon community. Rea wrote in 1665 that 'this common Anemone is by many Gentlewomen and others as ignorant, called Robin Hood, Scarlet, and John, and the Spanish Marigold ...'

### A. coronaria

Poppy anemone, de Caen, soft or narrow-leaved anemone

Mediterranean region to central Asia, with wild forms in red, blue, and white. In European gardens since at least the late sixteenth century. Parkinson grew almost thirty varieties, all of them single. Flowers especially admired had the boss, or 'thrum', of stamens in a colour contrasting with that of the petals. One grand-sounding sort had white petals and a red thrum; another, more subtle, had orange-tawny petals and a yellow-green thrum. In the late seventeenth century, the most expensive variety was aptly called 'the Perfect Curtizan', and had scarlet petals splashed with pink.

Curiously, single or semi-double poppy anemones were far more popular in Britain than the rather showier St Bavo types, whereas in continental Europe, the reverse was true. Nevertheless, British gardeners kept importing new types. By the middle of the eighteenth century fully double forms existed, mostly in either red or white, though blue and purple forms were beginning to come in from France (the doubles became known as St Brigid anemones). All were used for spring and early summer bedding, and the colours were mixed in the same way as for hyacinths and tulips.

By late Georgian times, hundreds of florists' varieties were in existence. Of the three hundred or so sold by nurseries, the best ones were valued at several guineas a root and had colour shadings of great beauty.

### A. × fulgens

A garden hybrid of at least early-seventeenth-century date. The richest vermilion and scarlet were the most treasured colours, a range scarcely expanded today. This is rather surprising, for the plant is a hybrid between the two foregoing species, both of whose colour ranges are wider.

As far as we can discover, no named florists' varieties of any of these anemones seem to exist. This is a tremendous loss, for the species absorbed enormous amounts of seventeenth- and eighteenth-century gardeners' time, and played a role in the garden quite as important as the tulip or the auricula. Worse, some of the basic types seem to have vanished as well. The forms found in modern seed and bulb catalogues are poor substitutes for period plants, but will have to do. For early gardens, it is worth weeding out unsuitable colours or, better still, marking special plants that you like, and building them up over several seasons (the roots are easily broken up once the plants are lifted), so that you can get exactly the look you want.

## NON-FLORISTS' ANEMONES

### A. appennina
Southern Europe. Perhaps mid eighteenth century. A lovely plant, with flowers of a soft yet glowing blue. Never widely grown, it was most popular from the 1890s onwards, as part of the 'woodland garden' ideal.

### A. blanda
Eastern Europe. Late nineteenth century. It is very closely related to the previous species, and new varieties continue to appear. All are lovely; 'White Splendour' is aptly named if you can plant it in quantity.

### A. nemorosa
Europe, including Britain. In gardens by at least the late sixteenth century. The plant is, even in nature, quite variable, though the oddities (sorts with flushed pink flowers, or with petals which are blue beneath) are rare. Gerard grew these, and also a double white (various lovely forms are still available) and a double purple (now, we think, vanished). It seems possible that all the 'antique' sorts may have been lost to gardens in the rest of the seventeenth century, for Miller was delighted to rediscover all of them, together with a double blue, and a large-flowered blue single, in woodland at Wimbledon. It is likely

that they were there because they had once been growing in the great garden once on that site.

Again, some of these forms got lost until rediscovered once more, this time at Pinner in the 1860s. One of them assumed the name of a great contemporary gardener (William Robinson), and still bears it.

Nowadays there are various named sorts of double white and single blue, indistinguishable from period sorts. They all are so lovely that they will look perfect wherever they grow – in a shaded part of the parterre, or in a woodland garden with rhododendrons and araucarias.

### A. ranunculoides

Northern and central Europe. Certainly in gardens by 1596, and probably much earlier. A charming bright yellow-flowered woodlander, though almost always grown, since the sixteenth century, in its double form. Not one of the garden's great plants, but still available and still worth having.

### A. hupehensis (*A. japonica* and others)

China and Japan. 1844 and later. In this case, the garden plant was sent to Europe long before the wild species from which it derived. The wildling was not found until 1908, whereas the Japanese garden plant, with purple semi-double flowers, was discovered in 1844 growing on tombs built on the ramparts of Shanghai. Robert Fortune, a collector of the very greatest taste, at once recognized its value, but got plants back to Europe only after hair-raising brushes with bandits and even pirate junks.

Once in cultivation, as is the plant's natural inclination, it spread rapidly. It was a common cottage-garden plant in Britain by 1849, and in America by 1870. Soft pink and perfect white forms were appearing in the 1860s, and new named sorts are still heralded today. Essential for every Victorian or Edwardian border, and certainly for any modern garden.

ANTHEMIS, see *Chamaemelum*.

# ANTIRRHINUM

Snapdragon, calf's snout, lion's mouth

Only one species (*A. majus*) has played much part in the garden scene, and though nowadays mostly treated as an annual, it is perfectly perennial (take cuttings in autumn), and was once widely propagated in named varieties.

It is native to south-western Europe and Sicily, though widely naturalized. In the wild the flowers are pink or purple, though some races have red flowers veined with yellow, or with a yellow throat. It may have been these plants that contributed to some of the most gorgeous of all snapdragons, popular in the nineteenth century but now apparently lost.

There seem to be no medieval records of it as a garden plant, though it was well known throughout Europe in the sixteenth century. Gerard and Parkinson grew purple, white, yellow and parti-coloured forms (Rea described the latter as white with purple feathering). Miller knew a similar range, but also seems to have grown the first properly striped one, much pre-dating the Victorian seed company who 'puffed' one called *A. hendersonii* (a fake species name) as the first ever striped snapdragon in the 1850s. By that date, most of today's groups of antirrhinums were fully fledged, from the nasty dwarf sorts used then and now for bedding plants, to ones with open and frilly flowers. However, by the 1880s, there were some wonderful plants to be had. The original *A. hendersonii* was striped like a carnation, with rose-pink stripes on a white ground. By 1887, the gardener could have orange striped with yellow, yellow mottled with crimson, white speckled with rose, or even cream with a violet belt behind the 'snout'.

All these were propagated by cuttings, though there were seed strains which offered approximations. We have not found anything comparable, though it is difficult to imagine that seedling descendants don't exist. Of the multitude of named double-flowered snapdragons, popular prizewinners at Victorian flower shows, no trace remains. They were sterile, and all propagated by cuttings, though today's seed strains are not too dissimilar if you feel like going well over the top.

If you do not like 'ordinary' snapdragons, look out for some of the species, such as the velvety-leafed *A. asarina* (sometimes placed in its own genus). This makes low tangles of greyish foliage, does well on walls, and produces fine crops of milky or creamy flowers, all yellow-throated. It has been grown, if not widely, since 1699.

# AQUILEGIA

Columbine, granny's bonnet

A genus packed with lovely flowers, many absolutely essential for any garden, let alone period ones. Before the mid seventeenth century, only one species (*A. vulgaris*) was grown in Britain, though it was grown in a multitude of forms.

A lost upside-down aquilegia,
from Gerard's *Herball* of 1633

New species began to arrive in our gardens once North America became widely settled. The Tradescants had collected, and were growing, one of the nicest of the new species by 1640, the glowing golden-scarlet *A. canadensis*.

10. The Plymouth strawberry, a wild variant of the native sort, popular in the early seventeenth century

11. *Eryngium alpinum,* grown since the late sixteenth century

▷ 13. *Dianthus* 'Damask Superb', perhaps eighteenth century

▽ 12. *Dianthus* 'Cockenzie', a charming Scottish pink; perhaps early eighteenth century

△ 15. *Dianthus* 'Sweetheart Abbey', a flecked variety, of seventeenth–century type

◁ 14. *Dianthus* 'William Brownhill', a heavily laced florists pink of the late nineteenth century

More arrived in subsequent centuries, until by the end of the 1800s breeders were experimenting with all sorts of crosses. Some Victorian aquilegia hybrids have long spurs and narrow flowers, and can still be seen in cottage gardens. They often have *A. formosa* blood in them and are very elegant. The striped columbine (often with white flowers streaked with pink and scarlet) seems to have vanished, though it was popular from the seventeenth century to late Victorian times.

Many twentieth-century strains of American origin involve *A. caerulea*. The long-spurred sorts, whether McKana or Scott-Elliott strains, are derived from it, as are the lovely clematis-flowered sorts developed in the 1930s, now becoming very rare.

Aquilegias cross with such ease that if you find something special, and want to save seed, keep it well away from any other columbines. Very special plants can be increased by division.

### A. caerulea

North America. 1864. The clematis-flowered sorts lack petals, and hence are spurless (rather like the 'starry' forms of *A. vulgaris*). They're extremely pretty and were originally available in white, blue and soft pink. We've not yet found the blue ones. The seed strain called 'Heavenly Blue' is derived from this species.

### A. canadensis

North America. In France from 1630, England from 1640. A plant so good that it is worth looking for the pure species, for many lesser columbines in dull red and yellow are given this name. The true species glows with intensity. It was an American cottage-garden plant throughout the eighteenth and nineteenth centuries.

### A. viridiflora

Siberia, western China. 1780 or so; the darker-flowered subspecies now widely grown was first distributed in 1825. One of the smaller columbines and early flowering, the green and brown flowers are at the least very interesting. It is not surprising that it was popular with artistic Victorian flower arrangers. William Robinson admired it in 1883.

### A. vulgaris

Much of Europe. Very variable in the wild; flowers violet, sometimes very deep, white or red, sometimes bicoloured. Single columbines, especially deep violet ones, can often be seen in medieval paintings and illuminations, or used as heraldic emblems. They appear in many early poems and stories, and even in some fifteenth-century cookery recipes (they were used as a source of colour – an alarming thought as all sorts are very poisonous). Double sorts were also widespread, at least by late medieval times, and there's one ancient illustration showing a plant very similar to today's 'Adelaide Addison' (it is probably a double variant of the bicoloured type mentioned above).

By the late sixteenth century, as well as singles in blue, purple, rose, purplish red, and white, there were 'starry columbines' in which the petals were suppressed, leaving a flat star-shaped flower, and 'rose columbines', in which the sepals are doubled and often with an attractive greenish tinge. Examples of these types still exist.

Gerard illustrates a fascinating upside-down aquilegia in which the petals are reversed, so that the spurs point forward instead of the more usual way. This was also popular in the eighteenth century, but we've not yet managed to find a comparable sort. Later in the seventeenth century only striped sorts were grown (plain colours were too ordinary). Striped sorts were still sold in 1862, though we haven't come across any survivors. The greenish 'rose' sorts were called 'degenerates'. They remained, even so, popular into at least the mid eighteenth century (Hill mentions what must have been gorgeous – a green and white one). It is difficult to find seed of good double, spurred forms. Most of them are suitable for any period garden, so have a look for ripe pods in friends' or neighbours' gardens. A few nurserymen offer the old 'starry' columbines (we've found them in red and white, and very pretty), but the following plants are more easily come by:

'Adelaide Addison'. A gorgeous blue and white double, with an offputting modern name, very similar to a medieval flower.

'Munstead White' (*A. vulgaris* var. *nivea*). Pure white and very vigorous, with large and beautifully held flowers. A Gertrude Jekyll selection, not all that different to earlier pure white forms, but very handsome.

'Nora Barlow'. Another recent name attached to an ancient type of 'rose' columbine – in this case a rosy-pink, with each sepal fading to green at the base.

# ARMERIA

Sea thrift, sea pink, ladies' cushion, sea cushion

Most garden thrifts belong to *A. maritima*, an exceptionally variable plant found throughout Europe. In nature, flower colour varies from purple to white, and includes various shades of red. The leaves vary greatly in width, and some races of the plant even make small shrubs. It is the neat and low-growing sorts that first came into the garden, probably in late medieval times. Parkinson writes that it was the first plant used to make the fancy patterns found in knot gardens, and was still in use as 'our ordinary thrift [used] to empale or border a knot, because it abideth greene winter and summer, and that by cutting, it may grow thick, and be kept in what form one list, rather than for any beautie of the flowers'.

Once knots went out of fashion, the humble but tenacious thrift remained as an edging to flower borders. In that capacity it was allowed to flower, so more interest was paid to the colour. Miller grew red and white sorts, both still to be found, and still making charming edges to paths and borders.

Not surprisingly, gardeners have looked at other species. The southern European *A. pseudoarmeria* (often known as '*A. latifolia*') was grown and lost by Parkinson (nice to know that it happened to him too), and is still occasionally seen. The large-scale and very attractive hybrids found in today's seed catalogues are closely related to *A. plantaginea*, a species grown by John Tradescant the Younger in the 1630s. The balls of pink flowers are held aloft by eighteen inches of remarkably wire-like stem. Well worth using.

# ARTEMISIA

This large genus has had representatives in the garden since at least Roman times. It is now wildly fashionable as it provides innumerable species with silver or grey leaves; indispensable in the garden as an easy means of avoiding errors of taste with the colours of flowers. In the past, such problems were of less importance, and artemisias were used in magic, in love potions (they don't work), in medicines, as moth killers, and as flavourings for endless beverages and foods. Interest in silver foliage developed strongly as part of the Victorian passion for bedding schemes, where white foliage plants that could be clipped were especially important. While several European artemisias were both ancient garden plants and suitable for these purposes, the most popular were *A. ludoviciana* (from North America) and *A. stelleriana* (Asia and America). Both were nineteenth-century introductions, Gertrude Jekyll being especially fond of the substantial white leaves of the latter. Both are still in use.

### A. abrotanum
Southernwood, lad's love, maiden's ruin, old man

So anciently grown that its place of origin is now lost, for it has been in gardens since at least the first century AD, and probably long before that. It is a lovely plant if kept in trim, with silver-green feathery leaves that have an aroma that some love, others detest. Its magical and medicinal properties were beginning to be discounted by the mid eighteenth century, though almost everyone still grew it; indeed, it was 'commonly propagated by the Gardeners near London, to furnish the Balconies and little Courts of the Citizens; for which purpose this Plant is well adapted, as it endures the smoke of London ...' It had reached American gardens by the seventeenth century.

### A. absinthium
Wormwood, absinth

Southern Europe. In gardens since at least the early Middle Ages. By late medieval times, the stories said that the bitter taste was the result of its having grown beside the path used by the snake to enter the Garden of Eden. It was administered to expel worms from the gut (hence one of its names) and poison from the blood. We do not know if the popular nineteenth-century potion, absinthe, had the same effect, whatever else it may have done. To keep moths away, bunches of dried stalks were hung in wardrobes and tapestries were whipped with the fresh stalks.

### A. arborescens
Mediterranean region and southern Portugal. Perhaps today the most fashionable species, and parent of several equally fashionable hybrids. An elegant plant with almost white leaves, grown indoors from at least the early seventeenth century, but found to be almost hardy in the middle of the eighteenth, at which time it was still a great rarity.

## A. pontica
Old warrior, small absinth

Central and southern Europe. In gardens from the early seventeenth century. A charming low-growing plant with fronds of white, threadlike leaves, and plumes of interesting but dingy yellow flowers. It runs strongly, and tends to get inextricably mixed up with other herbaceous plants. It looks well in elderly terracotta pots.

## A. vulgaris
Mugwort, moder of herbes, moderwort (mother wort)

Europe, including Britain. Probably cultivated since early times, and already with many vernacular names by 1526. It grew in American gardens by the mid seventeenth century. The wild plant is rather undistinguished, though plainly this did not worry the magicians and witches who were amongst its first users. In the garden, and in less exciting times, it had two very nice variegated forms, one in white, the other in yellow. Both were popular and widely grown in the eighteenth century, and may perhaps have been discovered in the previous one. We have found the white sort (of modest charm), but not the other. Pigeons decimate young shoots in spring, and need discouraging if you want to keep the plant.

# ASTER

A vast and complex group of plants, spread over much of the globe, with a huge number of species, an alarming number of which have been taken into the garden and further developed. Many of these developments are quite recent or are still in progress, especially amongst the ranks of Michaelmas daisies. We deal mainly with the basic species. Many are extremely tough plants, and have naturalized almost wherever they have been grown. Self-sown seedlings of Michaelmas daisies of all species can be found over much of Europe, and even the odd *A. macrophyllus*, with its coarse heart-shaped leaves and clusters of washy flowers has often completely taken over the wild gardens where it was planted by readers of William Robinson. It is excellent ground cover for the toughest places.

## A. alpinus

The mountains of Europe. In cultivation at least since the mid seventeenth century, and perhaps a few decades earlier. Wild forms have flowers in violet blue, pink or white, a range not much extended in the garden. It was a flower rather well suited to the parterre or flower garden, though of course it has become a popular rockery plant since eighteenth-century grottoes turned into nineteenth-century rockeries.

## A. amellus

Starwort

Southern Europe, especially Italy. Grown probably since Roman times, and the only important garden aster well into the seventeenth century. It was still grown in its pure form (flowers in red, white or blue) in Regency gardens, though by then largely supplanted by the American species. Nowadays the pure sort is hard to find, most varieties ascribed to it being of hybrid origin, like 'King George', widely popular after the First World War. It is worth growing if you can find it. The popular sort of Michaelmas daisy belonging to $A. \times$ frikartii should be grouped here. They began to appear in the early twentieth century as hybrids between $A.$ amellus and $A.$ thomsonii. Good new sorts are still appearing.

## A. novae-angliae

Michaelmas daisy

North America. Introduced in 1710. This is one of the most influential asters of the many introduced in the late seventeenth and early eighteenth centuries. It was found over much of Canada, and as far south as Virginia. Purple and pink forms were common soon after its introduction, and by 1818 it was a familiar sight in almost every garden. There is a wide range of selections and hybrids, mostly between this species and the following, and almost all developed this century. Many have the grey-green leaves of this species, and a similar colour range.

## A. novae-belgiae

Michaelmas daisy

Eastern North America, but now widely naturalized in all temperate regions. Introduced about 1710. This aster is part of a large group of very closely related species, but will also happily cross with many less related ones. It seems to have played a fairly small part in the garden scene until the later part of the nineteenth century, when plant breeders became interested in its possibilities. By the early years of the twentieth century, innumerable cultivars existed, in various shades of lilac, blue and purple, and in various degrees of doubleness and plant height. Many of these are now lost, and so some of the first Edwardian garden schemes devoted to them (Gertrude Jekyll was an early admirer) can no longer be re-created with much accuracy. Perhaps this is not too important, for the general look has not altered all that much in the intervening period. Many are inter-specific hybrids, nowadays of some complexity.

### *A. corymbosus* (sometimes still called *A. divaricatus*)

North America. Mid-1700s. Something of a rarity, even in the eighteenth century. It had a spell of considerable popularity in Regency gardens, and was then forgotten until revived (with every justification) by Robinson and Jekyll, for both the wild garden and the flower border. It has been forgotten again; a shame, because the cloud of tiny daisies atop wiry black stems (nice dried), contribute much to late summer and autumn.

### *A. tradescantii*

North America, particularly Virginia. 1632. As its name suggests, it was collected by John Tradescant the Younger in the wild, and grown at his garden at Lambeth soon after. It has a pleasant, if very modest, flower, that has always been grown by collectors, but is not really showy enough for less refined gardens. Its loose-branched sprays of spiky white daisies make an attractive foil to plants with bright autumn foliage or berries; they cut well, too. *A. turbinellus* is an amethyst-flowered equivalent of the same date.

  '*Aster chinensis*' now belongs to a distinct genus called *Callistephus*. As the old specific name suggests, the plants come from China and Japan. All are annuals, and many are spectacular. They began to appear in British gardens in the early eighteenth century, mostly via smart gardens in Paris, and then directly from their countries of origin a century later. They were popular in American gardens by 1740. Present-day seed catalogues are still full of them.

# ASTRANTIA

Masterwort

European plants of quiet beauty, often used as a foil for old roses, or amongst showier herbaceous plants (they are especially useful for toning down shrieking pink or amethyst). However, the flowers, or rather the groups of florets surrounded by a ruff of large jagged bracts, are worth looking at in their own right.

## A. major

(It is sometimes wrongly called *A. carniolica*, a different species.) Central Europe. In European gardens by the late sixteenth century, and in American ones a hundred years later. The flowers are mostly greenish white to pinkish green, with the colours subtly graded. Selected forms can be found with a dark reddish colour; rather gloomy-looking to some eyes. Something similar was grown in the mid eighteenth century, but Miller thought the plants neither useful nor beautiful. The plants are probably more widely grown today than at any previous period. The handsome variegated-leaf form is of recent origin.

## A. maxima

Eastern Caucasus. Introduced in 1804. A splendid plant, its flowers offering one of the most interesting shades of pink to be found in the garden. Probably more common now than ever before, and still not widely enough known.

# BELLIS

Daisy, daeyeseye, bonewort, brusewort, lesse consould

The common daisy of the lawn (one of several European, Asian, African and American species), is now made war upon and despised. Once it was a valuable herb used for cleaning or staunching wounds of various degrees, while the charming simplicity of its flowers made it a valued garden plant. Daisies can be seen strewn over the decorated pages of missals and books of hours throughout the medieval period. Over the centuries the basic species (*B. perennis*) has produced many variants, all of them prized since the sixteenth century, and still to be found.

The only other interesting species to make it over the garden wall is *B. rotundifolia*. From southern Spain and northern Africa, this is normally purplish red, though the form in cultivation is palest lilac, and late Victorian.

## B. perennis

By the late sixteenth century it existed with fully double flowers and in two forms; larger and smaller. There were red or white flowered ones, or ones with the two colours mixed. More extraordinary was,

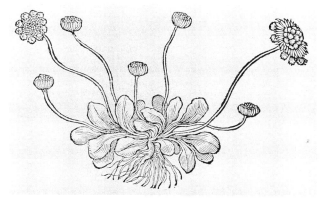

The charming hen-and-chicken daisy, still to be found,
from Gerard's *Herball* of 1633

and is, the 'proliferous' or 'childling' daisy, in which the flower (really a mass of tiny florets) throws out from its base up to a dozen or so stalks an inch long, each tipped with yet another tiny daisy. This one existed in several colours too, though the one most common today is pinkish with deeper flecks.

The range of ordinary daisies increased in the seventeenth century, with many forms speckled or streaked in various combinations of red, pink and white. There was even an 'abortive double green' one, which seems, not surprisingly, to have vanished.

In the eighteenth century, pure pink sorts evolved, as well as ones with crimson crested and twisted flowers. The late nineteenth century boasted a fairly nasty daisy with variegated leaves. Gardeners of the period also liked naming the variants, so although the 'modern' names of daisies are generally Victorian, the plants they are attached to are sometimes older.

In the sixteenth and seventeenth centuries, and for part of the eighteenth, daisies were scattered through the parterre and flower garden (and were no doubt happily hybridizing with the daisies in the grass, which they will still do if you let them). When 'wildernesses' became popular in the late seventeenth century, they were used to edge 'rural' walks (anything with a curve in them). In Victorian gardens, grand flowerbeds were often edged with the variegated daisy, while all the other sorts were to be found in cottage gardens, by the path edge.

European daisies had reached American gardens by at least the eighteenth century, and were cottage-garden plants in the following one. In the northern states, winter cold was a problem, and rare sorts like the hen-and-chicken or childling daisy were actually grown as conservatory or windowsill plants.

Nowadays there are a number of named forms, some of fairly local range, and some fairly modern. Seed catalogues list double daisies in various colours. Seed strains are all Victorian or later, and give large and rather blowsy flowers; fine, in lieu of anything else, for the loudest Victorian parterres.

'Alba Plena'. Possibly sixteenth century. A fine double white of great substance, rather broader in diameter than the ones in the lawn.

'Alice'. Probably nineteenth century, perhaps later. A quilled daisy, vigorous and fairly large, in a soft apricot pink.

'Dresden China'. Date not certain, often said to be eighteenth century, but if so, late. One of the smaller daisies, very double, and in a perfect soft pink. Very attractive indeed, and suitable for early Victorian gardens, if not earlier ones.

'Hen-and-chicken'. Perhaps sixteenth century. It is difficult to be certain that today's garden forms are of early date, as it is perfectly possible for the variation to occur at any time. When well grown, and with plenty of chicks, the flower looks very odd, but thoroughly charming.

'Rob Roy'. Nineteenth century. There are several plants circulating under this name, in slightly different shades of ruby red, but differing more noticeably in the degree of doubling. The most attractive ones are fully double and have no yellow eye. All are very much neater than the mop-heads from a seed packet.

'Robert' (or 'The Pearl'). Possibly nineteenth century. There are several slightly different plants under this name; all are tiny, with matching small-scale daisies, white and fully double. If you like bedding schemes, this is one to use for the most intricate detail.

'Aucubifolia'. Mid-1800s. A robust plant, the green leaves brightly flecked with yellow, the flowers best kept picked off. A novelty for high Victorian gardens, though not for the squeamish. We have not seen this plant, but believe it still exists.

# BERGENIA

Giant saxifrages

Ten species, all Asian. The first to be introduced was *B. crassifolia* from Siberia, so it is not surprising that it has become naturalized in parts of Europe. The plant was not especially popular until the late nineteenth century, and most of its varieties are modern. Another now-popular species (*B. cordifolia*) is also an eighteenth-century introduction from Siberia. Gertrude Jekyll loved the winter leaves, and put them in huge bowls mixed with Christmas roses or forced hyacinths. She even liked the summer ones, admiring their fine solid foliage, which she found useful for grand edgings to beds.

All the other cultivated sorts were introduced some time during the nineteenth century. Hardy forms of the Himalayan *B. ciliata* were available by 1820, though gardeners and breeders only started serious work on them in the 1880s. Early cultivars, if you happen to like bergenias, are 'Profusion' (1880), 'Progress' and 'Distinction' (both 1889). The varieties popular today, 'Abendglut' and 'Silberlicht', date only from the 1950s. Interest in the group continues apace, and posterity will no doubt collect forgotten sorts.

BRIZA, see Grasses.

# CALCEOLARIA

An extraordinary genus, mostly half-hardy. The most interesting species have curiously pouched flowers, some, even in the wild, decorated with bizarre fantasy. Calceolarias are one of the three or four genera that played an absolutely key part in Victorian gardens, in elaborate bedding schemes (usually providing intense yellow and bronze, sometimes scarlet) and in the conservatory, as well as in working men's garden clubs.

All the species come from South America, the first to reach these shores being *C. pinnata*, which arrived in Europe in 1773. *C. fothergilla*, which followed in 1779, is still widely grown and is lovely. Then a burst of new species turned up in Scottish gardens, sent home by Scottish emigrants (both in trade and religion) to that continent. A Mr Morrison, gardener to Lord President Hope, had four species in his glasshouse in 1829 and discovered a number of seed pods. Soon, he had distributed vast numbers of exotic-looking seedlings, forty of which were in commercial circulation by 1834. The whole bedding movement had just started, and the hybrid calceolaria and garden style became irrevocably linked.

New species continued to arrive, enriching the colours and markings of the hybrids, and by 1857 some of the original plants were thought of as 'old', and were even to be found in old cottage gardens.

Good sorts were easily propagated by cuttings, and most would happily overwinter under glass without much problem, especially if kept dry.

Calceolarias are still justifiably popular. The yellow shrubby sorts once so essential for bedding are still easily available, though the other shades are now rather scarce.

# CALENDULA

Marigold, Mary Gowles, goldes, ruddes

The common or pot marigold, *C. officinalis*, a plant, more or less annual, that has been in cultivation for so long, and is so widely naturalized, that its place of origin or domestication has been lost. Of the few other species, *C. arvensis*, a European annual, has only found an occasional place in the garden; odd perhaps, as the flowers of some strains are brown or violet.

References to marigolds are common in thirteenth- and fourteenth-century literature, especially the literature of doctors and cooks. It was a cheap, though flavourless, substitute for the saffron that flavoured many medieval dishes. It was also used to make a cordial thought good for curing depression (which seems to have been as common then as now).

Double sorts were popular by the late sixteenth century. Gerard describes the colour range of the ones he grew as 'of a light saffron colour, or like pure gold'. He also mentions a hen-and-chicken form, and says 'This fruitfull much-bearing Marigold is likewise called of the vulgar sort of women Jack-an-Apes on horsebacke ... for this plant doth bring forth at the top of the stalke one floure like the other Marigold, from which start forth sundry other small flowers, yellow likewise, and much of the same fashion as the first, which if I be not deceived, commeth to passe for accidens ...' He says, too, that it is not true from seed, in which he was deceived, for it is, and it is still to be found.

The seventeenth century saw no further developments, though 'the herbe and flowers are of great use with us among other pot-herbes and the flowers, eyther greene or dryed, are often used in possets, broths, drinkes, as a comforter to the heart and spirits, and to expel any malignant or pestilential quality gathered near thereunto ...' By this time, the marigold had also reached America.

In the eighteenth century, single-flowered sorts were used for flavouring (or at least colouring), butter, soups and stews. The doubles were kept to the flower garden, where they remain. Today's 'Art Shades' strain is a nice one.

CALLISTEPHUS, see *Aster chinensis*.

# CALTHA

Marsh marigold

Growing wild throughout Europe, it is only the double-flowered forms that have attracted gardeners much, though the wildling varies widely in stature and in habit. (Gerard mentions a dwarfish form in 1597, but it seems to have vanished from the garden thereafter.)

The story told by Clusius is that a double form, discovered near Salzburg in 1601, was grown in Vienna and then gradually circulated to gardeners throughout Europe. Gerard's editor illustrated it, but may not have actually seen plants. Parkinson did grow it, and thought it was marvellous. If you have a dampish border, it still is. There seem to be two double forms now, one full of petals, the other only half so. Why not grow the grandest you can find? Wild variants have recently started contributing to the garden, and there is now a single white, as well as a cream-coloured double.

# CAMASSIA

Quamash

In earliest summer, the camassias produce spires of narrow starry flowers (*C. leichtlinii*) or a low crackle of blue sparks (*C. esculenta*). None of them lasts for very long, but we always look forward to them, especially as they help to fill in the rather awkward gap between the late spring flowers and the delights of midsummer. All species are from North America, the roots of *C. esculenta* having once been an ancient and important food source for the indigenous Americans (we've not yet tried them). It was introduced here in 1827, and is now available in a number of forms. The rather grander *C. leichtlinii*, like most plants from the American wild west, was introduced in the 1850s. There are some gorgeous dark blue forms, as well as a good cream single, and an exceptional cream double.

Surprisingly, none have become really important garden plants, even though they are so tough that they will naturalize in grass or light woodland. They are perfect for upmarket wild gardens with an Edwardian or Victorian flavour.

# CAMPANULA

Bellflower

An enormous genus, only part of which has, even now, entered the garden. A handful of attractive and easily grown species have been grown since medieval times. They are all important garden plants, and one species even had its flower spikes trained into a sort of floral topiary. All were popular in America in the nineteenth century.

A few recent introductions are suitable for Victorian rockeries or alpine houses; two widely grown and pretty species, *C. portenschlagiana* and *C. porscharskyana*, were introduced from Yugoslavia in the 1880s; the charming and not quite hardy *C. isophylla* came from Italy at the same date.

### C. glomerata

Native. Showy enough for Elizabethan gardeners, who grew the unaltered wildling. A lovely white form, still to be found, was grown by the mid eighteenth century, and a hundred years later a double purple form (now apparently lost) was a common cottage-garden plant. A couple more forms are available today. All are attractive, especially in cramped situations where they do not run too vigorously. The white one is particularly telling at the front of a shady border.

### C. lactiflora

Caucasus, western Asia. 1814. Widely naturalized. Fashionable country-house flower gardens have used this species almost from its introduction. In nature the colour is fairly variable, and the smoky grey forms have been as popular as the more obvious blue ones. It was a popular cottage-garden plant by 1852, though either fashion or subtlety had hit it by 1872, when a writer in the *Gardeners' Chronicle* said that it was almost no longer to be seen. A good plant to follow on after and behind old roses, but it's essential to remove ripening seed-heads, even if that means throwing away some open flowers.

### C. latifolia
Great throatwort or giant throatwort

Native. Elizabethan and early Stuart gardens grew them in blue and, perhaps more telling, white. Both colours are still popular. Its toughness in the face of competition and difficult conditions make it a most elegant plant for wild and woodland gardens. We found the white one among the nettles when we took over our seventeenth-century walled garden.

### C. medium
Coventry or Canterbury bells

Much of southern Europe. Widely naturalized. This biennial sort, associated with two cathedrals (Coventry bells is the earlier name), has been grown at least from the days of their first building, and possibly long before. It may be a Roman introduction, perhaps as a food plant (the fleshy tap root is edible). Purplish-blue sorts were popular in medieval times. The white one seems to be seventeenth century, the pink forms nineteenth. The vastly inflated corollas of present-day strains seem to be a nineteenth-century innovation – earlier plants were more elegant. Some now lost eighteenth-century Canterbury bells were striped in blue and white. The 'Calycanthema', or cup-and-saucer types are, once again, Victorian novelties, though all sorts of modern Canterbury bells are far too inflated. If you save your own seed and want early-looking types, select narrow-flowered plants for a season or two.

## C. persicifolia
Peach-leaved bellflower, paper flower

Europe and western Asia. Sixteenth century or earlier. The lovely single blue, milky white or pure white forms look elegant in any garden, and were already popular when they were first recorded. John Rea wrote that he had heard of doubles in each colour, but that they were so rare he had not yet found them. This must have worried him, for he added 'if there be any such'. There were; they were well known by the mid eighteenth century, and had almost ousted the singles by 1770. Six varieties were common well into the nineteenth century – including some large-flowered single sorts heralded as new today (so 'Telham Beauty' will look fine).

The doubles need good soil and division every few years to flower well. The exceptionally pretty cup-and-saucer types seem impervious to bad treatment, and are of fairly recent origin.

## C. pyramidalis
Chimney bellflower, steeple bellflower

Northern Italy and north-western Balkans. Perhaps the most interesting, and certainly the largest of the garden campanulas. It was already well known in the late sixteenth century and has only really dropped out of favour in the last fifty years, though its 6–8 ft spikes of blue or white flowers are still occasionally seen in grand drawing-rooms or conservatories. In the 1820s it was almost the only campanula in the garden; few others seem to have been anything like as popular. Individual flowers will last for ten days or so if kept away from bees, but only a day or two if pollinated. It is not, therefore, an especially good plant for the open garden, however wonderful indoors.

◁ 16. *Dianthus* 'Madonna', modern and heavily perfumed

▽ 17. *Dianthus* 'Old Feathered', an early-seventeenth-century
type

△ 19. *Dianthus* 'Earl of Essex', a fine, sprawling,
nineteenth-century variety

◁ 18. *Dianthus* 'Allspice', an excellent modern garden
pink

21. *Lavandula stoechas*, stickadove, grown at least since the sixteenth century

20. *Polemonium* 'Lambrook Mauve', a hybrid from nineteenth-century introductions

22. A lush planting of nineteenth-century introductions at Crathes Castle, Aberdeenshire

If the central spike of flowers is removed when young, strong side shoots soon develop. These were sometimes trained to fans of wire or cane to make window or fireplace screens, or even around hoops or wire globes, but a well-grown and untortured plant in a twelve-inch pot makes a spectacular sight. They're easily grown from seed, flowering in the second summer, or they can be increased from rooted offsets.

Nettle-leaved bellflower (*Campanula trachelium*), from the *Botanical Magazine*, 1791

## C. trachelium
Nettle-leaved bellflower, throatwort, greater Canterbury bell, bats in the belfry, hawkesort

Native. Large numbers of common names often indicate the antiquity of garden plants and this one, with pendent and rather narrow bells of purple-blue or white, has been in cultivation since at least the

sixteenth century. Double forms in both colours are quite as old –
though the double white is now extremely rare (we have only just
found it).

# CARDAMINE

Lady's smock, cuckoo flower

Only *C. trifolia* and *C. pratensis* have really entered the garden, the
former on and off since the sixteenth century, the latter continuously
from at least the same date. The only form widely grown is the
double-flowered form of *C. pratensis*, a most lovely thing, even though
described in Hill's *Eden* as a 'Wantonness of Nature in a wild plant of
our Meadows'.

The flowers are usually a soft purple, though various other shades
were appearing by 1849, and various slightly darker sorts can still be
found. None has ever had a distinct name.

It has been widely grown in gardens of all classes since at least the
middle of the eighteenth century, was thought fit for the choicest
gardens in Regency times and was a popular cottage-garden plant in
Victorian ones.

Damp, shady sites suit it perfectly and, in its modest way, it will
soon colonize large areas. It will grow slightly less well in full sun,
but not at all in drought. In late-nineteenth-century plantings it looks
wonderful with hostas, ferns and lilies.

CARDIOCRINUM, see *Lilium*.

# CATANANCHE

Cupid's dart, buck's horne welde

The only species in cultivation, *C. caerulea*, is a native of southern
Europe and, with its sky-blue petals and silvery rustling bracts, it
is not surprising that it has been grown since at least 1596. For
some reason, Gerard placed it, quite absent-mindedly, amongst the
woads, like them to be used with honey to purge 'phlegme and choler
by the stools'. A lovely plant for late summer, growing happily
amongst shrubs or herbaceous perennials; the abundant flowers

shimmer atop tall wiry stems. They are often suggested for drying, though do remember that the petals shrivel away immediately, leaving you with a cone of papery and brown-tipped scales.

Seed-grown plants (Gerard got his from Padua; you can get yours from almost any seed catalogue), are usually single. Double sorts were grown in the eighteenth century. They must have been lovely, but seem to have vanished. They were propagated by cuttings. Now, though, there are variously coloured singles to be found, perhaps hybrid, though all are rare and of the late nineteenth century.

CELOSIA, see *Amaranthus*.

# CENTAUREA
Cornflower, blue bottle

A vast genus offering some plants with beautiful flowers, others with handsome foliage, annuals and perennials. The lovely annual sweet sultan, or sultan's flower, which, Parkinson wrote, 'is but lately obtained from Constantinople' and which became immediately popular, is the only scented sort. It is now correctly placed in the genus *Amberboa*.

Of the true centaureas, all the ones grown for their foliage date, in general, from the nineteenth-century interest in that aspect of gardening. The white-leaved *C. ragusina* was known in the eighteenth century, but only became *the* white-leaved bedding plant in the 1850s. (Now everyone uses the hardier *Senecio cinerea*.) The silvery *C. gymnocarpa*, often listed in seed catalogues today, dates from 1858.

## C. cyanus
Cornflower

South-eastern Europe, now widely naturalized. This handsome annual was popular in Tudor gardens, with dark blue, white and violet forms taken directly from the wild. Red and pink ones were grown by the early seventeenth century. All are available today, but some of the simple but intense blue ones are so handsome that there is rarely any point in using anything else.

### C. montana

Perennial cornflower

Mountains of Europe, but widely cultivated and naturalized. In gardens since at least the sixteenth century, and popular ever since. The present colour range, embracing white, various pink shades, and pure blue, does not seem to have changed much over the centuries; all are lovely flowers for borders.

### C. macrocephala

Caucasus, 1805. A vast and rather coarse plant which produces equally large-scale golden-yellow thistles, which attract and drug large numbers of bees. Spectacular when in bloom, but the show is soon over, leaving the wreck of a plant behind. Older, if you want a yellow centaury, is the Persian *C. suaveolens* of the seventeenth century.

### C. dealbata

Caucasus, 1804. A charming light-pink-flowered cornflower, now widely naturalized in Europe, and well worth growing in Regency gardens.

CEPHALARIA, see *Scabiosa*.

# CHAMAEMELUM

### C. nobile (still often called *Anthemis nobilis*)

Camomile

Western and northern Europe. In gardens since ancient times. One of those useful but modest plants that has always been surprisingly popular. Even in the thirteenth century it was used both as a medicine and as a turfing plant. For the former purpose, the single-flowered sort was the most potent, though the double has always been the most widely grown. It was in every American garden by the seventeenth century. In Europe, even in the 1850s and 1860s, it provided a popular tonic in 'camomile bitters', and a flavouring for both beer and sherry. Many acres were devoted to it outside London, and tons of flowers were harvested and kiln-dried every year.

Its scented leaves make it a good plant for turf seats; it makes a reasonable path, but looks best of all bordering one, softening the edges with gentle greenery and pretty double white flowers.

# CHEIRANTHUS

Wallflower, wall gilliflower, cheiri, heart's ease

Mediterranean Europe, especially variable in the Aegean. Introduced to northern-European gardens perhaps by the Romans, certainly by the Normans. It was widely naturalized in this country by the time Gerard wrote that the wallflower 'groweth upon bricke and stone walls, in the corners of churches everywhere as also among rubbish and other such stony places. The double wallflower groweth in most gardens of England.' It reached America with the earliest settlers, though by the 1850s it was thought rather tender, and was over-wintered under glass. Many of the modern garden wallflowers wander between this genus and *Erysimum*. The true wallflower is *C. cheirii*. Early references to it are easy to miss, for the plant was variously called violet, heartsease, gilliflower and even leucoium! Because it prospers in the tough conditions offered by stone walls, it was, from the fourteenth century, a symbol of faithfulness in adversity, though in more recent times to call someone a 'wallflower' has been a minor insult.

## SINGLE FORMS

Flowers in yellow, brown-red or the two colours striped together were common in Elizabethan gardens. The colour range increased slowly; straw-coloured and rust-red forms were available in the eighteenth century, and white, scarlet and reddish-black were popular in Victorian gardens. One, 'The Negress', the colour of a ripe mulberry, was so popular in 1852 that plants cost 5s. each – a large sum. Good forms were often kept semi-perennial by removing faded flowers. Varieties with variegated leaves (both 'silver' and 'gold') were popular in the mid eighteenth century, but seem to have been lost. Modern variegated plants all belong to *Erysimum linifolia*.

## DOUBLES

Late sixteenth century, perhaps earlier. At least one variety of that date seems still to exist. They were exceptionally fashionable in Georgian and Victorian gardens, and many seed strains existed that yielded good percentages of double-flowered plants. Miller derided the gardeners' belief that sowing seed at full moon yielded a better proportion of doubles. Seed strains of doubles are rarely commercially available today and the double wallflowers that exist are propagated by cuttings. Even in Victorian times, choice doubles were propagated in this way, seed-propagated sorts being supposed to have rather poor flowers. Grand-sounding plants in double black, scarlet, white and green all seem to have vanished.

'Harpur Crewe'. Though named after a mid-Victorian divine, the plant is well illustrated in Parkinson's *Paradisus*, and seems to have been widely popular in his day. Its abundant and deliciously perfumed flowers kept it popular at least until the mid eighteenth century, but presumably the Revd Edward Harpur Crewe had to rescue it from oblivion a century later. Plants need some winter shelter in cold and exposed gardens, and it is always worth having a few cuttings under glass. Plants available as 'Baden Powell' and 'Chevithorne' are so similar to 'Harpur Crewe' as to be scarcely worth growing.

'Old Bloody Warrior'. The colour of dried blood, double and heavily perfumed, wallflowers like this have been grown since the sixteenth century. This may well be a plant from that date. The flowers are widely spaced; in seed-grown sorts they are closer together. Plants from modern seed strains of doubles are difficult to propagate from cuttings, whereas this one is easy. Try it with nineteenth-century flamed tulips or better still with *Tulipa* 'Acuminata'.

'Miss Massey'. An exceptional flower, very double indeed and a lovely deep and warm yellow. She has a strong constitution and seems perfectly hardy, though as a precaution we overwinter a few plants under glass (plants flower wonderfully in the conservatory). A large double yellow similar to this is described in the seventeenth and eighteenth centuries.

# CHELIDONIUM

Greater celandine, swallow-wort

The only garden species, *C. maius*, is a common native throughout most of Europe, but its yellow flower and ochre yellow sap (once used to sharpen the sight), ensured that it was in gardens by at least the fifteenth century. In the wild, the leaf form is very diverse, and unusual variants have been collected since the early seventeenth century. The first double-flowered form seems to have been found by John Rea, at some time in the mid-1600s; he wrote that 'it differeth not at all from the common weed which grows in every hedge ... but onely that the Flowers of this are thicke and double; this Plant I found wild many years since, and setting it in my Garden, it much increased ... [I] am confident that most of the plants that are in England, came from that Root which I found.'

The plain double form still exists and is remarkably attractive but other, and even prettier, forms seem to have been found in the following century. Philip Miller describes an oak-leaved form with single flowers, but with petals divided into yellow fringes. He also grew an even nicer plant, with divided leaves as well as flowers. We grow yet another form, with laciniate leaves, and double laciniate flowers as well. Our one is splendid, as are the others, in rich soil in a fairly out-of-the-way part of the garden, where the plant's exceptional capacity for producing seeds isn't a problem.

# CHRYSANTHEMUM

The flower-show chrysanthemum, probably a complex hybrid between various species including *C. indicum* and *C. sinense*, is a late-eighteenth-century introduction. Before its arrival, the genus *Chrysanthemum* had already contributed many fine garden plants, all still admired. New developments continue.

## *C. segetum*
Corn marigold

Europe, probably introduced in Britain. An annual, well known in sixteenth-century gardens. By the eighteenth century it existed in various forms, white or yellow, with single, double or quilled petals. The double sorts were used as pot plants in 'Pleasure-gardens and Court-yards', and grew rampantly. They were propagated by cuttings, but seem to have vanished.

## C. coronarius

Southern Europe, and in gardens by 1629. Another rampant annual up to four feet high. The flowers had variations similar to the corn marigold.

## C. frutescens

Paris daisy, marguerite

The Canary Islands. In European gardens by the late sixteenth century. Introduced to Britain from Paris in the late seventeenth century, hence its common name. A marvellous and almost hardy plant for large tubs or vast earthenware pots, especially for those set along terraces or up steps. However, take care which variety you grow. Even as late as the mid nineteenth century, only the single white form was in cultivation, and that not widely. Nowadays, yellows and pinks, single and double, can all be found; they're almost modern florists' flowers on the continent of Europe, though scarcely yet in Britain.

C. parthenium, see Tanacetum.

## C. coccineum

Pyrethrum

Caucasus and Persia. 1804. The plant from the wild is an attractive dusty pink, and worth growing if you can find it. Nothing much seems to have happened after its introduction until it was taken up by the plant improvers at the end of the nineteenth century. In the early years of the following one, new varieties began to appear with flowers in a much fancier colour range and enlarged size. New forms continue to appear, most making good garden plants for modern gardens.

## C. leucanthemum

Marguerite, ox-eye daisy, moon daisy

A common perennial weed of the fields, native to all Europe. It was a favourite of medieval gardeners, and many contemporary references to daisies in fact mean this plant. Since that burst of fame, it is once again a weed.

## C. sinensis × indicum

The chrysanthemum. It probably originated in China, the plant being cultivated in that country probably long before 500 B C. Exported to Japan about A D 800, and to Holland in the late seventeenth century.

The first plants were soon lost. A few purple varieties reached Britain in 1790, though it is possible that these had been imported from Marseilles, which city they had reached a few years before. In Britain, they first flowered for a Mr Colvil of the King's Road in London, causing tremendous excitement.

In the early nineteenth century, new varieties began to arrive directly from China, first sent by Sir Abraham Hume in 1808. Between 1816 and 1823, seventeen new sorts were added. Experiments in crossing soon began, and by 1834 there were fifty varieties to be had, at least for those who could afford them. The range of types had increased dramatically, comprising singles, doubles, quilled and ranunculus-flowered types in rose, salmon, pink, yellow, buff, lilac and white. The first chrysanthemum society was formed at Stoke Newington in 1846, and society formation spread as enthusiasm for the plants increased. At shows, growers produced some incredible plants. A Mr Bowler of Ipswich won all the prizes with a plant in a sixteen-inch pot; it was twenty-seven feet in circumference and carried over a thousand flowers. The Chinese would have been horrified; they only allowed their plants four or five perfect blooms.

All the early introductions of chrysanthemum were of Chinese origin, and all had tightly incurved petals. The Japanese had developed their own distinctive plants, with a rather shaggy look, and the petals reflexed or only loosely incurved. These remarkable flowers began to arrive from Japan in the 1860s and caused yet another sensation. A few years later, these had been crossed with the Chinese types, giving a whole new range of flowers and plant forms. The variety count leapt to seven hundred.

Chrysanthemums could be tall or dwarf, and could be grown for vast specimen blooms or for showers of tiny ones. Soon whole gardens were devoted to them, and garden magazines of the 1870s often give planting plans for easily obtainable types.

Every cottage had at least some chrysanthemums by 1859, and almost every London garden was full of them, for they seemed not to mind the awful smoke of early autumn.

## GROUP SUMMARY

Not before 1790: quilled, feathered or tightly incurved blooms
Not before 1846: pompon types
Not before 1856: anemone-flowered types

Not before 1862: reflexed blooms
Not before 1890: early-flowering, spray chrysanthemums.

CHRYSOPLENIUM, see *Saxifraga*.

# COLCHICUM
Autumn crocus, meadow saffron, upstart, naked ladies

Any group of bulbs that not only produces handsome flowers, but flowers 'out of season' as well, often without any leaves being visible, must have fascinated all early gardeners with a passion for 'curiosity'. The pleasure still holds, and autumn crocuses are still very valued garden flowers.

Many of the species are extremely variable, and not always clearly distinguishable from one another. However, the common European sort *C. autumnale* does not grow in Turkey, so the sorts popular in sixteenth-century Constantinople, which eventually arrived in western Europe, were probably developed from some of the spectacular species of Asia Minor.

However, the wild European meadow saffron is itself very variable, producing flowers in many shapes, and in all shades of pink and purple, and in white. Some even have petals with a chequerboard of colours (called 'tessellated' by the botanist). Double forms can easily be found in the wild. Extracts from the plant had been used in medicine since at least Roman times (and not only for legitimate purposes; slaves took saffron potion to make themselves sick so that they could 'dog off' work; perhaps no one noticed if they overdid it and poisoned themselves terminally). It was so widely grown by interested gardeners that large numbers of variants were in cultivation in the sixteenth century.

Early descriptions and illustrations are rarely good enough to allow easy identification of the plants they describe, so it is difficult to know exactly what species gardeners grew. It confused them too, Parkinson wrote, rather as a way of getting round this problem, 'whereof we have some faire double flowers very delightful to behold, and some party-coloured both single and double so variable that it would make anyone admire the worke of the Creatour in the various spots and stripes of these flowers'. Modern taxonomists express similar sentiments. Both Gerard and Parkinson had a few plants brought from the Turkish capital, though these were almost certainly already garden hybrids involving *C. speciosum*, *C. variegatum* and *C. byzantinum*. A few decades later, Rea suggests that gardeners ignore the plain and single-petalled colchicums altogether, growing only tessellated and double varieties. However, he did have a grand 'great' double, which may have belonged to yet another oriental species.

By the middle of the eighteenth century, the range had rather contracted, *C. autumnale* being grown only in its white, double lilac, and two chequered forms. Various other species were still just about grown, including *C. byzantinum* and *C. bivonae* (Miller's 'broad-leaved' colchicum).

Many of today's grandest colchicums are hybrids, and sometimes show it in their rather blowsy flowers. In old gardens, stick to chequered flowers, or the smaller doubles. For Victorian wild gardens, or pieces of decorated woodland, try *C. speciosum*, in its varieties Rubrum or Album, both raised by Backhouse of York.

CONSOLIDA, see *Delphinium*.

# CONVALLARIA
Lily-of-the-valley, lily convally, may lily, ephemera

The only species in cultivation is *C. majalis*, a common native plant throughout much of Europe, temperate Asia and northern America (where it was popular in seventeenth-century gardens). In parts of central Europe, it is common to find plants with soft pink flowers. These were in British gardens by at least the late sixteenth century, but the marvellous smell of the ordinary white form had ensured the plant's presence in gardens since at least 1000 BC. Throughout medieval Europe, flowers were used to adorn Lady chapels and statues of the Blessed Virgin. Equally important, and as with many attractively and headily perfumed flowers and leaves, an extract (the flowers were distilled in water or brandy) was used to cure headaches, hysteria and faintings. This use persisted into Georgian times.

With such an ancient plant, various 'curiosities' exist, as would be expected. Gerard grew both the pink and white-flowered forms, but had not got hold of red-flowered plants. Seventeenth-century British gardeners admired the pink sort the most, and it is certainly very pretty. By the mid eighteenth century, the red one was common, but so was an odd-sounding sort with purple-striped flowers. By 1770, there were two double sorts grown, one with white, the other with striped flowers. The double white can still be found, though it has little elegance. A century later, gardeners could also grow, if they chose, plants with attractive variegated leaves, with either white or yellow markings. By the end of the nineteenth century, large-flowered selections, for those for whom the delicacy of the normal sort was not enough, were also on the market.

Not surprisingly, for such a splendid and tough plant, many of the old forms still exist. We have not yet found the red-flowered one, and the white-striped, variegated sort has also so far escaped us (we hope it is more interesting than the yellow one).

All are lovely plants, especially planted thickly around some favourite seat: one with sun in early afternoon or evening, when the warmth will draw every drop of scent from the flowers. They will save you doing too much weeding, so you might actually have time to sit down and enjoy them.

All sorts do especially well in earthenware pots, and look good too. A bit of gentle forcing will give you something nice and early to set on a windowsill indoors. Forced lily-of-the-valley was an important commodity in Georgian and Victorian London.

# CONVOLVULUS

Many of the loveliest flower paintings coming from Dutch and Flemish studios in the seventeenth century show, amongst the tulips, auriculas and jasmines, a charming convolvulus with white, yellow and blue flowers. This jolly plant is *C. tricolor*, an annual probably from some Mediterranean shore, but now naturalized throughout much of warmer Europe. It is still easily obtainable, worth growing, and was in every seventeenth- and eighteenth-century garden.

Another important annual, also widely grown from the seventeenth century, is *C. major* (though this wanders between *Convolvulus* and the closely related genus *Ipomoea*). It is a morning glory with purple flowers, though some seed labelled '*C. minor*' sometimes turns out to be an all-blue form of *C. tricolor*. If it does, don't complain; it is very pretty too, and has been grown since the eighteenth century.

Of perennials, the handsome silver-leaved *C. cneorum* has been in gardens since 1640, and the even lovelier pink-flowered *C. althaeoides* is of the same period. Neither seems to have been at all common until the nineteenth century. We admire even more the wonderfully serene blue flowers of *C. mauretanicus*, especially in pot-grown plants ranged up a sunny flight of steps. It was first marketed in 1861 as a hanging-basket plant, for five shillings; the basket came free.

CORTADERIA, see Grasses.

## CORYDALIS

### Hollowort, fumiterre

The holloworts have always hovered round the edges of the garden, either literally, like the charming yellow *C. lutea*, which colonized its walls, or metaphorically, because some (like *C. ambigua* with nascent blue flowers) are fairly difficult to grow.

Several European species were popular in Elizabethan gardens, *C. bulbosa* (once called *C. cava*) has hollow tubers with smoky purplish flowers, though forms still exist with reddish-purple or white flowers. *C. solida* has solid tubers, and only purplish flowers. The weedy though charming *C. lutea*, normally yellow, also has a white form which was once popular. It can still be found, and is very pretty if you can grow it in a damp and rather shady spot.

By the following century, some garden writers were being rude about the flowers; Rea, always good with a crisp phrase, wrote 'a Plant as low in growth as reputation'. He allowed only a large white and a reddish-purple sort (impossible to identify) to be worth growing.

In the eighteenth century, with increasing interest in grottoes, ruins and fancy rockwork, any plant that lent a look of venerable age to fresh masonry was admired, and so forms of *C. lutea* and *C. bulbosa* were once again fashionable.

The trend continues, and grand rockeries have all sorts of modern introductions.

## CROCUS

A vast genus, with endless numbers of charming flowers, with equally endless confusion about how many species there really are and what their names should be.

The most ancient of all the crocuses is the saffron, *C. sativus*, so ancient indeed that it seems to have no connection with any wild species at all. It's now quite sterile, yet still manages to be immensely variable – to such a degree that, even in the eighteenth century, gardeners thought that all the crocuses might simply be variants of it. (That is not the case, but it is still rather unclear quite what species the older garden crocuses belong to.)

Saffron is still widely used in some Mediterranean and many Asian countries, though now hardly used in traditional British cooking. This is a pity, for native-grown saffron was once thought the best flavoured of all. It was extensively grown, and not only as a flavouring; a vast book published in 1670, called *Crocologia*, was devoted to its equally vast range of medicinal properties. However, as a decorative plant, even the best forms of saffron are not the most beautiful of crocuses, though the styles are very conspicuous and a most thrilling shade of orange-scarlet. Nevertheless, any old garden ought to have a patch of it, which must be well fed if the bulbs are to flower. It is difficult to know when saffron was introduced to northern European gardens; it was so well known and so necessary to the Romans that they must have brought it with them wherever they colonized. It is supposed to have been a major crop around Saffron Walden since the fourteenth century.

The purely decorative crocuses pose major difficulties of identification. Many European species have albino variants, none of which can be adequately told apart. *C. vernus*, of central and eastern Europe, is the most variable of all, and one of the earliest in cultivation, being plain, striped or feathered, in shades of blue, purple-grey and white. *C. biflorus* provides not only the so-called 'Scotch crocus' (nothing to do with Scotland – it is a late Georgian name), but also the brilliant yellow ones normally assigned to *C. chrysanthus*.

Gardeners were selecting interesting seedling crocuses by the late sixteenth century, as well as growing plants collected from the wild in Europe and the Near East. By the seventeenth century, florists' crocuses could be had in white, purple, pale and deep yellow, large and small, and with the colours striped, feathered or flamed. Dutch gardeners were famed for their production in the eighteenth and nineteenth centuries, though by the end of the 1800s there were the beginnings of a crocus 'industry' in Lancashire. The range of basic types seems not to have increased much, and all sorts are still available.

Planting style is important. In the sixteenth and seventeenth centuries it was bad form to have plants of the same colour next to one another. Crocus beds were planted up in the same manner as hyacinths and tulips (see p. 156). During the eighteenth century it seems to have been possible to plant in rows or blocks of colour, but by the end of the century it was 'good form' to plant in irregular clumps of one sort, to achieve a supposedly 'natural' effect. Regency gardens in good taste used the now-familiar technique of scattering bulbs by hand, and planting them where they fell. 'Bad taste' was to plant them in fanciful stars or squares or, even worse, to have the sorts all mixed up (most modern gardeners would agree).

Of the autumn-flowering crocuses, Gerard seems to have grown both *C. medius* and *C. ochroleucus*, neither of much interest. Of the spring-flowering ones, some fairly well defined species were in gardens quite early, or came in in the eighteenth, nineteenth and twentieth centuries. Not all have been amenable to the florists' and hybridists' attentions, which is something of a relief, for many are of considerable beauty.

## C. susianus

Cloth of Gold crocus

The Crimea and Caucasus. At least late sixteenth century. A lovely flower, early, strongly scented of honey; it has a golden-yellow interior. The exterior is either a plain greyish purple, or is striped in various shades of the same colour. Both forms were widely grown in the seventeenth century, but less so today. It naturalizes well, and in a sheltered corner of the garden the perfume carries well.

## C. speciosus

Southern Russia, Turkey and Persia. In gardens since the late nineteenth century. The most gorgeous of all the autumn-flowering crocuses – the colour of a good form can make autumn worth while.

## C. tomasinianus

Hungary and Bulgaria. Late nineteenth century. A wonderful early spring crocus, naturalizing itself so easily that it almost becomes a weed. However, with its bluish-amethyst flowers, it is an essential weed, especially for late Victorian and Edwardian gardens.

## C. imperati

A garden hybrid, earlier than 1665. A marvellous small crocus, the outer three petals strongly striped in white and purple, the inner three an even and delicate purple. So fine that it has gone up in the world; in the seventeenth century it was called 'Episcopalis'.

*Cyclamen europeum,*
from the *Gardeners' Chronicle*, 1890

# CYCLAMEN

Sowbread, hogges meat, swynes meat, rose violet

The various names involving pigs date back to at least the fifteenth century, and may be much older. Roots of several species seem to have been used medicinally (for pigs) long before the plants were grown in the garden. None are native to Britain, though Gerard says that *C. coum* grew wild in Wales, Lincolnshire and Somerset. He may have been wrong; *C. coum* is naturalized, probably as a garden escape.

The showiest sort of cyclamen, found nowadays in chain stores, garden centres and flower shops, is a development of *C. persicum*. This reached European gardens in the early seventeenth century, from Syria rather than the country of its name (confusingly, the only Persian species of cyclamen is called *C. ibericum*). It was grown only by connoisseurs until Victorian nurserymen took it up and turned it into a popular flower from 1860 onwards. Some modern seed catalogues advertise small-flowered sorts which are probably closer to the basic

A frilled late-nineteenth-century *Cyclamen persicum*, from the *Gardeners' Chronicle*, 1898

species than today's monsters, and so would be suitable for a pre-Victorian windowsill. White ones, with a flush of purple or pink at the centre of the flowers were popular in the eighteenth century, and double ones in the 1600s. Neither the basic *C. persicum* nor its varieties is winter hardy.

All the hardy species are lovely, and have appealed to keen gardeners. John Rea, that early plant snob, thought them 'worthy to be received into the gardens of the best Florists'. He may have been thinking of the following four species: *C. coum* from southern Europe (Rea may have grown the popular white-flowered variant); *C. hederaefolia*, also a southern European of the seventeenth century and also with a lovely white-flowered form; *C. europeum*, and *C. repandum* (introduced in the early sixteenth century). Most species were in American gardens by 1725.

# DAHLIA

By the time that Spanish warriors were destroying the civilizations of Central America, the dahlia existed in Aztec gardens in many varieties. It may first have been domesticated for its edible roots (nineteenth-century British garden books give conflicting advice about its taste), but later it was valued for the intensity of its flower colours. Even by the sixteenth century fully double dahlias existed in a wide range of colours, including purple, rose, scarlet and yellow.

Surprisingly, dahlias were not amongst the Central and South American flowers and vegetables that took European gardens by storm in the sixteenth and seventeenth centuries. They seem to have reached Madrid in the eighteenth century, and began to be distributed to other European countries in the 1780s. The first seed arrived in France in 1789, but the resulting plants were almost immediately lost; Spanish plants arrived in London in 1798, but the same fate befell them. Eventually, between 1802 and 1804, various plants were introduced from France, and then, in 1815, a series of new garden hybrids were brought in from the same country – and dahlia mania began. By 1817, Lees of Hammersmith were selling fully double ball-flowered hybrids, though the flowers were so heavy that they hung their heads. In 1832 the first English hybrid appeared, and by 1836 there were almost one thousand varieties available, in plain colours or in dramatic stripes, with edgings or with spots and flushes. Most were fully double, though the still-favoured anemone-flowered types were also popular. In 1842, the first black flower appeared, and in the same year scarlet and yellow dahlias decorated the triumphal arches at almost every Scottish village on Queen Victoria's route through that country. One of the new dahlia societies was offering a prize of £100 (then a huge sum) for the best bloom of the season.

All excess produces a reaction. Double dahlias dropped out of fashion. In 1880 even popular garden newspapers were crying the virtues of the new single dahlias, or the even newer cactus-flowered forms that developed from *Dahlia juarezii*, introduced in 1872. In the garden, dahlias were used in large flowerbeds, sometimes called 'bouquets', or even in shrubberies. One popular way of using them was to plant in front of the equally popular hollyhocks (see p. 69).

Of course, as half-hardy 'bedding out' was the most popular form of gardening at the time, dwarf-growing sorts began to appear in the late 1880s, offspring of a dwarf species collected in Mexico in the previous century. The so-called 'orchid-flowered' dahlias began to appear in the 1920s, and breeding amongst many of the other types still continues.

The Royal Horticultural Society published a *Tentative Classified List and International Register of Dahlia Names* in 1969 which suggests that there are still very large numbers of nineteenth-century plants in cultivation. However, even some modern varieties look reasonably 'period': 'Bishop of Llandaff', of 1928, with its scarlet flowers and purple leaves looks similar to some of the *D. coccinea* seedlings of the 1820s, and even the charming 'Red Cross' of 1938 (single cream flowers, each petal having a broad crimson margin) looks like some of the 'laced' singles of fifty years before. It looks splendid in large pots in the courtyard.

There are also some useful dahlia species: the fairly hardy *D. merckii*, with its single purplish flowers, was introduced in 1840, and the grand and vast *D. imperialis*, a spectacular Mexican, well worth growing if you can overwinter it in the conservatory, dates from 1868.

# DELPHINIUM

Delphiniums, those towering spires of gorgeous blue, dove grey, soft pink or white, are only the most modern developments of this immense and fascinating genus. Perhaps the high point came in 1910, when Amos Perry staged an exhibition of them, and displayed thirty thousand spikes of flowers. Some of the older hybrids that remain are just about suitable for Edwardian gardens; for older gardens there are many good species.

Most of the annual delphiniums (or larkspurs) are now placed in a separate genus (*Consolida*).

### D. staphisagria
Staveacre, louse grass, pyllulery

Mediterranean area. In gardens from at least the fifteenth century. This is the oldest delphinium in the garden, and was probably first grown to drive bugs away from the gardener, rather than to decorate his flowerbeds. It was especially popular in the 1700s, probably because it is generally perennial and produces quite attractive but shortish spikes of purplish-blue flowers. Just possibly there was an increase in the louse population at the time. It is rarely seen nowadays.

**D. ajacis** (now correctly *Consolida ambigua*)
Rocket or branching larkspur

**D. consolida** (now correctly *Consolida tuntasiana regalis*)
Stockflowered larkspur, single-stemmed larkspur

Both these species were well known by the end of the sixteenth century, and were even then available in a wide range of colours, including red, pink and white, though both species are just plain blue in nature. Gerard and Parkinson both had double-flowered sorts, immensely popular in the seventeenth and eighteenth centuries and in American cottage gardens in the 1850s. They are still grown today. We have not yet found an equivalent to one popular in the 1750s which was purest white, but spotted with rose.

**D. elatum**

Central Europe and central Russia. Late sixteenth or early seventeenth century. Parkinson writes, 'the tall and upright single kindes have been entertained but of late years. The double kinds are more rare.' This perennial species, usually with muddy blue flowers in the wild, went on to great things, becoming part of the parenthood of today's garden delphiniums.

GARDEN DELPHINIUMS

*D. elatum*, with all its variability, only grows to about four feet high or so, and that was the maximum height for any common species of delphinium until at least 1850. However, large numbers of species from America and China had been introduced in the early 1800s; especially important were *D. chinese* and *D. grandiflorum* (this would grow to six feet high if heavily fed, and caused great excitement). By 1839, Sam Barlow, a famous florist, had started crossing some of the more dramatic species. By 1850, a Norwegian nurseryman had a vast collection of species in use as parent material. Some of the more interesting progeny were taken up, in 1860, at Kelways' nursery at

Langport in Somerset. By the 1890s, there were large numbers of gorgeous hybrids, singles and a few doubles, in amethyst, purples, blues, and milky whites.

None of the new plants were reliably perennial. The first that was seems to have been a variety called 'Millicent Blackmore' of 1910, with a branched flower spike and individual flowers three inches in diameter. The firm of Blackmore and Langdon still produces superlative delphiniums.

In the 1890s, groups of delphinium varieties began to be used for special purposes. The Belladonna group became important as cut flowers, though the first pure white sort only appeared in 1900. Double-flowered ones, given the fake Latin name of *D. ranunculoides*, appeared in the 1880s. These were, and are, especially sought after because, being sterile, the flowers last very much longer than fertile singles. The very rare 'Alice Artindale' (Mr Artindale was a well-known Sheffield breeder) dates from as late as 1935, and is very, very grand. The now-popular Pacific strains are of the 1950s.

If planting a late Victorian colour scheme, remember that yellow, cream and white were not available colours until 1895, and that there were *no* pinks until 1960.

# DIANTHUS

Of the immense tribe of *Dianthus* species, only a handful have contributed directly to the garden, although those few have been of immense importance and still give vast pleasure. Almost all of them have been in gardens for so long, and are so diverse, that several have lost contact with any known wild species, and all may be diverse because they have absorbed characters (especially flower marking, colours, and shape of petals) from species which have not themselves been important garden plants.

The diversity in *Dianthus* also makes classification hard. Every modern gardener will have a clear idea of what either a carnation or a pink looks like, and most garden books assign each to a proper species (*D. caryophyllus* for carnations and *D. plumarius* for pinks). Alas, pinks and carnations cross with the greatest of ease, and so there are all sorts of quite intermediate plants which are difficult to assign to either group. Indeed, Elizabethan and Jacobean gardeners recognized a third group, which they called the clove gilliflowers (a term often confusingly synonymous with carnations), which were intermediate in size and even social grandness between carnations and pinks; a sort of middle-class dianthus. The sweet Johns seem to have been a cross between the sweet william (*D. barbatus*), and either pinks or carnations. They were probably comparable to the rare and difficult-to-grow 'mule' pinks of today's connoisseurs.

All the main dianthus groups have, at one time or another, been florists' flowers, not only in western Europe, but also throughout the Near East, with Turkey being an especially important centre. It seems possible that the sudden emergence in European gardens of myriad forms of carnation and clove gilliflowers in the sixteenth century may have been caused by their wholesale importation from elsewhere. Even so, neither Gerard nor Parkinson connects his plants with the East. One of Gerard's gardening coups was to grow the first yellow gilliflower in England, and that was a plant sent to him by a friend in Poland.

Florists' groups, as we have suggested elsewhere in this book, always present problems. The first of these, with the dianthuses, is that each group developed an elaborate internal classification which changed over the centuries as new sorts evolved. In *Dianthus*, this is especially confused because carnations and pinks developed parallel groups (for example, the Painted Ladies), as well as single varieties which themselves later evolved into whole new clusters of varieties (the Malmaison carnations started life as a single variety, as did the Pheasant's Eye pinks). Some of these groups eventually declined to a single random survivor, often bearing the group name, but possibly not looking much like the variety that started the whole thing off. Most difficult of all, though, is the huge number of varieties (or at least names), that existed in the past, and their relationship to varieties that exist today. While, in general, we have adopted our usual solution by describing 'types' of flower and their period so that you can choose something that will look reasonably correct, there are so many lovely and supposedly old carnations and pinks in existence that we have included short lists of what we think are the very nicest varieties in commerce.

CARNATIONS, including clove gilliflowers.

## D. caryophyllus

Gylofre, incarnaytion

The carnation is of unknown origin, though often supposed a European. Medieval illuminations and portraits commonly show double scarlet, deep rose or white flowers with jagged petals and strong blue-grey leaves. Strongly scented and medium-sized ones, the clove gilliflowers, are often required in medieval charters and property documents, where rents are commonly (after an initial money

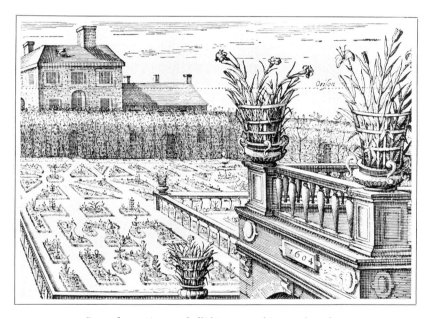

Pots of carnations embellishing an architectural garden

payment) paid as a single flower in spring, autumn or both (called a 'quit rent'). As most carnations flower in midsummer, this may have been more of a feat than is commonly supposed.

There were already large numbers of varieties, single, semi-double and fully double, in the late sixteenth century, in rose, red, purple or white, quite frequently spattered or streaked with one or more colours. All these were considered very choice, and were almost always grown in pots to be placed along walks or balustrades, by steps, pools and fountains. Many sixteenth- and early-seventeenth-century illustrations show neat open-work willow baskets set over the plants to support the flowers. The plants were taken indoors during the winter, and kept as dry as possible. No authentic sixteenth-century varieties survive (as far as we know), but it might be possible to re-create the look by taking seed from some of the old border carnations, and selecting sorts not hugely double, and with very jagged petal edges.

By the 1630s Parkinson grew nineteen carnations, and said that there were vast numbers of others. Certainly, breeding was taking place all over Europe. By 1665, John Rea was complaining bitterly that all modern plants came from Holland and Flanders. Though these showed dramatic colour combinations, and had marvellous names like 'General of the Indies', 'Incarnadine Bezond', and even 'Paragon Brewer', they easily reverted to plain colours and then swiftly died. He bemoaned the loss of all the old English varieties, which had been far tougher. Nevertheless, he still lists ninety or so of the newfangled plants as being worth growing. A decade later, there were three hundred and seventy sorts equally fit for the garden, mostly still streaked, but including some very grand ones, basically white, but with spots of colour (called 'piquettes').

These were immensely popular in the early eighteenth century, but 'flakes' took over in the 1750s. In these, the irregular stripes of colour radiate outwards from the centre of the flower. Proper 'flakes' are made up of only two colours. The 'bizarres' (and they lived up to their name) were streaked with three or four colours. In the 'painted lady' group, the petals were coloured on the upper surface of the petal, white below. Miller, like Rea, also complains about new French varieties, which had 'rose-edged', or smooth rather than serrated, petals. However, he does say that some of the English varieties had been rediscovered, and were being marketed at high prices.

In America, carnations began to arrive in the early years of the eighteenth century, and became common by 1740. By this date in Britain, the carnation was a show plant, and Miller gives elaborate directions for bringing flowers to absolute perfection.

In the nineteenth century, flakes or bizarres remained popular, but by 1840, the picotees, now white flowers with the narrowest band of colour along the smooth petal edge, were supreme. Some, now alas vanished, were of extraordinary elegance; 'Zenobie' had petals edged with ruby, others had edges of purple or even black.

Though elegant, the picotees were perfectly hardy and much less expensive to buy than the tender flakes and bizarres – a nurseryman at Walworth was selling, in the 1840s, picotees at £3 10s. for twenty-five pairs, but 'proper' carnations for a pound more (that year's carnation was Twitchett's 'Don John' at two guineas a pair of plants!). The hardiness of the picotees seems to have been bred into other carnation groups to produce hardy border types – while glasshouse enthusiasts, particularly in France, produced more or less continuously flowering carnations. A seedling of one of these became the famous 'Souvenir de Malmaison', which itself was developed to provide the whole Malmaison group by the end of the century. These have the spectacularly large, if still refined, flowers that were essential in Edwardian drawing-rooms or on Edwardian bosoms. A few sorts can still occasionally be found.

Various seed strains were developed about the same time, often free-flowering enough to be treated as annuals. The Chaubaud strains can still be found in seed catalogues.

Amongst the hardy border carnations were some wonderful plants. Only a few, it seems, still exist, including 'Raby Castle' (popular by 1870) in salmon pink, with slightly darker flecks, which is still easily available. Others, much rarer, include the supposedly seventeenth-century 'Fenbow's Nutmeg Clove'.

Carnations, both glasshouse or border, are still essentially florists' flowers, and breeding continues. No doubt almost every modern variety will go the way of the 'wheat-ear' – an oddity popular in late Georgian gardens with a series of overlapping calyces. In 1871, the Revd Harpur Crewe published a letter appealing to anyone who grew it, perhaps the owner of 'some of those dear old-fashioned gardens whose owners have stood bravely out against the bedding mania, and have zealously propagated and zealously preserved these choice gems of floral antiquity'. He seems not to have had a reply.

## PINKS

### D. plumarius

Pink, sops-in-wine, pheasant's eye

The basic species is a charming plant with small white or palest candy-pink flowers, with five fringed petals and a delicious clove-like smell. It is native to much of central and southern Europe. Double forms in white and several shades of pink, including 'Old Fringed White', 'Old Fringed Pink', 'Houston House', 'Cockenzie', make excellent garden plants, and although some sorts are supposed to date from the eighteenth century, similar plants have been grown since the sixteenth century, and are probably much older.

Rich scarlet pinks, both single and double, are quite commonly seen in medieval illuminations, and the variety called 'Caesar's Mantle' may just perhaps date from this period. Scarlet doubles were still fashionable in the Renaissance, and many provincial portraits show sitters grasping a single bloom.

The feathered or 'starre' pinks described by Gerard form another important group. The flowers are single, larger than those of *D. plumarius*, have very frilled petals and often a darkish pink 'eye'. Some forms have a very strong smell indeed. It seems likely that they are hybrids between *D. plumarius* and some other species. They remained popular into the 1660s (John Rea approved) and we've found comparable plants at the sites of two ruined and ancient gardens.

In the early seventeenth century, gardeners (entranced with the variations to be found amongst the pinks in their gardens) began to develop flowers with elaborate patterns of colouring. New designs evolved swiftly over the next two hundred years and so, though it is impossible to say that a particular pink in cultivation today is a cutting from a plant that originated two or three centuries ago, it is possible to say that it belongs to a type fashionable at a particular date.

An early-seventeenth-century sort of flower has the old 'starre' pink shape and frilling, and the petals are streaked radially with deep pink rose or mulberry. 'Ragamuffin' or 'Cedric's Oldest' belong to this class. They are comparable to some of the 'bizarre' carnations. By the late seventeenth century the 'pheasant's eye' type had evolved. These were usually single, but if double, had a ragged cluster of small petals near the centre of the flower. Markings normally consisted of a dark central blotch, and a soft irregular band of colour along the jagged margin of each petal. 'Pheasant's eye' became the name for a vast group of varieties, and it was sometimes even used for every sort of pink. All remained fairly popular until the late eighteenth century. 'Pheasant's Eye' and the modern 'Sweetheart Abbey' represent the type today. When planting pinks now, it is worth remembering that in the seventeenth and early eighteenth centuries, 'pinks were of many sorts and little esteem, they serve only to set the sides of borders in spacious gardens, and some of them for posies, mixed with the buds of Damask Roses'.

'Pheasant's eyes' were completely ousted from the garden by the fully 'laced' pinks that began to appear in the 1780s. These were fully double, and each petal had a continuous and hard-edged band of colour along the margin, and an equally strong blotch at the base. Most early forms (all, alas, vanished) had quite strongly frilled petals, but because the petals were graded in size, the flowers were of exceptional beauty. There were endless debates about the 'correct' sort of flower (how thick the lacing should be, or how highly 'domed' the flower) but by 1800 florists had decided that the frilled edges had to

Smooth-edged laced pinks from
*The Florist*, 1852

go. Selection was so intense that smooth-edged petals had evolved by 1824, perhaps bringing in the character from the carnations, giving rise to new enthusiasm – and new controversy between northern and southern breeders over what constituted the perfect flower. 'Dad's Favourite', 'Paisley Gem' and 'William Brownhill' resemble plants of this period. All are remarkably beautiful.

While using florists' pinks to give a garden a particular period look, it's important to remember that they were specialists' flowers. There were many other sorts of pinks that less fussy gardeners still liked, and these showed no particular sort of evolution. Several sorts of single flowers are reasonably dated to the eighteenth century (when rabid florists only cherished doubles), for instance the small velvety crimson 'Irish'. Alternatively, wildly flamboyant doubles, which the florists must have hated, were popular from the late eighteenth century to the present day, whether the pale pink 'Earl of Essex' (nineteenth century), the dark-eyed 'Sam Barlow' of the 1860s, or the still widely grown 'Mrs Sinkins' (first marketed in 1872 at three shillings a pair).

Interest in 'old' pinks is on the increase, so do look for suitable plants. Plants with names that include 'London' are modern but are often reasonable fascimiles of laced pinks. 'Allwood' pinks are also modern, with long flowering periods, as they're usually hybrids between old forms of pink and perpetual-flowering carnations. Few are of much delicacy.

However, any history of the pink has problems. Anyone who does grow them will be aware how prolific they are of seed, and how attractive the seedlings. Stories of ancient plants found in gardens should always be regarded with some suspicion. In some ways more important is the sentimental aura attached to pinks, at least since the 1850s. Perhaps because pinks were a flower of humble gardens (even the most sophisticated of the florists' plants), sentimental gardeners have always wanted to believe that any nice, fragrant pink must be old. By the 1850s, pinks were almost seen as a national flower, associated with old trees, mossy lawns and mixed borders. 'For then', in that golden age, 'the wife was head-gardener, and little feet in satin slippers made many a rustling amongst the sweet-smelling flowers and the medicinal herbs.' Don't let Shirley Hibberd's remarks put you off pinks; whatever their age and provenance, all but the crudest of modern ones are delightfully worth growing.

## SWEET WILLIAM

### D. barbatus

Sweet william, sweet John

The Pyrenees and the Balkans. In cultivation in several forms at least since the early sixteenth century. Singles had always been, and still are, popular. However, doubles were more choice (and are now very rare; seed strains are occasionally available). A scarlet double was in cultivation by 1634; today's 'King Willie' may perhaps be a descendant. Gardeners, even into the 1880s, found the plant very easy to propagate and to flower; we find it neither. Late in the seventeenth century there were enough doubles in cultivation for the singles to be considered rather common, and even the double red was 'well known to every country woman'. They obviously managed better than we have. One variety that was less common had a red and white flower and was called 'London Pride'.

Single sweet williams, being nice tidy plants, became popular once more in Victorian bedding schemes, and there still exist many seed strains from that period. Almost all are sold as colour mixtures, so if you find a plant in a colour that you especially like, remove all flowers, keep removing any flower stalks that try to form, and treat the leafy side shoots as cuttings.

Sweet Johns were usually sterile (unusual for a dianthus hybrid), and so had to be propagated by cuttings. As one parent was always a double pink, the children that were kept in the garden were double too. 'Mule' pinks are very similar, though supposed to be crosses between sweet williams and carnations, not pinks. However, they remain small in stature. 'Napoleon 111', 'Emile Paré' and a few others can still be found, representatives of a once large group of plants popular in the 1880s. The first 'mule' is said to have been made in the early eighteenth century.

### D. chinensis
Chinese or Indian pink

Eastern Asia. Single and double forms, all annual, were known in both Europe and America by the mid eighteenth century but were not especially popular. Modern forms are mostly complex hybrids with other species.

### D. superbus

Central and southern Europe. In gardens by the sixteenth century, but not important until the 1850s. In the wild, flowers are pink, purple, or white, with petals that are all fringe and almost no centre. The perfume is heavy. An attractive hybrid strain easily available is called 'Loveliness'; the flowers are about an inch across, rather larger than those of the wildling, and with a perfume strong enough to fill the garden. Lovely in pots; modern, but essential.

OTHER SPECIES

The Cheddar pink (*D. gratianopolitanus*), the Deptford pink (*D. armeria*), and the maiden pink (*D. deltoides*), have all been grown, if rather rarely, since the late sixteenth century.

# DICENTRA

Bleeding heart, ladies' lockets, Dutchman's breeches

A horticultural success story, for though most of the important species were not introduced to European gardens until Regency times, they were soon found even in cottage gardens, and by 1877 were thought of as 'old-fashioned', comparable to pinks, auriculas and other genuinely ancient garden plants.

*D. cucullaria*, an American, arrived first in 1731, but remained in obscurity. *D. eximia*, also American, arrived in 1811, but has only become an important garden plant in the last couple of decades. It was left to the Chinese *D. spectabilis*, with its showy pink sepals, to take gardeners by storm. It first appeared in the West in 1810, was lost, then re-introduced from 'the Grotto garden on the Island of Chusan' by Robert Fortune in 1846. By 1852, some gardens already had clumps that were thirty feet in diameter, and up to five feet high; of course, horse manure was easily available. Various attempts were made to use it as a bedding plant, all doomed to failure as the plant would not stand up to a wind.

Presumably, all the lower-growing species were of no use because of their less bright colours; even the plain pink *D. spectabilis* has now fallen out of fashion rather, though the gorgeous white form is still much sought after. In America, bleeding heart was a popular cottage-garden plant by 1877.

# DICTAMNUS

Burning bush, bastard dittany, fraxinella

Southern Europe and temperate Asia. In gardens by the late sixteenth century. The wild plant (*D. albus*) is rather variable, and several colours of flower were known early on. Gerard thought it a 'verie rare and galent plant', and though now not rare (it is easily grown from seed), it certainly is gallant. Parkinson grew it in four different colours in the seventeenth century, though only purple and white are much seen today. He said, correctly, that 'the whole plant as well roots as leaves and flowers, are of a strong scent, not so pleasing for the smell, as the flowers are beautiful to the sight'. A well-grown clump in full flower is certainly worth travelling some way to see. No one seems to have tried to set their plants alight until the nineteenth century; the pungent smell, not at all unpleasant, noticed by Parkinson is supposed to be a flammable gas, given off in such quantities that on a hot still day it can be ignited. (Our plants may never have been warm enough.)

# DIGITALIS

### Foxglove

Every gardener knows the handsome native sort, purple and spotted, or perfect white, but of the dozen or so other species a surprising number are also used as garden plants, and have been for several centuries. Nowadays, there are even various hybrid sorts, several of them of unusual beauty.

## D. *purpurea*

Europe, including Britain. In gardens since at least the fifteenth century. By the end of the sixteenth, the white-flowered sort was much admired, in borders rather than in the knot or parterre. In the eighteenth century, it was essential in the wilderness, and in the next century in the wild garden. It had first become popular in America in the 1740s. It is so fine, even if only for a few weeks, that it ought to be in everyone's patch. Self-sown seedlings can be purple flowered; look for young plants whose leaves have midribs which are brownish or pale purple. Throw those away.

There are a number of rather gross strains of foxgloves, some with immense spires, some with heavily spotted flowers, or flowers evenly distributed around the stem. Much nicer is a form with apricot flowers (probably a hybrid). It is a remarkably handsome seed strain, once distributed by Suttons, and does not seem much earlier than the early twentieth century.

### D. × mertonensis

This is an attractive hybrid of 1926. The spikes are rarely more than three feet high; the flowers are voluminous, and of a wonderful crushed-strawberry colour. It is reasonably perennial, but easily grown from seed.

### D. lutea

Western and central Europe, as well as southern Italy. In gardens by the sixteenth century. The rather thin spires of pale yellow foxgloves are not exactly devastating, but have undeniable charm, looking wonderful in light shade if you can afford space for a big clump. It is perennial and seeds itself around with discretion.

### D. grandiflora (often still called D. ambigua)

Eastern central Europe. Sixteenth century. Nice open gloves of an intriguing greenish yellow, and a slightly pointed lower lip. They hang quite thickly upon the three-feet-high spire. The plants are fairly perennial, and not too productive of seed.

### D. ferruginea

South-eastern Europe and Turkey. Sixteenth century. Lovely rusty red flowers, on spikes up to six feet high. Biennial and very much worth having.

# DODECATHEON

American cowslip, shooting stars

Only one species is of much importance in the garden. *D. meadia*, first seen in Europe in the early 1700s, flowered in London in 1709 at Fulham Palace. It seems then to have been lost until re-introduced in 1744, after which it became a popular garden plant in shaded borders or in light woodland.

Various forms exist; white (absolutely gorgeous), violet and large flowered, though all these are probably modern. In any case, the basic species is perfectly lovely.

# DORONICUM

Leopard's bane

The main species, *D. pardalianches*, European but now widely naturalized in Britain, has been a garden plant since the sixteenth century, and probably long before (it was naturalized even by 1594). It is not clear why it should be associated with leopards; the usual story is that the plant's roots were used to poison them.

Any plant that can naturalize itself needs watching when in the garden. *D. pardalianches* is certainly quite invasive, but does produce its bright yellow daisies early in the season.

*D. plantagineum* is another European species, also found in sixteenth-century gardens. There are various pleasant hybrids and selections that you might prefer to the species. One of these, called 'Harpur Crewe', is of 1896.

DUCHESNIA, see *Fragaria*.

# ECHINOPS

Globe thistle

Stately plants with handsome and large-scale leaves, and stout stems up to six or seven feet high, topped with balls of narrow, silvery, tightly packed and almost too tasteful flowers. They look elegant even when dead and brown, and you will probably leave them in the border. If you do, the first November gales will shatter the heads, scattering hefty seeds near and far.

### E. ritro

Southern Europe. Sixteenth century or earlier. The plant is variable in nature, and taller and shorter sorts were in cultivation by the early seventeenth century. Head size also varies, as does flower colour; this can be mid to lightish blue, purplish in some modern garden varieties, or white (even more stylish). The plant was never really popular until the late nineteenth century. Miller said, in the eighteenth, that it had no particular beauty.

### *E. sphaerocephala*

(Sometimes called *E. paniculata*.) Europe and Russia. Eighteenth century, but only popular from the early nineteenth century. Regency writers thought it quite impressive, but their plants were perhaps better than ours.

# EPIMEDIUM

Barrenwort, bishop's hat

Attractive groundcover plants in shade, retaining their leaves in winter. Only one species was introduced early, *E. alpinum*, from south and central Europe; it was grown by Gerard in 1597. He had this 'rare and strange plant' from 'the French King's herbarist Robinus'. Parkinson, with less grand contacts, liked it too, and 'cherished [it] for the pleasant varietie of the flowers'. Most other species arrived in the nineteenth century, including *E. grandiflorum* (sometimes called *E. macranthum*) from Japan in 1830, *E. perralderianum* from Algeria in 1867 and *E. pinnatum* from Persia in 1849 (the form *E.p. colchicum*, from the Caucasus, arrived later).

# ERANTHIS

### *E. hyemalis*
Winter aconite

South-eastern France to Bulgaria, but naturalized in many countries, including Britain. The date of introduction to Britain is unknown, but was probably before 1578, being plentiful in London gardens by 1597. Classified by the herbalists as an aconite, and with some reason (it's very poisonous). It was still proving fatal centuries later; a newspaper of 1822 gives the story of a Mrs Gorst, who died after eating a tuber, having mistaken it for horseradish.

Two forms were known to gardeners by 1665, a rich and a pale yellow (nowadays we have just one). It is an attractive and useful little plant. As Hill says, 'it accompanies the Snow Drop, painting the face of Winter, and foretelling the approach of Spring'. The flowers are very temperature-sensitive, opening when it's above 10°C. It's easily naturalized where it's not disturbed, and eventually makes magnificent carpets of yellow.

# ERIGERON

Fleabane

A large and widely distributed genus, with a number of interesting species for the garden. Even the earliest of these only dates from the eighteenth century: the lovely *E. philadelphicus* (with clusters of soft pink daisy flowers) arrived from North America in 1778, and *E. macranthus* (with violet-blue flowers) arrived from the Rocky Mountains in 1841.

More soon arrived. The most popular is the pretty little *E. karvinskyanus* (often still called *E. mucronatus*), which arrived from Mexico in 1836. It looks wonderful on walls and suitable steps, and has become naturalized in parts of south-west Britain and the Channel Islands. The much larger *E. multiradiatus* was brought from India in 1880.

However, many of the most popular erigerons are selections and hybrids of *E. speciosa*, from western North America. Good ones include 'Superbus' of 1889, and 'Quakeress' and 'White Quakeress' of the 1890s.

# ERYNGIUM

A fascinating genus, with long-lasting teasel-like flower-heads, splendid in the garden, for flower arrangements and for drying. Some of the species have a surprisingly long garden history. There are two native ones, *E. maritimum* and *E. campestre*. All the species thrive in a well-drained soil, many putting up a good display in dry conditions.

*E. maritimum*, sea holly, the more attractive of the two natives, is mentioned in *The Grete Herball* of 1526 as the 'thystle of the sea' or 'yringe'. It was a popular aphrodisiac, Gerard tactfully suggesting that it is for 'people that have no delight or appetite to venerie, nourishing and restoring the aged and amending defects of nature in the younger'. It was taken as a sweetmeat, 'the roots condited or preserved with sugar'. These are the 'Eryngoes' which are mentioned by Falstaff in *Henry IV*, part 2.

Gerard also grew other European species: the very handsome *E. alpinum*, which has the largest flower heads of them all, and *E. planum*, with small light blue flower heads, good for cutting. *E. amethystinum*,

also from Europe, was grown by John Tradescant the Younger by
1634 (and was grown at Oxford by 1648).

E. *bourgatii*, from the Pyrenees, with its steel-blue flower-heads
surrounded by silvery and spiky bracts, was grown by 1731. The
hybrid E. *oliverianum*, later a favourite of Gertrude Jekyll, seems also
to have been grown by this date. Another favourite of Jekyll's was a
nineteenth-century introduction, the biennial E. *giganteum*, which
came from the Caucasus and Iran. It now has a common name of 'Miss
Willmott's ghost', owing to that lady's habit of secretly scattering seed
about gardens she visited.

The American species are quite startlingly different from the round-
leaved Europeans, having long narrow evergreen leaves. E. *yuccifolium*
was the first to arrive from North America, in 1699. The statuesque
E. *agavifolium*, with its dramatic and sharply toothed leaves and large
flower heads, is listed as a new arrival from the Argentine in Jackman's
catalogue of 1886.

# ERYSIMUM

The so-called 'perennial wallflowers', often low-growing and mat-
forming plants popular for rockeries, belong to this genus, though
most have at some time or another been placed in *Cheiranthus*.

The Siberian wallflower, for instance, is usually listed in catalogues
as *Cheiranthus* × *allionii*, but is probably an *Erysimum*. A hybrid raised
in 1846, it is commonly grown as a biennial. The perennial types of
erysimum are rather more fun, though not all are fully hardy.

The plant best known as E. *mutabile* was introduced in 1777 from
Morocco, and has exciting flowers which turn from pale yellow to
buff to purplish. E. *linifolium*, from Spain and Morocco, has linear
grey leaves and deep mauve flowers. A modern selection, handsome
and bushy, made by E. A. Bowles, (variously called 'Bowles' Mauve'
or 'Bowles' Purple'), is often available. E. *alpinum*, from Scandinavia
in 1823 but not widely grown until the 1890s, has yellow flowers
('Moonlight' is a modern and pale-flowered cultivar).

Most of the erysimums available, however, are hybrids, often (to
make things difficult) with various species of cheiranthus. They are all
perennial, but tend to be short-lived, and can be propagated by seed
(there are some reliable seed strains), or by cuttings.

# ERYTHRONIUM

A bulbous genus, with a pair of leaves at ground level, lying beneath nodding flowers with pointed and reflexed petals. Only one species is native to Europe and Asia, *E. dens-canis*, the 'dog's-tooth violet', so-called from the shape of the corm. All the others are without exception North American, mostly from the west. They are not difficult to grow, needing moisture-retentive, fairly humus-rich soil, doing well in semi-shade. Leave them alone to increase.

*E. dens-canis* is widespread throughout Europe and across Russia to Korea and Japan. It was introduced to this country in the late sixteenth century and grown by l'Obel (Lobelius), later botanist and physician to James VI and I. Gerard calls it 'a goodly bulbous rooted plant' and says it 'hath not long been found out'. He had two colours, purple and white, to which Parkinson added a red sort. By the mid seventeenth century, it was being produced for sale in quantity in France and Flanders, but these imported corms often did not grow well, probably because they had dried out in transit, something which it heartily dislikes. The species is quite variable, and by the late eighteenth century there were many different sorts available. The leaves are usually splendidly mottled or blotched with grey or brown. The flowers are of the greatest elegance. Named cultivars are becoming difficult to get hold of today.

The first American species, *E. americanum*, was introduced well in advance of the others, being in a list of plants received by the Tradescants in 1633. We can assume that it was some time before they saw it in flower – it is rather shy to do so in this country, needing to be well established in damp soil. Phillipps recommended planting it 'in the shade of the purple rhododendron [he meant *R. ponticum*], as it loves the same soil and flowers at the same season'. Other species were introduced slowly throughout the nineteenth century, including *E. revolutum*, *E. tuolumnense*, and *E. oregonum*. The named cultivars generally available today are modern hybrids between the three above species. Many are lovely; try 'Pagoda'.

# EUPHORBIA

It is the often handsome foliage and the bracts, rather than the insignificant flowers, which attract modern gardeners to this genus. As an example, Gertrude Jekyll writes in glowing terms of *E. characias* subsp. *wulfenii*: 'a wonderful plant of May ... It adapts itself to so many ways of use, for, though the immense yellow-green heads of bloom are at their best in May, they are still of pictorial value in June and July, while the deep-toned grey-blue foliage is in full beauty throughout the greater part of the year.'

However, twentieth-century gardeners (and flower-arrangers) were not the first to appreciate these plants. Some species are recorded quite early; 'Spourge' (probably *E. lathyrus*), and 'Spourge gyant' (probably *E. palustris*), are in Turner's *The Names of Herbes* of 1548. *E. lathyrus*, 'caper spurge', was of course cultivated for its seeds, used as caper substitutes, and was probably not thought of as a decorative plant. It is native to the east and central parts of the Mediterranean region, but is now widely naturalized. This may mirror its erstwhile popularity. Gerard thought that it was 'the best knowne of all the rest and the most used'.

*E. palustris*, from Europe and western Asia, is a splendid plant, and it is easy to believe that early gardeners must have appreciated its great heads of sulphur-yellow bracts and the leaves, which colour so well in autumn. This species needs a damp soil, not necessary for the other giant, *E. characias*, from the western Mediterranean, so fashionable now, but mentioned in the Tradescants' plant list of 1629 to 1633. Also listed in 1634 is *E. dulcis*, a small species from Europe, with rich autumn colouring.

Parkinson describes no euphorbias, probably not thinking them worthy of inclusion in a book of garden plants, but Gerard's *Herball* has many, including the native wood spurge (*E. amygdaloides*, of which the attractive purple and variegated-leaved variants are modern) and the European cypress spurge, *E. cyparissus*, rather a menace, with invasive roots. However Gerard was, of course, looking at plants from a medicinal, rather than a decorative, point of view.

In the eighteenth century, interest centred mainly on the half-hardy shrubs and succulents, which were 'stove' or greenhouse plants. The hardy sorts were, according to Miller, 'rarely admitted any-where but in the Physic-gardens'. In the early nineteenth century, two species were introduced which have become familiar greenhouse and house plants, the poinsettia (*E. pulcherrima*, from Mexico in 1834) and the crown of thorns (*E. millii*, still sometimes called *E. splendens*, from Madagascar in 1828).

Hardy sorts now widely grown are *E. epithymoides* (often in catalogues as *E. polychroma*), from E. Europe in 1805, and *E. robbiae*, from north-western Asia Minor, also introduced in the nineteenth century. The subspecies of *E. characias* of which Gertrude Jekyll was so fond, *E.c.* subsp. *wulfenii*, arrived in 1829. *E. griffithii* is a mid-twentieth-century introduction.

FERULA, see *Foeniculum*

# FILIPENDULA

Closely related to spiraea, the filipendulas generally need a damp soil, apart from *F. vulgaris*, the dropwort, native, growing on chalky grassland. It is mentioned in *The Grete Herball* of 1526, but the more decorative double form doesn't seem to be recorded until the eighteenth century. Miller also mentions a single sort, 'larger in every part', which he himself brought from Holland in 1727. This was perhaps similar to (or may be the same as) the modern 'Grandiflora'.

## *F. ulmaria*
Meadowsweet

A British native of swamps, marshes and river banks. It is called by Gerard 'Queene of the Medowes ... the leaves and floures farre excell all other strowing herbs ... for the smell thereof makes the heart merrie, delighteth the senses'. That is almost enough to make one 'strow' today! There is a splendid sort with golden-green leaves, *F. ulmaria* 'Aurea', but we cannot find where and when this was first recorded. There are also variegated-leaved and double-flowered sorts, not quite so desirable, neither mentioned in early garden literature. *F. rubra*, Queen of the Prairie, came from the United States in 1765, and *F. palmata* from Siberia around 1823. Both of these have pink flowers.

# FOENICULUM

### F. vulgare
Fennel

Native to the Mediterranean region and possibly elsewhere in Europe, including Britain, but widely naturalized. It has been grown since early times, primarily for culinary use, but it also makes an attractive garden plant. The red- or purple-leaved version is mentioned by Parkinson in 1629.

'Giant fennel' is in the genus *Ferula*. *F. communis*, 'Fenel Gyante', is mentioned by Turner in 1548. The stalk of this was the original schoolmaster's ferule.

# FRAGARIA

Strawberry

Apart from the large-berried garden hybrids, which amply deserve their place in the kitchen garden, there are several species which look good amongst shrubs as ground cover.

### F. vesca
Wild strawberry

An invasive native, perhaps best confined to the wilder parts of the garden. It has been cultivated at least since Roman times. Gerard grew red, white and green sorts (red and white ones can still be found). Parkinson had an amusing oddity called the 'prickly Strawberry', found by John Tradescant the Elder in a garden in Plymouth. It is intriguing; the berry is covered in green leafy growths, making it, as Parkinson says, 'plesant to behold, and fit for a Gentle woman to wear on her arme, etc., as a raritie in stead of a flower'.

There are other eccentric forms too, such as the double-flowered *F. vesca* 'Flore Pleno', and the one-leaf strawberry, *F. vesca* var. *monophylla*, which was introduced from France in 1773. More common than any of these nowadays is the 'alpine' strawberry, *F. vesca* var. *semperflorens*, a non-running sort, apparently known since the sixteenth century, though not much cultivated till the middle of the eighteenth century. We think the white-fruited form the best tasting.

Parkinson also grew several other species, including the central European, *F. moschata*, and the eastern North American, *F. virginiana*, both of which are extremely vigorous. *F. moschata*, which he called the 'Bohemia strawberry', needs both male and female plants to bear the fruit, which is large and knobbly, with a delicious musky flavour. It was popular before the development of the larger hybrids.

*F. chiloensis*, from South America (with *F. virginiana*, a parent of

The delicious musk strawberry,
now known as *Fragaria moschata*,
from a late-eighteenth-century print

the modern hybrids), was introduced in 1727. It is not as vigorous as the others and so is more useful for decorative ground cover. It has glossy green leaves and large white flowers. *F. indica*, now renamed *Duchesnia indica*, was introduced from India in 1804. Quite rampant, with yellow flowers and red non-edible fruit (both occurring rather attractively at the same time), it was used for Regency hanging baskets and was recommended by Loudon for ground cover. The variegated-leaf strawberry, *F.* × *ananassa* 'Variegata', is a Victorian. The first mention of it is in 1859, when it was recommended for use to drape the sides of flower 'baskets' and urns; it is said to associate well with fuchsias.

# FRITILLARIA

A genus containing many flowers of exceptional beauty, which have been collected and highly valued for hundreds of years. Two species are common in gardens, and several others can easily be grown in the open border.

### *F. imperialis*
Crown imperial

South-eastern Turkey eastwards to the western Himalayas. This plant, long cultivated in Turkish gardens, was introduced to Europe around 1570, and from thence came to Britain. By 1597 Gerard has it in 'great plenty'. It is the first plant Parkinson describes in the *Paradisus* because 'The Crowne Imperiall for his stately beautifulness deserveth the first place in this our Garden of delight.' Both he and Gerard, incidentally, placed it among the lilies. They mention the double and triple crown imperial (ones with a second, and sometimes a third, row of flowers above the first), Gerard thinking the variation to be a product of age, or the 'fertilitie of the soil'. Parkinson thought them 'but meere accidentall'. Both also noticed the nectaries at the base of each petal (Gerard saw them 'resembling in shew faire orient pearles'), and that 'The whole plant ... do savour or smell very like a Fox.' They do.

Seventeenth-century gardeners only had the common brick-coloured form, but by the mid eighteenth century there were many sorts, including a truly double-flowered one in yellow, as well as a yellow single, and two sorts with variegated leaves. American gardens boasted red and yellow singles by 1740. Most of these are still around today, though only the yellow-flowered one is at all easily available. *F. imperialis* is not difficult to grow, liking well-drained soil in a sunny, warm place, though we have seen it do splendidly in semi-shade. It is best left undisturbed for several years.

## F. meleagris
Snake's head, fritillary

A native plant, though this was not realized until the eighteenth century. Foreign plants were introduced from France in the late sixteenth century and called the 'Chequered Daffodill or Ginny-Hen Floure'. It was, according to Gerard, 'greatly esteemed for the beautifying of our gardens and the bosoms of the beautifull'. As with any plant people like, variants were soon collected and began to proliferate. Doubles were grown by the end of the seventeenth century. By 1829, Loudon has nearly twenty varieties 'with red, white, purple, black, striped and double flowers', besides one said to be a cross between this and *F. imperialis*, an extraordinary-sounding combination. Some forms, including the double, are said to be still around today, though many are very rare. The species is very easy to grow, and can be naturalized in grass or under shrubs.

Three other easily grown species have been popular in Europe since the seventeenth century.

## F. persica
Southern Turkey to central Iran. Long cultivated in Persia and Turkey, the very robust form 'Adiyaman' probably dates from the seventh century. The flowers are a lovely dusky purple. It was introduced into Britain in the late sixteenth century and is described in Parkinson and Gerard as the 'Persian Lily'. The young shoots emerge early, so it is best in a sheltered position.

## F. pyrenaica
Pyrenees. Mentioned by the Tradescants in 1633, and by Parkinson, this is a very easy species, with dark, green-lined bells. It does well in semi-shade.

## F. latifolia
Caucasus, Turkey. Similar to *F. meleagris*, but shorter, and with fewer leaves. In the nineteenth century it was a popular garden plant with many garden varieties; it is now very scarce.

# GALANTHUS

Snowdrop

### G. nivalis

Probably native, widespread in Europe. All the other species are confined to the eastern Mediterranean region. Described by Theophrastus, around 320 BC, as growing on Mt Hymettus, and spoken of by St Francis as the emblem of hope, it is difficult to understand why the snowdrop failed to generate enthusiasm amongst early gardeners in Britain. It was called the Candlemas bell in the Middle Ages, but does not seem to have been a garden favourite and is not mentioned in Chaucer or Shakespeare. Gerard and Parkinson do describe it, along with *Leucojum*, as the 'bulbous Violet', and are not aware of it as a native flower. The name 'Snow drop' does not appear till the Thomas Johnson edition of Gerard's *Herball* in 1633. The double-flowered version, *G. nivalis* 'Flore-pleno', does not seem to be recorded before the eighteenth century, and in the nineteenth century numerous other species and varieties began to arrive. The snowdrop has, of course, made up for early indifference by becoming enormously popular, and an obsession with collectors. Amongst the nineteenth-century introductions were: *G. plicatus*, from the Crimea in 1818; *G. byzantinus* (now thought to be a subspecies of *G. plicatus*), from western Turkey in 1893 (perhaps a re-introduction, as Parkinson records a 'lesser early bulbous Violet' from Constantinople); *G. nivalis* var. *scharlokii*, from Germany in 1868; and *G. elwesii*, from Asia Minor, in 1875.

# GENTIANA

The genus, known to both the ancient Egyptians and Greeks, is named after Gentius, King of Illyria, who is supposed to have been the first to use it in medicine. If so, he used the roots of *G. lutea*, a European species not at all typical of the genus, being much larger than all the others, and bearing tiers of star-shaped yellow flowers.

Gerard grew it, as well as two other species; the lovely *G. acaulis*, the trumpet gentian (now considered as a group of species, but all with only slight differences between them), and *G. cruciata*. He also grew two related British wildlings, the marsh gentian (*G. pneumonanthe*) and the field gentian (actually now *Gentianella campestris*, grown at least by 1400).

More native species were still being grown in the early seventeenth century. The native G. *verna*, perhaps the most beautiful of all gentians, was popular, as was the handsome willow gentian (G. *asclepiadea*).

The first of the now popular Asiatic species, and one of the easiest to grow (G. *septemfida*), came from the Caucasus in 1758. Most of the others are recent introductions, and so are of no use to the period gardener.

# GERANIUM

The hardy geraniums have always been loved, but have perhaps reached new heights of popularity in modern times, when labour is expensive and problematical, giving full rein to their merits as groundcover plants. Their emergence into prominence (as with many hardy plants) is probably due to the influence of William Robinson. Many geraniums have good foliage and often beautiful flowers, most growing happily in sun or shade.

There are three native species which make good garden plants; G. *pratense*, G. *sanguineum* and G. *sylvaticum*.

## G. pratense
Meadow cranesbill

Grown by Gerard and Parkinson in its white and striped forms (G. *pratense* 'Album' and G. *pratense* 'Striatum', both still available). There are various modern and improved forms or hybrids of the type plant such as 'Johnson's Blue' or 'Mrs Kendall Clarke'. The handsome double forms, of which there are three (in white, lavender-blue and, best of all, deep violet-blue), were first described in the late nineteenth century. All make wonderful, if vigorous, border plants. The basic species is widely naturalized in America.

## G. sanguineum
Bloody cranesbill

This, with bright purplish-crimson flowers, was grown by Gerard and Parkinson. The form G.*s.* var. *lancastriense*, found on the Isle of Walney, has pink flowers, and was growing by 1732 in Dr Sherard's garden at Eltham. Other variants are more modern, the white being used in gardens since around 1900, and 'Glenluce' being introduced by A. T. Johnson around 1935.

## G. sylvaticum
Wood cranesbill

First used in the garden in the nineteenth century, it is quite close to *G. pratense* and, like it, is naturalized in North America. A double form, which we have not found, was grown by 1878.

Several European species, including *G. phaeum* and *G. macrorrhizum*, were introduced to Britain before the end of the sixteenth century, and are now widely naturalized: *G. phaeum* is the dusky cranesbill or mourning widow, a good plant for shade (now in pink, purple and white), and the pungent-leaved *G. macrorrhizum* is a splendid weed-suppressor for sun or shade.

Plants common in gardens now, and reasonably easily available, include:

*G. nodosum*, introduced from southern Europe in 1633. Has attractive lilac, violet or pinkish flowers, and grows well in shade. Naturalized.

*G. maculatum*, from North America in 1732.

*G. ibericum*, from south-eastern Europe and south-western Asia. Introduced to our gardens in 1802 (better known for the late Victorian hybrid *G.* × *magnificum*, a splendid plant called by Gertrude Jekyll 'the best of the large cranesbills').

*G. endressii* came from the Pyrenees in 1812 (there are several forms and hybrids of this plant, all modern).

*G. wallichianum* from the Himalayas in 1820 (best known for the late Victorian 'Buxton's Variety').

*G. psilostemon* (often called *G. armenum*) was brought from Armenia in 1874.

*G. himalayense* (sometimes listed as *G. grandiflorum*) came from Sikkim in the 1880s (the best-known forms being *G.h.* 'Gravetye', presumably a William Robinson plant, and *G.h.* 'Birch Double', of unknown date).

The pretty-leaved *G. renardii* is modern, from the Caucasus in 1935; the common cultivar 'Russell Pritchard', probably a *G. endressii* hybrid, was raised around 1915.

# GEUM

A large and widespread group of plants, only a few of which are in the garden. The common wildling herb bennet (*G. urbanum*) with its ordinary yellow flowers, was grown in medieval times, and probably earlier, because the root was used as a substitute for cloves, and an infusion of the leaves was good for 'stitches and griefe in the side'.

A double-flowered form of *Geum coccineum*,
from the *Journal of Horticulture
and Home Farmer* of 1907

Sixteenth-century gardeners also grew *G. rivale*, the water avens, some forms of which had (and have), flowers up to an inch in diameter. They can vary in colour from cream (actually a greenish rather than a yellowish white), to pink. Gerard mentions a 'mountain aven' with a bright red flower, which may be *G. coccineum* from the mountains of Greece, though it seems to have dropped out of use by the eighteenth century. Philip Miller, in 1754, says that avens are good plants for damp shady borders where nothing else will grow. That suggests a slight failure of his horticultural imagination, but bear G. *rivale* in mind, for some of the colour forms look very attractive amongst other damp-ground vegetation.

However, the geums of present-day gardens, gaudy, often double, in scarlets, oranges and some good yellows, are mainly offspring of the Chilean G. *chiloense*. This was introduced in 1824, with various other species of the genus from the same region. Almost all the hybrids that are still in commerce are modern.

GLAUCIUM, see *Papaver*.

GOMPHRENA, see *Amaranthus*.

# GRASSES

Plumes of the once-proud pampas grass can now be bought dyed the most awful shades of bottle green, bronze and madder. *Cortaderia selloana* will no doubt survive the indignity, and eventually regain the place of one of the most elegant of all Victorian grasses. Grasses were the subject of a mild rage from perhaps 1840 onwards, and the floras of the Far East and the Americas, as well as the natural flora of northern Europe, were raided for interesting finds.

Earlier, grasses had been little regarded. Parkinson describes only three, including one still very widely grown today. 'Gardeners' garters', 'ladies' laces' or 'ribbon grass' (*Phalaris arundinacea* 'Elegantissima') were the rather prosaic British names for something the French called '*aiguillette d'armes*', as the leaves resemble the striped pennants used by knights at war. The grass remained popular in eighteenth-century gardens, and was widely grown in Victorian Britain.

The only other old sorts are the lovely 'feather grasses' (species of *Stipa*). Parkinson describes two, lesser and greater, the lesser and older one being the most fun: 'for I have knowne, that many Gentlewomen have used the former lesser kind, being tyed with tufts, to set them instead of feathers about their beds, where they have lyen after childebearing ... when as they have been much admired of the ladies and gentles that have come to visit them'. This was probably *Stipa pennata* (still easily obtainable). It is not clear which species was called the 'greater' feather grass; perhaps *S. calamagrostis*.

23. *Cheiranthus* 'Miss Massey', a popular Victorian double wallflower

24. *Cheiranthus* 'Harpur Crewe', grown at least since the late sixteenth century

25. *Cheiranthus* 'Old Bloody Warrior', strongly scented and possibly Elizabethan

26. *Erysimum alpinum*, a 'perennial' wallflower, introduced in 1823, but popular in the late nineteenth century

▷ 28. *Dictamnus albus* 'Purpurea', which John Gerard thought 'verie rare and galent' in the late sixteenth century

▽ 27. *Helleborus orientalis* hybrids from species introduced in the nineteenth century

29. Verbascums and a *Rubus* species combined in an attractive tangle with nineteenth-century salvias and roses at David Bromley's Shropshire garden

These three remained the only decorative grasses throughout the eighteenth century. As botany became a polite occupation, interest in grasses began to pick up. By the late 1820s, some natives like quaking grass (*Briza media*) or southern Europeans like the lovely *Helictotrichon sempervirens*, were beginning to appear in the gardening literature, but not yet in lists of common border flowers.

The most important of the pampas grasses arrived from South America in 1848, but it was only when people became interested in exotic foliage ten to twenty years later that it became a popular plant.

By the 1880s grasses had found their way into many departments of the garden. Some, like the variegated form of the common foxtail (*Alopecurus pratensis*) were used, carefully clipped, as edgings to flower-beds; the Japanese *Miscanthus sinensis* was often used with common lilies, providing height in the same place. The vast tribe of bamboos soon became essential in the wild garden. In the early twentieth century, grasses of all sorts were dried for winter decoration, and the foliage of plants like the yellow form of *Milium effusum* ('Bowles' Golden Grass') or the striped *Phalaris* began to play a part both in formal and informal plantings.

# HELIANTHUS

## Sunflower

All are from North or South America, so even the oldest ones in European gardens date largely from the sixteenth century. Several species have much more ancient histories in the Americas, where all seem to have been food crops.

Naturally, anything as spectacular as the annual sunflower (*Helianthus annuus*) will have attracted sixteenth-century gardeners, and it was widely grown. It remained popular for the next hundred years, though it began to go out of fashion in the more fastidious Age of Reason. In that century, new species of sunflower, ones with more natural elegance, were still pouring in. Even so, it was still grown as the central plant in 'bouquets' (eighteenth-century flowerbeds of moderate size, planted up in as gorgeous a manner as possible). Incidentally, the perennial forms that were supplanting it were most sought after in London gardens where, even by the 1750s, the smokes and fogs were so bad that many other garden plants refused to grow. The following three species are all perennial.

### H. atrorubens

South-eastern United States. Early eighteenth century. Still popular, this was the favourite flower in the famous Dr Sherard's garden in 1732, but thereafter became rare until its re-introduction to Regency gardens from Louisiana. It then took off, as it will in your garden too.

### H. × multiflorus

Origin unknown, but in cultivation by the late sixteenth century. Most of the named sorts now available, lovely things for a spacious border, are of the late nineteenth century at the most. Beware, as they are invasive.

### H. × laetiflorus

Possibly North America, perhaps of garden origin. This is a rather complex hybrid, but certainly involving *H. rigidus* (introduced to Europe in 1810), and the far-famed Jerusalem artichoke (*H. tuberosus*). This had a considerable vogue in the seventeenth century as a vegetable, and then all Europe realized its disadvantages and it dropped to its present minor status.

# HELICHRYSUM

The helichrysums encompass both the tender and showy 'everlasting' annuals, the hardy and shrubby 'everlastings' that decorated ladies' hats in the eighteenth century, and the familiar grey- or white-leaved sorts, like *H. angustifolium* (the familiar curry plant), and *H. splendens*.

## IMMORTELLES, LIVE LONGS, GOLDEN FLOWER GENTLE, ETERNELLE FLOWER

There are many sorts of everlasting flowers, but the oldest in cultivation is *H. orientale*. This seems to have been introduced from Crete or Turkey in the seventeenth century, though its dried flowers were known earlier. By the eighteenth century, apart from its use by milliners (charming, no doubt) its clusters of straw-yellow flowers were used to decorate fireplaces in summer and vases in winter. (It was widely used in America for the same purposes.) It seems to have dropped out of use in the following hundred years. Also now rarely seen is *H. stoechas* (goldy-locks or golden cassidony), a fifteenth-century arrival from southern Europe. As its pleasing names tell, the flowers are a shiny golden yellow.

However, the plants now most widely called 'everlastings', and available in many colours and heights, belong to *H. bracteatum*. This was only introduced in the early nineteenth century, and from Australia. Its showy flowers were soon immensely popular, used for winter flower decorations, for funeral wreaths and bouquets, and in those finicky craftworks with which idle Victorian ladies filled their empty hours.

HELICTOTRICHON, see Grasses.

# HELIOTROPIUM

Heliotrope, cherry pie

Soft velvety leaves and sprays of small blue flowers are both made memorable by the flowers' heady perfume; a mixture of almonds, vanilla, lemons and perhaps some cloves. High Victorian gardens in summer, and their conservatories in winter, were where the heliotrope reached its greatest perfection and variety. It is essential in any garden of that period. New varieties appeared almost every year, each heralded as new and improved; most were hybrids between *H. corymbosum* (from Peru) and *H. peruviana*. The latter came to Europe in the 1750s, but made little headway with its obscure flowers. *H. corymbosum*, of Regency gardens, had much showier blooms, and, together with other South American plants (see *Verbena*, *Calceolaria* and *Petunia*), soon made a hit.

The hybrid heliotropes were in all shades between deepest violet blue and pure white, and sometimes whole parterres were filled with them. Good forms were propagated by cuttings and overwintered under glass (you can still do this if you find something special amongst seed-grown plants). If you garden in the north, though, you will find that plants do best even in summer under glass; they will not grow much if bedded out, and so will not flower. Under glass, feed them and support them with canes, and you can have quite large bushes.

Seventeenth- and early-eighteenth-century references to heliotrope refer either to weedy European plants of little interest, or to the Jerusalem artichoke, which because its flowers follow the sun, was called 'the Indian heliotrope'.

*Helleborus niger*, the Christmas rose, from the pages of *The Garden*, 1883

# HELLEBORUS

A group of handsome and very fashionable plants, with elegant rather reptilian leaves and flowers; it is no surprise that they are all very poisonous. All species hybridize with ease, both in the wild where they meet, and even more easily in the garden. Interest in the hybrids, though presumably some may date from the nineteenth century, is a recent phenomenon, and fully justified. The species themselves fall fairly neatly into 'ancient' and 'modern', or at least nineteenth century.

## H. niger

Black hellebore, lyons fote, pedelyon, Christmas rose

Eastern Alps, but widely naturalized. Used by mankind since neolithic times, and probably as a garden plant since Roman days. Prehistoric burials sometimes contain seed and capsules, but usage may have been as an arrow poison (it was still used as such by the Gauls), or for religious, medical or magic purposes. Some of these survived until recently; it was a cure for madness, melancholy and hypochondria well into the seventeenth century, and was planted into modern times by cottage doors as a protection from spells.

Parkinson thought that the 'flowers have the most beautiful aspect, and the time of his flowering most rare, that is, in the deeps of Winter about Christmas, when no other can be seen upon the ground'. The flower remained, and remains, popular. Large-flowered selections are all modern.

## H. foetidus

Black nisewort, setterwort, bearsfoot

Europe, including Britain, and Asia. Handsome bunches of bright green flowers (best in the second or third year from seed), make it a fashionable flower today. Some Italian forms are especially grand; a good one was grown by E. A. Bowles. Today's vogue for green flowers was certainly echoed by late-seventeenth-century gardeners; in earlier times the plant may have been used medicinally. It seems not to have attracted eighteenth- or early-nineteenth-century connoisseurs, but came back into fashion in the 1880s, when its leaves became popular for dressing the fruit dish (alarming thought, as the juice is poisonous). A splendid plant altogether.

## H. viridis

Bearsfoot, wild blacke hellebore

Europe, including Britain. Reportedly used by sixteenth-century horse doctors, though presumably not for curing melancholia. Rare in nature, rarer in the garden (it will not flower in ours).

## H. lividus

Balearics. 1880s. One of the later introductions, included here as a connoisseurs' plant of the mid nineteenth century. Flowers vary from green to truly livid (pale pinkish grey, 'the colour of a corpse', but attractive all the same), and have a slight perfume on warm days in the conservatory, where it needs to be kept in cold areas.

### H. orientalis

Greece and Turkey. It is often said to be a nineteenth-century introduction (it was described in *Edwards Botanical Register* of 1842 as 'vastly rare', and was, like the foregoing species, kept under glass). However, Miller grew a tall, reddish-flowered plant that must have been this one, and even Parkinson grew something similar 'from beyond the sea', which 'perished quickly after'. Not much grown until early this century, it is now popular, with vast numbers of hybrids. The early flowers of some forms are damaged by hard frosts, so find a sheltered site for it, and it will enliven January strolls in the garden.

### H. corsicus

Corsica, Sardinia and the Balearics. Mid 1800s. Very rare until recently, now immensely fashionable, admired for its large green flowers and spiky foliage.

# HEMEROCALLIS

Lily asphodel, day lily

For all the seven thousand or more present-day varieties, in shades of pink, scarlet, apricot, with waved petals, fancy 'throats' and the rest, one of the sixteenth-century day lilies is still, to our minds, much the most beautiful. This is usually called *H. flava*, but now correctly has an older name, *H. lilioasphodelus*. This is probably native to Asia, as are all the other species, though this one has been in Europe for so long that it was once thought to be native to the foothills of the southern Alps. Its flowers are an unsullied and rather lemon yellow, elegantly trumpeted, and with a ravishing perfume. Some forms have rather floppy leaves and flower stems, but their languid elegance is more fun than some of the others that have rather perky upright stalks. It seems happy almost anywhere in the garden, and is particularly good by doorways and flights of steps. We used to grow it under glass for early flowers, and the perfume was almost too strong.

It is widely cultivated, and was 'common in every country garden' in the 1660s. It emigrated early, and was popular in American cottage gardens by the 1800s. In America and Europe it was often seen in Victorian flower arrangements, teamed with red and white peonies.

The other 'antique' species is *H. fulva*. Chinese, and an ancient garden plant there, it was grown both for the beauty of the flowers and for their edibility. It was known, with Chinese elegance, as 'the flower of forgetfulness', and was supposed to cause loss of memory and therefore of sorrow. No such effects seem to have been noticed in prosaic Europe; Gerard, who grew this 'orange tawney' day lily, reports their use for curing 'hot swellings of the dugges' after child-birth; probably not the sort of forgetfulness the Chinese had in mind. The plant was well known in the 1570s throughout Europe, and was connected with Phoenicia; perhaps it arrived here along the old spice routes. Certainly, it was considered just as choice. It had brownish-red flowers, rather upright growth, and was sterile. This strain (technically called a clone), naturalized itself far and wide, and can still easily be found in commerce under the name 'Europa'.

By the end of the seventeenth century, when the two first arrivals were common, 'choice' sorts were available with flesh-coloured flowers, and there was one so pale as to be almost white (though this may have been a *Crinum*). Nothing much more happened to the genus in the eighteenth century, except that gardeners started calling *H. lilioasphodelus* 'the yellow tuberose', because of the similarity of perfume.

Not a great deal more happened in the nineteenth century, until 1860. A double form of *H. fulva*, crowded with petals, was brought from Japan, where it had been noted by European travellers since 1712. It was being sold by the London nurseries by 1861. A marvellous variegated form arrived in 1864, and soon became popular (the leaves are splendid, and even the double flowers appeal to some gardeners). Both are known as 'Kwanso' types. Another dramatic sort, with a deep bronze patch on each of the petals (now known as *H. maculata*), arrived in 1897.

New species began to flood into Europe towards the end of the century, and some arrived in America directly from Japan, to be then re-exported to Europe. American conditions suited them, though the first attempts at crossing species started in Britain. A Mr Yeld produced one called 'Apricot' in 1892, and there were many more by 1900. Amos Perry produced some exceptional sorts in the early twentieth century, and so American gardeners naturally wanted their own. They soon surpassed European efforts. The grandest modern sorts are all from that country, where it has become almost a florists' flower. In several hundred years' time, collectors will be agonizing about all the vanished varieties . . .

# HEPATICA

'Jon the Gardener', in his early-fifteenth-century list, describes the liverwort as a herbal flower (as the vernacular name suggests). Medicinal use seems not to have lasted; by the 1440s, the name trinity flower becomes as important, or even 'mount trifoly' a hundred years later. The leaves are, of course, deeply tri-lobed, giving rise to the old Latin name of *H. triloba* (now more correctly *H. nobilis*).

This lovely plant is a native of much of Europe and North America, generally with clear blue flowers. In Italy and Austria, however, there are populations with purple, white or pinkish ones, and sharp-eyed gardeners have discovered doubles in all these shades.

Gerard grew red, white and blue singles in 1597, and his editor added the double blue, once 'a stranger in England . . . now plentiful in many gardens' by the 1630s. Parkinson notes that this lovely plant was introduced from Italy. Gardeners then must have found the doubles easy to propagate, for just ninety years later the singles were almost disregarded. Double purple and blue were widely grown, and connoisseurs had red, pink and white.

In the early eighteenth century Hill wrote, 'It is a plant . . . that needs nothing, but to have been more scarce, to have been esteem'd extremely . . . but it is doubtless in the deep blue double State that the plant glows in its full lustre', and he was entirely right. By the 1750s, even some of the doubles were common enough to use as edges to flower-garden borders, though the double white was still rare. Pink was often used in Scottish kitchen gardens.

By the 1820s, all sorts of hepatica were mixed with plantings of snowdrops and eranthis. By the 1840s a sort of class attitude to hepaticas had emerged, with doubles being thought appropriate to grandish gardens, and the cottage dwellers only aspiring to singles. It is not clear if this applied in America as well, where hepaticas were widely grown in mixed flower borders.

In 1851, a writer in the *Gardeners' Chronicle* had discovered that the double white was fertile, and suggested that serious breeding of new types could now begin. It did; only six sorts were common in the

1860s, but by 1870, this number had doubled. The traditional sorts had become cheap. Astonishingly, some nurseries offered double pink, blue and red at about 50s. per hundred plants, with reductions on a thousand. One even had double red at 12s. per hundred!

We still hear of local gardens with paths once bordered by doubles, and a chance visitor said hers still was. Yet doubles seem now impossible to grow; ours just about manage to come up each year, wan with the effort. It is difficult to know what has happened. If doubles were so cheap in the late nineteenth century, perhaps everyone thirty or forty years later got bored with them and threw them out. Perhaps the doubles became virused and difficult to propagate. For whatever reason the doubles are now rare and should be treasured.

The other garden hepatica is *H. transylvanica*, with larger rhizomes and larger and fancier-shaped leaves. In the wild only blue shades exist, though there is a pink and possibly hybrid form in the modern garden. The species was introduced in the late nineteenth century and was soon being selected and hybridized for improved forms. Plants like 'Ballardii' represent the best of these and are certainly lovely.

HERMODACTYLUS, see *Iris*.

## HESPERIS

Sweet rocket, dame's violet, close sciences

The ordinary single *H. matronalis*, whether white, pale or deep purple, is one of the pleasures of early summer evenings.

The species has an enormous range throughout southern Europe, eastwards to Siberia, and is quite variable. The forms in gardens nowadays seem to be French, which may suggest that the first gardeners to use it were from that country (though this may not have been the sort widely grown in fifteenth-century gardens).

By the end of the sixteenth century, a double white appeared, and remained rare until the 1640s. By the late seventeenth century, every country garden grew single white, purple, and striped sorts, while posh ones had the double white, or the very new double purple. Both were said to root easily from any sort of cutting. By the mid eighteenth century even the striped form had doubled, and the double white was so common that it was easily to be had in the London flower markets.

However, gardeners had noticed that all forms were getting harder to root. The white double sort had reached America by 1725, though it is surprising that the plant survived the crossing.

The striped sort seems to have vanished by the 1820s, though the double white was still in every cottage garden; it would not grow in smoky cities. It was popular all over Europe, and there were apparently sheets of it on the west coast of Scotland. By 1884, the purple had virtually vanished, and even the double white was being sold at 1s. 2d. a plant because it was 'now almost lost to commerce'.

The position remains the same today. The double white is now exceptionally difficult to propagate, even though it exists in at least two forms (they differ in the hairiness of the leaf). However, if you ever come across it, and you really do have time to look after it properly, snap it up. Gerard was right when he wrote 'within this two or three yeares hath been brought to our knowledge a very beautiful kinde of these Dames Violets, having very faire double and white flowers'. He knew an exceptional plant when he saw it.

*H. matronalis* is rather vaguely perennial. *H. tristis*, its yellow flowers with a purple flush, is decidedly biennial. It has been in gardens since at least the early seventeenth century, though never widely grown. It is fine in the wild garden, but better on old walls if you have them.

## HIERACIUM

Of this colossal groups of hawkweeds, the only one for old gardens was described by Gerard as 'a stranger and onely to be found in some few gardens.' This was the golden mouse-ear, Grimme the collier or the orange hawkweed (this last being its boring and rather belittling modern name). Technically, it is *H. aurantiacum*, though the flower is not a flat orange shade, but is excitingly suffused with rose madder. It is quite invasive and seeds rather too, but has nice dark spotted leaves, and was the only old plant we found in the ruined gardens of one of the most romantic castles in all Scotland. It is a native of much of northern and central Europe.

Grimme the Collier, from Gerard's *Herball* of 1633

# HOSTA

A group of plants already deep into a florists' boom, with dozens of new hybrids appearing each season at high prices, and old ones appearing in general cultivation at much lower ones. Soon every garden will have its group of hosta forms, whereas a decade or so ago they were only in flower arrangers' or dowagers' gardens. Lovely though many are, they are not of much use to the period gardener. Though hostas (once more amusingly called 'funkias') began to appear from China and Japan in the 1780s (*H. plantaginea* and *H. ventricosa*), they were not much grown until the late 1830s. By this time the wonderful *H. sieboldiana* was common in London gardens (it did not mind the smoke). None was especially amenable to the carpet-bedding craze (though some modern ones would have been excellent), so they were relegated to the woodland garden by the 1890s. By that date, too, one then called '*Funkia ovata*' (probably *H. plantaginea*), or the white day lily, was thought of as an old-fashioned American garden flower.

In the last years of the nineteenth century Gertrude Jekyll started looking seriously at hostas, and began to exploit their visual possibilities with great imagination. She planted the glossy-leaved *H. plantaginea* 'Grandiflora' (a sterile Japanese hybrid introduced in 1841) in huge Italian pots, combined with white lilies, ferns and hydrangeas. Elsewhere, she used the blue leaves of *H. sieboldiana* as a foil to soft pink moutan peonies.

HYACINTHOIDES, see *Scilla*.

# HYACINTHUS

Common hyacinth

Native to western Syria and Turkey, but widely naturalized elsewhere. In the wild the flowers are grey, violet blue or white, but garden forms in a wider range of colours may have existed in Constantinople long before their introduction to western Europe, probably in the mid sixteenth century. Gerard grew blue, white and purple singles at the end of the century, and a greenish-flowered double was added in the 1633 edition of his *Herball*. He was not doing too well, for other European gardens already had blue, white and pink doubles by 1613.

Doubles became popular, if expensive. There were seven sorts in

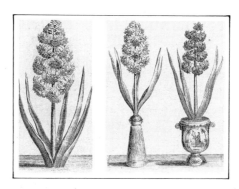

Early-eighteenth-century double hyacinths
from George Voorhelm's
*Traité sur la jacinthe*, 1773

Europe by 1687 (most were produced by Dutch breeders) with, in England at any rate, a double white being the most choice (they still are).

By 1754, Miller lists twelve sorts and, though giving a long section on their cultivation, does not explain that hyacinths have become an object of speculation just like the earlier tulip mania. A good variety like 'King of Great Britain' could cost £100 a bulb, and rarer ones still fetched twice that sum. These costs are astonishing, bearing in mind the numbers of bulbs required for a mid-eighteenth-century bedding scheme.

These old doubles had rather loose flower spikes, often with nodding flowers. The flowers themselves were either semi-double or double, with a mass of tiny petals forming a button in the middle of the flower (sometimes of a different colour), or just fully double.

By the 1800s or so, the price of doubles had dropped to a few shillings a bulb, and gardeners almost lost interest in the singles (though singles remained essential to provide the pollen for breeding new doubles). Doubles remained immensely popular throughout the rest of the nineteenth century, until by its end new developments in the single sorts began to reverse the trend. Singles began to appear with flowers so densely packed in the spike that they almost made 'drum-sticks' of colour. These were cheap to produce, and perfect for bedding schemes. The breeders of doubles tried to emulate this development, but the visual difference between tightly packed singles and doubles proved not dramatic enough to cope with the difference in price. The doubles were doomed, and today only a few sorts remain; we have not found any of the ones with differently coloured buttons.

Using hyacinths in the garden always presents a problem. Almost all modern singles have tight flower spikes in the first year. In the second year, if you have starved them a bit, the flower spike will be much looser, and will look much more like a seventeenth- or eighteenth-century hyacinth. You are unlikely to find enough doubles to make a hyacinth bed (we grow our few precious ones in pots for the house), but try using singles. Numerous plans were published; here is a grand one of 1766 designed by the Haarlem bulb raiser, George Voerhelm, and a simpler and rather earlier one by J. Krebs:

In this one, the bed is seven rows deep (allow three inches between rows), with a single bulb at each 'station'.

| pink | white | pale blue | pink | white ... | | |
|---|---|---|---|---|---|---|
| blue | blue | blue | blue | blue ... | | |
| pale blue | white | pale blue | pink | pink ... | | |
| blue | blue | blue | blue | blue... | ... ... ... repeated |
| pink | white | pale blue | white | pink ... | | |
| blue | blue | blue | blue | blue ... | | |
| pink | white | pink | pale blue | pink ... | | |

or what about this five-row bed which, continued, gives a zigzag of colours:

| pink | white | white | white | pink | blue | blue | blue |
|---|---|---|---|---|---|---|---|
| blue | pink | white | pink | blue | pink | blue | pink |
| white | blue | pink | blue | white | blue | pink | blue |
| pink | white | blue | white | blue | white | blue | white |
| pink | pink | white | blue | blue | blue | white | pink |

In the top scheme, we have substituted 'pale blue' for what is, in the original, a blue-centred white flower.

As with the tulip, planting schemes were remarkably conservative, and the examples we give could be used for seventeenth-century as well as for early-nineteenth-century hyacinth beds. Some general ideas for Victorian plantings are given (pp. 53 ff.) for anything later than that.

If you do come across some double-flowered hyacinths (there are only two or three still just about in commerce), you will find that the flower spikes are still a bit tight. Starve them, and you will get something that looks perfectly authentic. Better still, starving them extremely reduces the doubling, and you might find that you have fertile plants (at least female fertile). If you do, take pollen from some other single hyacinth in the garden, and use it to pollinate the fertile 'double'. Many of the seedlings should give double or semi-double flowers; bulbs take about five years or so to get to the right size.

Mid-Georgian flowerbeds would also combine hyacinths with other bulbs in flower at the same time. This increases the colour range a bit. Yellow hyacinths all date from the late nineteenth century at the earliest.

### H. amethystinus
Spanish hyacinth

Pyrenees. Cultivated sporadically from the early seventeenth century, but only general in gardens from 1830 or so. Exceptionally attractive, especially in the white form. Good in the wild garden.

## HYSSOPUS

A shrubby herb, of no use in the kitchen, but attractive in flower, in various shades of blue, as well as white, and a bluish pink. It is native to much of southern and eastern Europe, but has been cultivated for so long that it is also widely naturalized. It was in almost every garden in the fifteenth century, and as even the wild form is very variable, it is not surprising that there were many varieties in the garden, mostly now lost.

Gerard grew all the present-day flower colours, but had a variegated sort 'very goodly to behold'. Parkinson went one better and had a golden-leaved one. By the mid eighteenth century, Miller went several better again, having a curled-leaf one, one with cut and jagged leaves, and even one smelling of musk. Parkinson talks of hyssop being a country medicine, used for green wounds, falling sickness and aches and pains. It was still widely used as a tisane in the eighteenth century, though thereafter it dropped from use.

Old bushes develop nice gnarled trunks and lend a picturesque look to gardens with plenty of lavender, sages and roses. The bushes clip well, and they were used to make 'knots' in Tudor and early Stuart gardens. They still make excellent edgings in formal gardens. Clippings were once used to strew on floors.

## IBERIS
### Candytuft

Candy is the old name for Crete, and it is from that lovely island that Gerard received seed 'By the liberality of the right honourable the Lord Edward Zouch'. He did well too, getting plants 'sometimes blew, often purple, carnation or horseflesh, but seldom white'. His plant was *Iberis umbellata*, a common annual today, and once again with various pinky-purple or reddish shades (no modern seed catalogue would now dare call them 'horseflesh').

Gerard must have lost the pinkish strains, for Parkinson only had white and purple, and that remained the colour range into the present century.

The other common *Iberis* species are perennial and more recent. *I. semperflorens* appeared here in the late seventeenth century, and did well despite its Sicilian origin. It seems to have been used in the 'wilderness' and in early-nineteenth-century shrubberies, 'where it is particularly well adapted to enliven the sombre appearance of ever-green plantations during the winter season'.

*I. sempervirens*, growing on Mediterranean sea cliffs, reached the gardens of northern Europe in the mid eighteenth century, and was used on grottoes and rockwork.

## IRIS

A genus so widespread in Europe, Asia and northern Africa that all nations of gardeners have admired both their own, and their neighbours', irises. Some of the most ancient garden irises have not only lost any contact with wild species, but are now grown in temperate gardens worldwide. Since the sixteenth century, interested gardeners have always grown a wide range of species and varieties: here we deal only with the most popular sorts.

### Iris germanica
German or bearded iris and, possibly, fleur-de-luce

Modern studies suggest that *I. germanica* and its forms are sterile hybrids between *I. aphylla* and *I. variegata* and, though similar in apppearance, are quite distinct from the fertile and fairly modern bearded irises. Perhaps *I. germanica* originated in southern Europe, or even the Near East; it is so ancient that it is naturalized over much of Europe (including Germany), western and central Asia. It is found in various colour forms, from deep blue through to almost pure white (palest in *I. florentina*). The commonest form in many gardens is in two shades of blue, though it is not related to the bicoloured 'bearded' types. It has an undemonstrative beauty missing in some of the showier 'bearded' irises. Medieval sources stress the medicinal uses of all the German irises, though that function seems largely to have vanished by the sixteenth century. The dried roots are still used as orris root, sweetly scented of violets, and put into pot-pourri or used as a base for scented powders and cheap perfumes.

The form of German iris called '*I. florentina*' is still to be found, and a gorgeous thing it is, being justly popular well into the eighteenth century. The milky white flowers have perfect form and a delicious perfume, and also last reasonably well. It is not clear whether the irises that were symbols of regality, used by the pharaohs of ancient Egypt and the kings of ancient Crete, were this plant or the rather similar *I. albicans*. It was this equally pale iris that the followers of Muhammad adopted to plant by their graves, so spreading it all along northern Africa, into eastern Europe and to Spain.

## BEARDED IRISES

These seem to be based on hybrids between the pale-blue-flowered *I. pallida* and the yellow and brown *I. variegata*. None seems to be much earlier than the seventeenth century, when quite a number of iris species were living at close quarters in gardens all over Europe. Gardeners here were certainly raising them from seed by 1601, and becoming excited by the new colour range, though the additions were

◁ 30. *Erigeron philadelphicus,* a marvellous introduction of 1778

▽ 31. *Verbena* 'Silver Anne', similar to nineteenth-century bedding varieties

32. The prettiest of the Parma violets, 'Marie Louise', of 1865

33. Catmints, *Chrysanthemum coccineum,* and other nineteenth-century flowers at Mottisfont Abbey, Hants

▷ 35. *Erythronium* 'Pagoda', a fine modern hybrid

▽ 34. *Hemerocallis* 'Kwanso Flore Pleno', an ancient
Japanese garden plant introduced to Europe by 1881

△ 37. *Hemerocallis flava* and golden sage, both known since the la[
sixteenth century

◁ 36. *Salvia patens,* introduced in the early nineteenth century,
and once used for bedding

rather dingy-sounding yellowish whites, greeny mauves and one or two fancily striped sorts.

The eighteenth century saw pure yellow selfs, as well as bicolours. Deliberate crossing began in the 1820s. Flowers with waved petal edges (the *plicata* group), were around by 1844, and by 1870 or so there was quite a large range of colours, including browns, and blues so deep as to be almost black (one Victorian flower arranger used to team straw and deep blue irises with the buds of *Papaver orientale*). Massive breeding programmes were under way by the 1890s in Europe and a decade later in America. Gertrude Jekyll made use of these new plants and designed a number of iris gardens.

## OTHER IRISES

### I. foetida

Native. The roast-beef iris or stinking gladdon. This has been in gardens since the sixteenth century and was grown for its marvellous orange-scarlet seeds; the variegated-leaf form (very handsome) was discovered in the eighteenth century. Subtler still are the forms with either yellow flowers or yellow seeds, or both, though these seem to be no earlier than the late 1800s.

### I. sibirica

Central and eastern Europe; Russia. Popular in gardens by the late sixteenth century. A connoisseurs' flower in the seventeenth and eighteenth centuries. Selection of forms started in the nineteenth century, but only late on, with the growth of the herbaceous border. Most named sorts are modern. Foliage, flowers and seed pods are all immensely useful in the garden when slender and very linear elegance is necessary.

### I. xiphioides
English iris

Supposedly discovered in Bristol in the sixteenth century, but actually native to the Pyrenees. However it was so common in England that even continental botanists and gardeners thought it must belong here. Widely grown ever since. Even in the seventeenth century it was a florists' flower, available in many colours and markings – the rarest were pale reddish purple and white striped with violet. The present range is no larger. Differing from the next species in that the seed pods are large enough to let the seeds rattle.

## *I. xiphium*
Spanish iris

Southern France to Portugal and Spain. Again, widely grown by the sixteenth century and in a similarly wide range of colours. The so-called Dutch iris is a hybrid between an early-flowering Spanish iris and another species. It is now more popular than either Spanish or English, and is a florists' flower in the modern sense of that word.

Interesting irises for sixteenth-century gardens include the deliciously plum-pie-perfumed *I. graminea* from central and southern Europe, the wonderfully elegant and also perfumed *I. pallida*, the ancient *I. pseudacorus* (though the handsome variegated form is modern), and the mysterious-looking *I. tuberosa* (now usually placed in the genus *Hermodactylus*; Gerard called the flowers 'goose-turd green', but don't let this put you off).

For more modern gardens, try *I. kaempferi*, introduced from Japan in 1857, *I. tectorum*, grown on Chinese roofs to preserve houses from lightning and with suitably electric-blue flowers, from 1872, *I. unguicularis*, eastern Mediterranean and northern Africa, late nineteenth century, and the handsome *I. chrysographes*, Chinese and introduced in 1911 (look for the gorgeous velvety black sort). The pretty little *I. reticulata* from the Caucasus, Turkey and Iran arrived in the mid nineteenth century. All named forms are modern.

KNAUTIA, see *Scabiosa*.

# KNIPHOFIA
Torch lily, red-hot poker

These spectacular denizens of large Victorian herbaceous borders, now mostly grown in subtle pale colours, still look slightly foreign in northern Europe. They are all African; the first species to be introduced was *K. uvaria* in 1707. Surprisingly, it does not seem to have made much impact. *K. pumila*, also from South Africa, followed in 1774, but it was not until the Abyssinian *K. leichtlinii* arrived in 1880 that things took off. Before then the garden writers had been rather rude about them, but William Robinson, with his usual perspicacity, was enthusiastic, especially about the dramatic hybrids that soon appeared. After that, there was no stopping them, until even the most insensitive gardeners began to groan. Of the sixty or so hybrids available in 1900, most are lost. If you want to use them, they can look wonderful, especially up against stone walls.

*Lathyrus rotundifolius,*
a perennial and unsweet pea,
from *Gardeners' Chronicle*, 1880

# LATHYRUS

### Lathyrus odoratus

Some time in the year 1699, Franciscus Cupani, a Sicilian monk, sent a few seeds to Dr Robert Uvedale of Enfield. Amongst the plants that came up was a twining pea that produced reddish-blue and deep-violet flowers, and had a quite overpoweringly sweet smell. The sweet pea, as it soon became known (though various other species are, if less spectacularly, perfumed), may have been grown earlier, for something like it can occasionally be seen in the medieval illuminations produced by Continental monasteries. However, this time it caught on, as Dr Uvedale passed seeds around. The plant was being sold commercially by Benjamin Townsend in 1724, and a few years later various different

A Victorian dwarf sweet pea, 'Cupid', first shown at the Crystal Palace in 1897; from *Gardeners' Chronicle*, 1898

colours began to appear. Miller grew a pure white one (now sadly lost) and the lovely pink and white 'Painted Lady' (still with us). The seeds were sown in late summer, the young plants put out in autumn, and by next summer huge plants produced thousands of flowers. We have not yet tried this, nor have we yet used the traditional place for them, which was along the espalier rails of fruit trees in the kitchen garden.

There were five varieties by the close of the eighteenth century, six by 1837. Forty years or so on, Henry Eckford began serious selection and crossing of the strains, soon producing the improved large-flowered sorts still sometimes to be found as 'Giant' or 'Grandiflora' sweet peas. These had, too, an improved colour range. In 1899, a certain Silas Cole grew some of Eckford's 'Prima Donna', and found a single plant with waved petal edges – the beginnings of the Spencer strain. These waved sorts had ousted all others by 1910 or so, and have stayed on top ever since. Modern developments include some horrid dwarfs used as bedding. None of the Spencer types have as powerful a scent as the older ones which, if there are too many indoors, can be almost disagreeable.

All the sweet pea types are annual. However, there are some very fine perennial peas.

### L. latifolius

Central and southern Europe. Cultivated at least since the fifteenth century, and widely naturalized. In nature, the flowers are purple or pink, and Gerard and Parkinson had these colours. A pure white sort appeared in the early nineteenth century, and nowadays a large white called 'Snow Queen' shares pride of place with various pink or rose shades. All are attractive, and are good for rambling through shrubs, especially roses. The flowers have no scent.

### L. grandiflorus

Sicily and southern Italy, the Balkans. Probably introduced in the early nineteenth century, and a popular cottage-garden flower by mid-century. The large rose-pink and mauve flowers have an agreeable smell and pick well. The plant is rampageous once established.

### L. vernus

Southern Europe. Early seventeenth century. Flowering early, old forms have lilac and blue flowers.

# LAVANDULA

### L. angustifolia
Lavender, spike, spike lavender

Mediterranean region. An ancient garden plant, and one essential for every garden, whatever its period. The usual lavender (*L. angustifolia*, once called *L. spica*) was used by the Romans and brought by them to northern Europe; it is referred to in all sorts of medieval sources. It was in every garden from the sixteenth century at least, yielding essential oils for perfumery and medicine, as well as purely garden pleasures. Not surprisingly, various other species in the genus have been taken into the garden at various times and, though lovely, none has become so widely grown or given so many varieties.

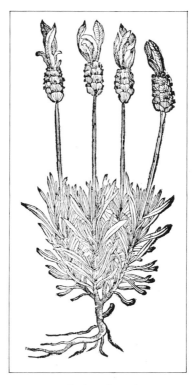

Stickadove lavender,
from Gerard's *Herball* of 1633

By late medieval times it was used as low hedges in knot gardens and later in parterres. Though all these need clipping to keep them neat, the plants must have been allowed to flower (the flower-heads are the 'crop' for distillation anyway), for a number of flower variants were grown by the late sixteenth century. Gerard grew the handsome white-flowered form, and had seen, in some royal garden, a dwarf and deep-blue-flowered sort, supposedly with a strange smell. White-flowered sorts were admired by Queen Henrietta Maria; now there are both large and short forms, the former by far the more attractive though young plants need some support before they become established. The usual blue sort had crossed the Atlantic by the seventeenth century, though it needed protection from cold North American winters.

By the eighteenth century, the range had grown. 'English lavender' was the sort generally agreed to make the best lavender oils and waters, and this remained so well into Victorian times. In 1852 an ancient crop at Mitcham near London yielded £200 an acre of oils – the first distillation having the best aroma. A lovely pink-flowered one is probably of recent origin.

### L. stoechas
Stickadove, French lavender

Southern Europe from Spain to Greece. In gardens by the sixteenth century. Variable in nature, there are many forms in the garden, the best having especially large and intensely coloured tufts of bracts at the top of each knot of flowers. They are very pretty, though not hardy in northern Europe, hence a common pot plant for many centuries.

## OTHER LAVENDERS

Many sixteenth-century gardeners loved variations on themes, and so were keen on cut-leaved lavenders. *L. dentata* was the commonest, with a tuft of blue or white bracts at the tip of each inflorescence, just as popular as *L. stoechas*, though we find the smell less attractive; it hails from Spain and the Balearic islands. The gorgeous *L. lanata* with broad white leaves, effective and long-lived against a warm wall, and with a good smell, was introduced to Regency gardens from southern Spain.

# LEUCOJUM
Snowflake, snow flower, bulbous violet

Of the snowflakes, the spring, summer and autumn types were in European gardens by the late sixteenth century. They were widely grown, and are now equally widely naturalized. *L. aestivum* grows wild from Ireland to the Crimea, *L. autumnale* grows from Portugal to the Ionian islands, and *L. vernum* is common in central Europe.

By the late seventeenth century, even tender sorts from Portugal were admired – though it is not clear if these included the pink forms of the autumn snowflake.

The plants have undeniable elegance (during the short flowering periods), but are rather undemonstrative. Miller lists them in the index of the 1754 edition of *The Gardeners Dictionary*, but forgets to do much else. Even Phillipps noted that they were much less cultivated than in Gerard's time. However, with the kindling of interest in the wild garden from the late nineteenth century, the fortunes of the genus revived considerably. Gertrude Jekyll thought *L. vernum* one of the gems of March, and planted it amongst drifts of blue *Iris reticulata*. William Robinson loved the whole genus, and especially admired a group of well-fed plants of *L. aestivum* backed by rhododendrons at Longleat. Perhaps, though, it was a particularly vigorous clone. He may have been offered a piece: the most vigorous and floriferous sort is now called 'Gravetye Giant' after Robinson's estate. Should it have been called 'Longleat'?

# LILIUM

Two species of this gorgeous genus are amongst the oldest of domesticated garden plants, perhaps not so much because of the wonderful elegance of their flowers but, more basically, because their fleshy bulbs are edible. It seems now rather sacrilegious to dig up a lily and eat it, but early hunter-gatherers will have had no such qualms. The madonna lily (*L. candidum*) was grubbed up in Anatolia and *L. tigrinum* in the Far East.

In European gardens, the madonna lily reigned alone until the early sixteenth century, but the list included a few other European and Turkish species and their variants by the century's end. One or two Americans arrived at about that time, but made little impact. A few more arrived from that continent in the eighteenth century, including *L. philadelphicum* and *L. superbum*, but lapsed into gentle gardening obscurity. Perhaps lilies were not especially admired, for even some of the old, even ancient, garden variants were beginning to disappear. Miller said of these (and there were eighteen), with some regret, 'so when they are once fix'd in a Garden, they are not very subject to decay ... therefore from such places [he meant old gardens in the countryside] there may be Hopes of retrieving those flowers again'. However the first Asian lily (*L. dauricum*) had just arrived when he wrote. It was a harbinger of a flood of Japanese, Chinese and Korean lily types that came in in the nineteenth century, many of quite astonishing elegance. Lilies became a rage, and breeders began to look at the possibilities. Groups like the Mid-Century Hybrids were formed in the 1860s and 1880s (some are still around), and new lily hybrids still appear every year, mostly based on oriental species. Beautiful though they all are, the period gardener will find that when well grown, the old types can be just as beautiful, and far more romantic. We describe only the most important species.

## L. candidum

White lily, madonna lily

Possibly of Anatolian origin, but now grown throughout Europe, Asia and temperate America. It seems to have been known throughout the ancient world, probably just as a food crop. The ancient Greeks imported it from Asia Minor for a more sophisticated use as a salve or ointment. It was so admired, or was so important, that it soon became sacred to several Greek goddesses. The Romans took over the goddesses and the flower, and distributed it throughout their empire. Pliny recorded some elaborate recipes for turning its flowers purple, so he may have known the purple-streaked variant.

Its six-fold symmetry appealed to the Moors, who distributed it along the north coast of Africa and into Spain and Portugal, where its vernacular names are, to this day, corruptions of the plant's Arabic names. It has been associated since early times with the mother of Christ, though that is perhaps not surprising in view of its pre-Christian connections. It reached America by 1630.

In nature the species is fairly variable, and there are a surprising number of garden forms, many once widely grown, but all now either very rare in Europe, or extinct. These include the purple-striped form introduced to Britain in the mid eighteenth century, the variegated-leaf one of a similar date, and the sixteenth-century 'Sultan Zambach', a form with narrow-pointed petals and an exceptional perfume, perhaps selected from wild populations. A double madonna lily seems to have been known by the mid seventeenth century and was popular in the early eighteenth century. It must have survived into Victorian Britain, as a nurseryman was advertising for bulbs in

1871. He wanted a thousand bulbs; perhaps Britain did not hold so many. We have not found it.

## LILIES OF THE SIXTEENTH AND SEVENTEENTH CENTURIES

### L. martagon

Martagon, Turk's cap, mountain lily

Europe, possibly native to Britain as well. Popular in the sixteenth century in mauve or purple. The lovely white form was admired by 1634. Double forms in both colours were grown by 1754, and remained in gardens until at least 1840, but are exceptionally rare, and perhaps extinct.

### L. chalcedonicum

Scarlet Turk's cap lily

Asia Minor. Gerard may have grown the first bulbs, imported from Constantinople. What a lucky man he was to see the first one in flower – one of the most thrilling reds in the garden. A double was popular in the eighteenth century, though it is difficult to imagine that it could be more elegant than the single. It is now lost. Victorian flower arrangers liked the single, combined with the madonna lily and black helleborine (*Veratrum nigrum*). American gardeners grew it by 1740.

### L. bulbiferum

Eastern and central Europe. Gerard knew this in several forms, all with upwards facing flowers, but with or without bulbils, and in various shades of red. Seventeenth-century connoisseurs sneered at it rather, saying it was in every countrywoman's garden; nevertheless it survived in popularity until the fabulous orientals displaced it in the late nineteenth century. It is not common now, however handsome.

### L. pyrenaicum

This handsome clear-yellow martagon from the Pyrenees is so elegant that most gardeners, whether of the sixteenth century or modern times, are prepared to ignore the rather offensive smell.

## L. pomponium

Southern Europe. John Rea adored this, boasting in the 1660s that his plants had eighty to a hundred flowers on each spike.

## L. canadense

North America. There are various dates given for its entry, all in the 1620s or 1630s. Rea thought it was not fully hardy, though later gardeners discovered the falsity of this, admiring the elegantly pendent yellow, orange or scarlet Turk's caps. Popular in the 1820s. Still sometimes seen.

### LILIES OF THE EIGHTEENTH CENTURY

Two important American additions are the correctly named *L. superbum*, from eastern North America, introduced in either 1727 or 1728, and *L. philadelphicum*. Neither made much impression until the 1820s.

### LILIES OF THE NINETEENTH CENTURY

Almost the 'century of lilies', this century saw large numbers of species come from Japan, China and the western states of America. Important oriental ones include *L. tigrinum* (from Canton in 1804), *L. speciosum* (from Japan in 1832), *L. auratum* (from the same country in 1862, with a double form arriving in 1873). From California in 1875 came the gorgeous spotted leopard-lily (*L. pardalinum*). Now no longer in the genus *Lilium*, the astonishing giant lily (*Cardiocrinum giganteum*) was introduced from the Himalayas in 1850 or so. The first bulbs were available commercially in 1851 and cost three guineas each.

### LILIES OF THE TWENTIETH CENTURY

The supply of new species has slackened off; the most popular of all easy garden lilies, *L. regale*, from the China–Tibet border, made its dazzling entry in 1904.

# LOBELIA

In the summer of 1862, for the first time at Kew Gardens, the humble blue lobelia (then called *L. speciosum*, now *L. erinus*) was planted alternately with white alyssum as a margin to a bed of the variegated-leaf geranium 'Flower of the Day' and a verbena called 'Lord Raglan'. The results caught the public imagination and made a sadly indelible impression. Blue lobelias and alyssum can still be seen throughout the country in parks and humble private gardens as testimony to the longevity of gardening tradition.

It was Paxton who first suggested, in 1839, that some of the new low-growing lobelias coming from South Africa and Australia might be suitable for the equally new summer bedding. The first arrived in 1752, but was treated as a tender perennial. It became a cherished pot plant, used to grace the front edge of greenhouse shelves. These early plants were all pale blue, but by the sixties or seventies trailing lobelias existed in all shades of blue, pure white and various blue-greys. More amusing were some of the doubles, one of which, 'Katherine Mallard', still exists, and is remarkably pretty (though easy to lose). Both it, and the singles, should you find a plant whose colour you particularly like, are best propagated by suppressing the flowers for a few months and then breaking up the plant into cuttings, at any time during early or mid summer.

However, there are two species of lobelia that are much older (and grander) garden plants than the common blue sort. The oldest of all is the blazing scarlet cardinal's flower (*L. cardinalis*). This gorgeous thing – though the colour is difficult to use (except in tubs or vast pots, or in drifts along the pond-side) – has been grown in Europe since the early seventeenth century. It was imported from Virginia. Well grown, it will reach five feet high and can be spectacular indeed. The now-common purple-leaved sort is probably of nineteenth-century origin and is closer to *L. fulgens*. A white-flowered variety, now lost, was popular a hundred years earlier.

The rather subtler *L. syphilitica*, once believed to cure syphilis, was in Europe by 1665. It was American (as the disease itself may have been). The plant has never made much impact, even in its lovely white form, though it was one parent of a group of hybrids popular in the 1880s and 1890s. All now seem to have been lost, though modern breeders are experimenting with the same cross.

The Mexican *L. fulgens* became the rage soon after its introduction in 1809. It was forced in cucumber houses and taken indoors during the summer. Often five feet tall, it was matched with potted plants of *Campanula pyramidalis* (see p. 96) and, like them, its flower spikes were sometimes pinched into fancy shapes, most often a pyramid. Every Regency drawing-room had to have it.

*L. × vedrariense* is a handsome purple-flowered hybrid, hardy, and probably a late-nineteenth-century cross between *L. syphilitica* and either *L. fulgens* or *L. cardinalis*. It is well worth growing.

# LUNARIA

Of the two species, one biennial (even though it is called *L. annua*), the other perennial (*L. rediviva*), the first has been cultivated for so long that it is naturalized throughout the temperate gardening world. It may be native to Italy, certainly to southern Europe, but Chaucer mentions it in connection with wild flowers, and Gerard believed it a British native. When he was writing it had an astonishing range of vernacular names, including white satin flower, balbonac, penny flower, money flower, silver plate, prick-sangwort, satin, but 'among our women it is called Honestie', perhaps because of the unbroken and translucent septum. Their name triumphed.

There are almost as many variations as names; flowers vary from pure white, through bluish purple, to deep red, and the leaves can be variegated. Pod shape can vary from circular to elliptical; Gerard illustrates both types and Miller mentions them one hundred and fifty years later. Though the white-flowered one occurs in nature, neither it nor any of the other forms appear in old garden literature, so we presume that they are all newcomers. It is reputed to be one of the first European garden plants to reach America.

The perennial honesty has smaller but fragrant flowers, in various shades of purple, some pale and lovely. It first appears in garden books in 1597, but as the roots of both species were eaten in salads, it seems likely to have been an early introduction from central and southern Europe. It is attractive, but is now rather rare.

# LUPINUS

Phillipps was subject to one of the many ironies of garden history when he wrote that lupins 'scarcely deserve a situation amongst choice flowers and we should therefore recommend them to the shrubbery'.Only a few years later, David Douglas began to send back some of the fourteen or so new species he was collecting in the north-western states of America. *L. polyphyllus* arrived in 1826, and hybridization started soon after.

The tree lupin, a favourite nineteenth-century introduction,
photographed in 1890

Before the influx of American species began, garden lupins were all derived from European annual crop species. *L. albus*, from the Balkans and the Aegean, was grown by the Romans for its oily seeds and nutritious fodder. In the wild the flowers are white or blue. *L. luteus* from south-western Europe was also a crop plant, but because the flowers are deliciously perfumed, was more popular in gardens. Both have been part of the garden flora since at least the late sixteenth century and probably long before.

The first perennial species introduced to Europe was the Virginian

*L. perenne*, brought back by John Tradescant the Younger in 1637, and this became fairly popular by the mid eighteenth century, though because it was so rampant it only found its way into the largest gardens. Later, its poor colour led to its unlamented loss.

The tree lupin, *L. arboreus*, arrived from California in the late eighteenth century. It first flowered in Ireland for Lord Mountmorris, and it was soon creating a stir. Early sorts were all yellow flowered, but a white form (given the name of 'Snow Queen') was rare and desirable in the 1880s, and was taken up by all the gardening grandees, including Gertrude Jekyll. It made even more of a stir in the next decade when hybrids between it and *L. polyphyllus* began to appear.

*L. polyphyllus* arrived from the west coast of America in 1826, with flowers in a rather ordinary lupin blue-purple. The first hybrids, made by James Kelway of Langport, gave large perennial plants, with tall flower spikes in various shades of blue, pale blue and dingy yellow. These were crossed amongst themselves and about 1912 there was a colour break, providing a seedling with rose-pink flowers. Offspring of this gave all shades of pink, lilac and mauve. *L. bicolor* was used to add flowers that showed two distinct colours – the modern lupin had arrived. In the 1930s, George Russell began to add various improvements, and many splendid varieties of that date still exist. Curiously, some of these hybrid lupins are so luxuriant that in parts of Europe they have begun to displace the ancient annual lupins as fodder plants, which might please some gardeners quite well.

# LYCHNIS

A small genus, since the catchflies are now found under *Viscaria* and some of the campions (having dallied with *Melandrium*) are now under *Silene*. This leaves us with *L. chalcedonica* and *L. coronaria*, both consistently popular in the garden for hundreds of years, and one or two others.

### L. chalcedonica
Jerusalem cross

A name common to most European languages – an early introduction date is assumed. It was a common plant in ancient Turkish gardens, so perhaps it really was introduced at the time of the Crusades. At any rate, by the late sixteenth century it was 'very common almost everywhere'. By 1629, there was a double-flowered scarlet sort, as well as white and blush-coloured singles (both still available). By 1722, a double white was popular, though this seems to have vanished by the 1920s. The singles come happily from seed, but the luxurious double must be propagated by division or by leaf-stem cuttings.

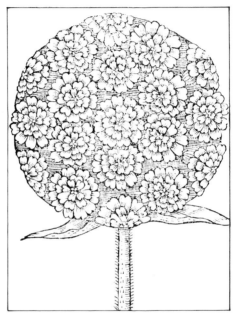

*Lychnis chalcedonica* reduced to a decorative
ideal in Parkinson's *Paradisus*, 1629

### L. coronaria

Rose campion

Southern Europe. The date of introduction is unknown, but it is mentioned as a garden plant in the mid fourteenth century. By 1597, the rare white was being grown, as well as the now more common purplish-red. By 1614, there was a double red sort and by 1665 a double white. They became increasingly popular until, by the eighteenth century, they were grown almost to the exclusion of the others. In spite of this they seem now to have vanished. 'Spotted' versions of the single flower were around by 1629, no doubt similar to our

'Oculata' (white with a pink eye) – gorgeous, and not nearly common enough.

### L. flos-cuculi
Cuckoo flower, ragged robin

Europe, including Britain, and north Asia. The double form of this delightful native was grown in gardens by the sixteenth century, was common in the nineteenth century, and was described as a good border plant as late as the 1950s. Is it still around today? There were variants with white flowers and one with a white flower and a purple eye.

### L. flos-jovis
Like a small-scale and more graceful version of *L. coronaria*, this was introduced from the central Alps in 1726. The flowers of the type are reddish-purple. There is, however a white-flowered sort, and the lovely modern 'Hort's Variety' has clear rose-pink flowers.

*L. dioica*, see *Silene dioica*.

# MALVA

The native musk mallow, *M. moschata*, seems to have been grown in both European and American gardens by the seventeenth century. We do not know whether they had the very attractive white-flowered form, or just the usual, but no less fine, rose-pink flower of the type. In 1871 William Robinson, a connoisseur of wildlings, called it 'the very best of the Mallows' and 'a very good garden plant, especially the white form'. Both are tough; we found the white one thriving amidst the jungles when we took over a derelict garden.

The annual *M. crispa*, 'French curled mallow', from Europe and Asia, was introduced by 1573, and is now widely naturalized.

*M. alcea*, a European, is perhaps the most popular today. It did not arrive in gardens until 1797, and the erect form, usually called 'Fastigiata', not until 1820.

# MATTHIOLA

### *M. incana*
Stock, stock gilloflowre, leucoium

Coastal southern and western Europe. Like many heavily perfumed flowers, they were immensely popular in the sixteenth century, and probably long before. The type plant is sub-shrubby, hardy, perennial, with grey-green leaves and pink or purple flowers. Selection and hybridization over the centuries (probably with *M. sinuata*, a native species, and *M. fenestralis*, introduced from Crete in 1759) has led to the formation of markedly different types.

By the sixteenth and seventeenth centuries, stocks were single or double flowered, and purple, white, red or striped. The doubles were much admired. Parkinson explained that the double-flowered plants set no seed and so if the gardener wanted to increase or preserve his plants (they are doubtfully perennial), he had to save seed from a patch of mixed single- and double-flowered plants. Doubles had crossed the Atlantic during the seventeenth century.

The plant from which the ten-week stocks, *M.i.* var. *annua*, are descended was described in the sixteenth century. However, the first record of the name 'ten-week stock' occurs in James Justice's *The Scots Gardener's Director* of 1754. Brompton stocks, originally raised by London and Wise in the early eighteenth century, are first mentioned by Miller in 1724.

Another ancient group are the East Lothian or intermediate stocks. Modern strains sold now come, like the Brompton stocks, in shades of red, pink, purple, yellow or white. If you can find genuine old East Lothian stocks, you will have plants that look identical to those shown in sixteenth-century illustrations; we have only found them in purple and white. There is an interesting semi-double plant in commerce which may be old. Modern breeding techniques have led to seed strains which can produce almost 100 per cent double flowers.

Though stocks are in the main treated as annuals or biennials, some strains can in fact be reasonably perennial. They can easily be propagated from cuttings, though it was noted in the eighteenth century that 'Plants thus raised are always weaker than those raised from seeds, and never produce their flowers near so large and fair.' True.

MECONOPSIS, see *Papaver*.
MELANDRIUM, see *Silene*.
MILIUM, see Grasses.

# MIMULUS
Monkey musk

Though they seem archetypal cottage plants, and some are naturalized throughout the country, mimulus are comparatively late introductions, nearly all arriving in the nineteenth century. Most modern garden forms are hybrids between *M. luteus* and *M. guttatus*, and sometimes also with *M. cupreus*. All need a damp position in sun. For those with dry gardens, they make splendid pot or tub plants.

*M. luteus* was the first to arrive, in 1763, from Chile, followed by *M. guttatus*, from western North America, in 1813. Though there seems to be considerable confusion between these two species (perhaps because of the extensive hybridization), the general consensus seems to be that, while both have yellow flowers and red-spotted throats, *M. luteus* also has larger red blotches on the petals. *M. cupreus* from Chile (1861), the other partner in hybridization, has flowers that open yellow and then turn copper-coloured. There is an attractive hose-in-hose variant, one flower placed inside another.

*M. moschatus*, at one time a common denizen of cottage windowsills as a pot plant, was collected by David Douglas from western North America in 1826. It was once much cultivated for its penetrating scent of musk, which was found in some wild populations but not others. Inexplicably, around 1914 the scent disappeared completely from every plant in the world, including those in the wild. People who still remember the scent say that one plant was enough to perfume a whole room. Even without the powerful scent, it makes a pretty plant, whether indoors or in a suitable place outside.

# MIRABILIS

## *M. jalapa*

Marvel of Peru

Tropical America. Seeds were brought from Peru to Spain in the sixteenth century, and from thence to England. The flowers are usually vivid crimson, but pink, white and yellow sorts can be found, sometimes attractively streaked. They do not open till late afternoon, and they close by noon on the next day. During that time the perfume is a delight. The plant is easily grown from seed, but may be treated like a dahlia and lifted every year, or as Gerard puts it: 'At the first frost I dig up the roots and put up or rather hide the roots in a butter ferkin . . . to stand in some corner of the house.' Any other receptacle will do just as well.

MISCANTHUS, see Grasses.

# MONARDA

Only two species are grown, *M. didyma* and *M. fistulosa*. The first is the more attractive, with large hooked scarlet flowers, but it needs a moist soil. *M. fistulosa* has smaller pale purple flowers and will grow happily in dry conditions.

### *M. didyma*
Scarlet bergamot, bee balm, Oswego tea

North America. The name 'bergamot' comes from the supposed resemblance in fragrance to the bergamot orange, an early Italian orange-lemon hybrid. The first seeds were sent by John Bartram to Peter Collinson in 1744 from Oswego on Lake Ontario (where the leaves were indeed used to make a tea). The cultivar most often grown is 'Cambridge Scarlet', which appears to date from the early 1900s.

### *M. fistulosa*
Also from North America; it was grown in France by 1635 and probably reached Britain soon after. It was certainly in Britain by 1656. Many modern strains of bergamot are hybrids between the two species.

# MYOSOTIS
Forget-me-not, scorpion grass

Our beautiful native forget-me-nots do not seem to have been used much as garden plants in early times, though the Tradescants thought highly enough of them to include them in their plant list in 1634, the species being *M. arvensis* and *M. sylvatica* (or *M. discolor*). However, in Victorian times these plants began to come into their own. William Robinson recommended their use in the wild garden, for which they are still particularly suited. He makes special mention of *M. dissitiflora*, from the Alps, 'not inferior to any of our handsomest native kinds'. They were, and are still, used for bedding, grown as biennials, though they are mostly perennial (but short-lived). As well as the usual blue, there were pink, white and striped sorts (now lost) grown before the end of the nineteenth century. Most of the modern cultivars are hybrids, combining *M. alpestris*, *M. dissitiflora* and *M. sylvatica*.

# NARCISSUS

One of the garden's most popular flowers. *N. tazetta*, the bunch-flowered narcissus, was known in ancient Egypt and Greece, and even found its way as far as China and Japan, presumably along the early trade routes. Most species are found in the Iberian peninsula, but some can be found all round the Mediterranean. Because many have been in cultivation for so long, and in so many places, natural populations are often interbred with long-established and naturalized intro-ductions. A surprising number of species and natural hybrids were described by the late sixteenth and early seventeenth centuries. Many of them are still available today.

Deliberate hybridizing did not begin until the latter half of the nineteenth century, since when the number of cultivars available has exploded. Most of these are of no relevance to the period gardener, who, with some exceptions for the nineteenth century, must look to species, or to natural hybrids, for the flowers of past gardens.

## THE PSEUDONARCISSUS GROUP

### *N. pseudonarcissus*
Lent lily

This species is immensely variable even in the wild. Many of the forms have, at one time or another, been given separate species names. It occurs throughout much of Europe, including Britain, where the name is first recorded in 1557. Certainly, it was widely admired by the end of the sixteenth century, and it was sold in great quantities at the market in Cheapside.

## N. hispanicus

Northern Spain and Portugal; south-western France. This, the largest of the group, was in gardens by 1576. It is the parent of most of the modern yellow trumpet cultivars, and was used extensively for breeding in the nineteenth century. The most spectacular result of this is 'King Alfred' (still available). The common double daffodil of gardens, N. 'Telamonius Plenus', is sometimes thought to be derived from N. hispanicus (or another member of the pseudonarcissus group). No corresponding single form of it is known. The double has been grown since the late sixteenth century, and is now widely naturalized. It was popular in American gardens by 1779.

## N. obvallaris
Tenby daffodil

An attractive pale daffodil, related to N. pseudonarcissus. It is of uncertain origin, and hardly known outside Britain (though a similar plant is found in northern Italy). Whether it is a true native or an early garden escape, it has been grown since at least medieval times.

Minor members of the pseudonarcissus group include N. alpestris, N. moschatus and N. pallidiflorus, all late-sixteenth- or early-seventeenth-century introductions. There is a gorgeous double form of N. moschatus, in silvery yellow, probably of the sixteenth century.

## THE POETICUS GROUP

## N. poeticus

Southern Europe. In one form or another, it has a history stretching back to ancient Greece, and is mentioned, along with N. tazetta, by Theophrastus in 320 BC. The date of its introduction to this country cannot even be guessed at, but the 'Whyte daffodyl' or 'Whyte Laus tibi', mentioned by Turner in 1538 must be this one.

The species is so variable that the name 'Pheasant's Eye' is sometimes applied to the whole group of species, subspecies and varieties, though sometimes it is restricted to the form N. poeticus 'Recurvus' (an early-nineteenth-century plant, occasionally called 'Old Pheasant's Eye'). All make splendid garden plants, flowering several weeks after the yellow sorts have faded. Most have a ravishing perfume.

## *N. majalis*

By the eighteenth century, it was the only member of the poeticus group to have become naturalized in Britain, so try it in a wilderness or wild garden. If you need a late Victorian member of the group, look out for the one introduced by the famous firm of Vilmorin in 1870 called *N. poeticus* 'Ornatus'; it is worth having.

## OTHER GROUPS

Two naturally occurring hybrid groups were important early garden plants. The first of these was *N.* × *incomparabilis*, the 'nonpareille', or 'great nonesuch'. A hybrid between *N. poeticus* and *N. pseudonarcissus*, this was grown by the late sixteenth century. It almost vanished, but was rediscovered and revalued by nineteenth-century narcissus enthusiasts. Other lovely crosses between the same two species include cultivars like 'Sir Watkin' or 'Welch Peerless', found in an old garden in 1886, and the properly Victorian Barrii and Leedsii strains. Another important early hybrid group has been called *N.* × *medioluteus*, a cross between *N. poeticus* and *N. tazetta*. Well-known by Elizabethan times, this is the 'Primrose Peerlesse' that Gerard said was 'most common in our countrey gardens'. It was naturalized by the early seventeenth century, and can still be found. Just to confuse matters, intentional crosses were made between the same two species in late-nineteenth-century Holland, and were named Poetaz varieties.

*N. tazetta* itself was cultivated in Britain before 1597, in both single and double forms. A related species, *N. papyraceus* or 'Paper White', also seems to have been grown in Britain by the same date, though its heyday came in the early nineteenth century. Then, between two and three hundred varieties were grown by Dutch nurserymen, and the bulbs were sold at 4s. per dozen. In spring, it could be found in every Victorian drawing-room. Nowadays, it is rather expensive, though worth every penny. The perfume is wonderful.

## *N. jonquilla*

Jonquil

Spain and Portugal. In gardens by the late sixteenth century, in both single and double forms. The double form, planted at Blenheim, became known as Queen Anne's jonquil. We find it difficult to keep, though the perfume makes any trouble worthwhile. *N.* × *odorus*, a lovely and rather similar hybrid between *N. jonquilla* and *N. pseudonarcissus*, was grown by the early seventeenth century.

### N. triandrus
Angel's tears

Spain, Portugal. Grown since the late sixteenth or early seventeenth centuries. The remarkably beautiful double-flowered *N.* 'Eystettensis' or *N.* 'Capax Plenus', with its six ranks of palest cream petals, is perhaps a Triandrus hybrid from the late sixteenth century, and can still be found.

Other double daffodils grown in the seventeenth century include one easily available today, 'Van Sion'. Parkinson gives the history of this plant, which came from the garden of 'Vincent Sion, borne in Flanders, dwelling on the Banke side, in his lives time, but now dead; an industrious and worthy lover of faire flowers'. As with *N.* 'Telamonius Plenus', any single form has been lost. Grander still is 'John Tradescant's rose Daffodill'. This was still common at the end of the nineteenth century, but has become rather rare. E. A. Bowles may be responsible, for he called it 'a heavy-headed, overloaded flower'.

Of the dwarf species often planted in rock ·gardens today, *N. bulbocodium*, from southern France, Spain and Portugal, was known early, and had been introduced to Britain by the early seventeenth century. However, the charming miniature daffodil *N. asturiensis*, from Spain, and *N. cyclamineus*, from Portugal (often crossed with larger trumpet daffodils) were not introduced until 1885.

# NEPETA

### N. cataria
Kattesminte, catmint

Native to most of Europe, including Britain, and naturalized in North America. It was growing in English gardens by 1265. Five hundred years later, Miller recommends propagating the plant from seed, rather than from division, because 'if this is transplanted into a Garden, the Cats will surely destroy it'. The cats, according to Miller, roll on the plant, then gnaw it and eat the tops 'which occasions a sort of drunkenness'. Unsatisfied, they then tear it to pieces with their claws 'and when the whole plant is destroyed, they will roll upon the Ground till they have smoothed the Surface, as if a Roller had passed over it'. Have people been planting catmint for over seven hundred years just so they could watch this extraordinary feline ritual?

The plants we grow today as catmint derive from *N. mussinii*, which was introduced from the Caucasus around 1804. The improved forms usually grown, called *N.* × *faassenii*, are sterile hybrids between *N. mussinii* and *N. nepetalla*. *N. nervosa*, with handsomely textured leaves, was introduced from Kashmir in 1927.

# NIGELLA

Three species of *Nigella* have been widely grown for hundreds of years. Only one is likely to be seen in modern seed catalogues. All are attractive hardy annuals, with decorative horned seed pods.

## N. damascena
Love-in-a-mist

Southern Europe. This still-popular plant is supposed to have been introduced from Damascus in 1570. Gerard mentions a single blue and a double white flower. Parkinson has double blue and double white. Both seem to have vanished. A variety frequently grown now is 'Miss Jekyll', a bright cornflower blue.

## N. sativa

Northern Africa to Ethiopia and Asia Minor. A food crop grown by the ancient Egyptians. Said to be the 'fitches' mentioned in Isaiah, this plant was valued for its aromatic seeds. It is recorded in *The Grete Herball* of 1526 as 'cokyll' or 'gith' and was grown at Syon before 1548.

## N. hispanica
Fennel flower

Spain, southern France. This first appears in a garden list of 1620, a double form being grown by 1693. It was still cultivated in the nineteenth century, but is rarely seen today. A shame.

# OENOTHERA

The evening primroses are mostly American, though several species are now naturalized throughout Europe. Biennials or perennials, they are all lovers of well-drained soil and plenty of sun.

The first to arrive was *O. biennis*, sent from Virginia to Padua in 1619, and described by an English botanist in 1621. Known as the tree primrose, its propensity to become 'a troublesome Weed' when allowed to seed (as it does prolifically), was noted by Miller in the eighteenth century. However, it was regarded as a proper plant for city gardens, as it would thrive in 'the Smoke of London'. Incidentally, in France, at the end of the first season, the fleshy roots are sometimes eaten like salsify. *O. erythrosepala* (sometimes called *O. lamarckiana*), another biennial, and similar to the above, seems to have been grown since the mid nineteenth century.

*O. acaulis*, a dwarf perennial species, with white flowers turning pink, was recommended in late Victorian times as an edging for shrub beds. Other species commonly available include the perennial *O. missouriensis*, again fairly dwarf, introduced in 1811, the biennial *O. stricta* (often called *O. odorata*), introduced by Sir Joseph Banks in 1790, with yellow flowers turning red as they fade, and *O. tetragona*, introduced in 1800, which has several good garden cultivars.

# OMPHALODES

### O. verna
Blue-eyed Mary

This native of southern Europe was introduced in 1633, and grown by the Tradescants. Often depicted in paintings and embroideries since then, it always seems to have been valued in the garden for its early flowers (from February to May) and its usefulness as a path edger and in shade. Though the normal plant is blue-flowered, there is a most lovely white-flowered sort, of a slightly different habit.

Several other species are grown in gardens, notably *O. linifolia*, called Venus' navel-wort, an annual species introduced from south-western Europe before 1722, and the handsome perennial *O. cappadocica*, with intense blue flowers, introduced from Asia Minor in 1814.

# ORNITHOGALUM

A large genus of bulbs, though only a few species have ever been in general cultivation. Three were grown in gardens by at least the early seventeenth century, and the first two have remained common.

### O. umbellatum
Star of Bethlehem

Native to most of Europe, including Britain, and Asia Minor. Mentioned as 'Dogges onion' or 'Dogleke' in 1548, it is 'Our common Starre of Bethlehem' in Gerard. Offsets are rather too readily produced, so it is best to plant it where you'll be glad to see it increase.

### O. nutans

Balkans and Turkey. Naturalized in places throughout Europe, including Britain; certainly grown here by the seventeenth century. The plants, with subtle silvery-white and pale green flowers, do well in shade.

### O. pyrenaicum
Bath asparagus

Europe, including Britain, and Morocco and the Caucasus. The young flower shoots were used as a substitute for asparagus, and grown and sold in Bath. It has pale greeny-yellow flowers, not as showy as the other species.

Other *Ornithogalums* were grown by the seventeenth century, at least by collectors. Parkinson, for example, grew *O. arabicum*, a lovely species difficult to grow well in this country, as he notes, and *O. unifolium*, a curiosity in that it has only a single leaf, which rises well above the flower spike.

### O. thyrsoides
Chincherinchee

South Africa. Known in Europe by 1757. This is well known as a cut flower, and is more rarely grown as a garden plant. Since it is not hardy, the bulbs must be lifted in winter if grown outside, or else grown in a cool greenhouse or frame.

# PAEONIA

It is useful for the period gardener to divide this genus, which contains so many beautiful garden plants, into two distinct groups: the species native to Europe, and those from the East. The Eastern species, principally *P. lactiflora* and *P. suffruticosa*, did not reach Europe or America until the late eighteenth century, so before this time the only species that could possibly be grown were *P. officinalis*, *P. mascula* and, perhaps, *P. peregrina*. Since this time, of course, new species as well as old garden cultivars from the East have kept arriving, but the picture has been changed mainly by the enormous amount of hybridization which has gone on. This started in the 1820s in France, and switched to Britain in 1864, when James Kelway began breeding, and in more modern times, to the USA. Because peonies are such long-lasting plants (they will happily survive without division for fifty years or more), many of the nineteenth-century cultivars are still easily available. They are not difficult to grow, needing rich, well-drained soil, in sun or light shade.

Both groups have ancient histories. The European ones are described by Theophrastus *c.* 320 B C, and by Pliny and Dioscorides in the first century A D (though whether the description refers to *P. officinalis* or *P. mascula* is not clear). These early writers were concerned with the medicinal uses of the peony. It was invaluable, offering many cures, but especially relief of pain, whether of mind or body. We do not know when peonies first arrived in Britain, but they are mentioned in medieval documents from A D 1000 onwards. They are described by Neckham in the twelfth century and a bill of 1299 has the infirmarer of Durham Cathedral Priory buying 3lb of peony seeds for 3s. 2d.; they are also mentioned by Piers Plowman in 1362, and so on.

## *P. officinalis*

Southern and central Europe. Called the 'Female Peionie'. By 1568 this plant was said to be common throughout England. Originally with a single red flower, the form that every gardener now knows is the double red. This was once highly prized; plants in Antwerp in 1570 cost twelve crowns each. By 1629, according to Parkinson, it was already 'so frequent in everie Garden of note, through every Countrey, that it is almost labour in vaine to describe it'. It seems to have been introduced into Britain in the 1560s.

Gerard describes a single white form, and also a double white (which he did not grow, but expected from Flanders). By 1665, Rea had a carnation pink one, as well as a red one with white streaks. The plants, he says, are 'commonly set in great tufts in the middle or corner of knots or on borders'. Most of these forms have persisted to the present day and are still available. *P. officinalis* has also been one of the species used in peony breeding from the 1820s onwards. The medicinal uses seem to have persisted too, at least until the eighteenth century, when Hannah Glasse has a recipe for the distillation of peony roots in alcohol (for weak hearts and stomachs).

### *P. mascula* (sometimes known as *P. corallina*)

Southern Europe. Called the 'Male Peionie'. There is a naturalized population of this plant on Steep Holm, in the Severn estuary, near the site of an Augustinian priory established in the late twelfth century. It is reasonable to assume that the plant may have been introduced there by the monks. It is uncommon now, and probably was never as common as its more glamorous partner. A subspecies of this, *P. mascula* subsp. *arietina*, is now more likely to be seen. There is some doubt about the introduction date of this. It was certainly in Britain by 1824, but may have arrived earlier. The colour of the species, and the subspecies, can vary from deep purple-red to shades of pink and to white.

### *P. peregrina*

Balkans. In Britain by 1629. Known as 'Paeonia femina Byzantina'; it had come to northern Europe by way of Constantinople. It has deep red single flowers and is often sold nowadays under the cultivar names 'Fire King' or 'Sunshine'.

The second group of peonies come from the Far East and have a far longer and more distinguished history than their European counterparts.

### *P. suffruticosa*

Tree peony

China, Tibet. This species was cultivated in ancient China. A garden variety register was begun in AD 700, and there were said to be thirty-nine garden varieties by the tenth century. They were exported to Japan about AD 734, where another cycle of breeding and selection soon began. They remained fashionable, and expensive, in these countries for centuries. The first successful introduction into Britain seems to have been around 1790.

## P. lactiflora

Central China and Siberia. This is the herbaceous peony on which the modern cultivar structure is built; it reached Britain initially in 1784 and was re-introduced by Banks in 1805. Again known in ancient times, in China some strains were used as food in A D 536 (the roots were eaten), but breeding to improve the flowers began around 1086. By 1596, thirty varieties were listed in Chinese nurseries. The species has huge single white scented flowers, but is rarely seen now (the plant known as 'The Bride', or 'Whitleyi Major', is close). Chinese garden varieties began to come in quite quickly after the first introduction (Loddiges's nursery was instrumental in this), and then breeding began, using *P. officinalis* crossed with *P. lactiflora*. This took place primarily in France, by breeders such as Calot, Dessert and Crousse, all still commemorated in cultivar names. By 1850, peonies had become so popular that nurseries couldn't keep up with the demand. James Kelway began breeding in 1864, and the firm bearing his name still sells fine peonies today.

Early cultivars include: 'Duchesse de Nemours' (1856) and 'Festive Maxima' (1851), both double whites; 'Marie Crousse' (1892) and 'Baroness Schroeder' (1889), both blush pinks; 'Sarah Bernhardt' (1906) and 'Auguste Dessert' (1920), pale pink; 'Madame Calot' (1856), 'Félix Crousse' (1881) and 'Kelway's Lovely' (1929), deeper pink.

The 'Imperial' peonies are single sorts in which the stamens have turned into narrow petals, and make a huge, colourful centre, sometimes yellow, sometimes the same colour as the outer petals.

In the twentieth century, the impetus for peony breeding passed to the USA.

Among the other species which have been introduced in the nineteenth and twentieth centuries, some became connoisseurs' plants; these include *P. emodi*, from north-west India in 1862, *P. lutea*, from China and Tibet in 1886, and its more robust form, *P.l.* var. *ludlowii* (double yellow tree peonies, such as 'Chromatella', are *P. lutea* × *P. suffruticosa* hybrids), *P. delavayi*, introduced in 1908, and the formidably named *P. mlokosewitschii*, from the Caucasus in 1907.

# PAPAVER

Poppy

## *P. somniferum*

Opium poppy

Europe, Asia. A very variable hardy annual, anciently cultivated for its seed and for the latex obtained from the immature seed capsules (the drug opium), as well as for its fine flowers. Some European decorative forms may be three thousand years old. There are separate subspecies for producing poppy seed and poppy-seed oil (*P.s.* subsp. *hortense*), and for producing opium (*P.s.* subsp. *somniferum*). The first has dark grey to black seeds; the second, white seeds. Both have been grown as crops in this country, the opium sort mostly in the nineteenth century. *P.s.* subsp. *hortense* is naturalized in some areas, such as the Fens, as a relic of this cultivation. Both of the subspecies must have been introduced early into this country, perhaps by the Romans. The species is recorded in *The Grete Herball* of 1526 as the 'blacke poppy' and 'white poppy', a reference to the seed colours.

By Gerard's time, there are garden varieties with double flowers in 'white, red, darke purple, scarlet, or mixt of some of these'. By the seventeenth century, there was a sort with laciniate leaves, and another with laciniate petals (Parkinson's 'Double feathered Poppies'). Opium poppies had reached America by the same date. Many garden varieties are mentioned in the eighteenth century, amongst them a double black and a 'double jagged Poppy, with beautiful striped flowers'. Various strains of *P. somniferum* are readily available today.

## *P. rhoeas*

Field poppy

Europe, including Britain, northern Africa, temperate Asia. Another hardy annual, which is also very variable (a feature gardeners have used to breed more attractive forms). It is mentioned in *The Grete Herball* as the 'reed' or 'wylde' poppy. By 1629, there is a double form, and by the eighteenth century, a whole suite of garden variants. Fairchild, in 1722, mentions a strain called 'Dutch Poppies', which were derived from *P. rhoeas*, and Miller a few decades later gives a description of 'very double (firy) flowers, which are beautifully edged with white'.

In the 1880s, the Revd Wilks of Shirley must have used something similar to create, by repeated selection, the Shirley poppies. They are characterized by the lack of the usual black blotch at the base of the petals, and in having yellow anthers. Originally a single strain, and then later double, they are still available in shades of pink, rose, salmon, crimson and white. Many are quite close to those known in the eighteenth century.

### P. orientale
Oriental poppy

South-western Asia. This plant arrived in Britain via Paris and was grown here before 1714. A hardy perennial, the pure form has brilliant vermilion flowers with a dark central blotch. Several closely related species arrived later, including *P. bracteatum*, from the Caucasus and Persia in 1817 (eventually crossed with *P. orientale* to produce some of the garden hybrids), *P. pilosum*, from Asia Minor in 1852, *P. rupifragum*, from Spain, and *P. atlanticum*, from Morocco in 1889.

Gertrude Jekyll used *P. pilosum* and *P. rupifragum*, and mentions a hybrid between the latter and *P. orientale*, which she said occurs when the two are planted together. She also recommended planting gypsophila beside *P. orientale*. By the time the poppies have died down (they do so early – one of their disadvantages), the gypsophila will be full grown, and will cover them. Perfectionist that she was, she then went on to recommend planting nasturtiums to cover the brown seed pods of the gypsophila. Many of the available cultivars of *P. orientale* are quite modern, a number of them bred by Amos Perry.

Other species of garden interest, short-lived perennials often treated as annuals and both useful for eighteenth-century gardens, are *P. nudicaule*, the Iceland poppy, from northern sub Arctic regions, introduced around 1730, and *P. alpinum*, the tiny and soft-coloured alpine poppy, from Austria and Switzerland, introduced in 1759.

Additional members of the family Papaveraceae we might also mention here include *Glaucium flavum*, the yellow horned poppy, a native, and *G. corniculatum*, the red horned poppy, from southern Europe and the Mediterranean. Both were grown in British gardens by 1597. *Meconopsis cambrica*, the Welsh poppy, another native, was grown by the Tradescants, and is mentioned in their plant list of

1629–33. There are some exciting modern variants. Doubles in orange and yellow, much discussed in the garden press in the 1890s, can still be found.

# PELARGONIUM

Commonly called geraniums. A half-hardy genus used for summer bedding, and for pot plants in the garden, greenhouse and windowsill.

The first species to be introduced was *P. triste* (the 'sad-coloured' pelargonium), in 1631. From South Africa, as are most species, this was sent to Paris on a Dutch ship, and came from thence to England. Tuberous-rooted, with sprays of delicate yellow and brown flowers, it is powerfully and sweetly scented at night (and was called 'Nocte Olens'). Highly valued in the seventeenth and eighteenth centuries, it was the basis for a group of nineteenth-century hybrids, apparently now extinct, but beautifully illustrated in Sweet's *Geraniaceae*. The species is essential for every period windowsill.

There was a slow but steady trickle of introductions throughout the eighteenth century, and by the early nineteenth century it became a flood. The nineteenth century also saw a huge increase in breeding and hybridization. The stage was set for the pelargonium to become 'the chief of flowering plants suitable for the parterre' and a period-indicator plant of the Victorian era.

Though the Victorian parterre came and went (with only a diminishing amount of municipal park bedding to remind us of its variable delights), the popularity of the pelargonium has scarcely abated. Breeding has continued, and it is now possible to sow F1 hybrid pelargonium seed to give flowering plants the same season. This may unfortunately reduce people's enthusiasm for overwintering older cultivars, even though most are far more attractive. Here, we shall concentrate on five main groups: zonals, ivy-leaved, scented, uniques and regals.

## ZONAL PELARGONIUMS

Known as *P. × hortorum*, these are complex hybrids of *P. zonale*, *P. inquinans* and various other species. *P. zonale*, which is not itself strongly marked, was introduced in 1710, and *P. inquinans* by 1714. Sorts with marked leaves were probably introduced into the zonal stream quite early. Miller refers to a painted-leaf geranium in 1724, and there is a further scattering of eighteenth-century references. White-margined-leaf sorts were around by 1785, and there were many more by 1840. *P. violarium*, which is tricoloured, was introduced in 1792. Silver- and golden-variegated sorts, ones with tricoloured leaves and ones with 'butterfly' marks were all being produced by the 1850s. By 1860, these foliage varieties had become a passion with 'carpet-bedding' gardeners. The flowers, brightly coloured, were often removed to stop them detracting from the beauty of the leaves. There are many varieties still to be found, including; 'Happy Thought', 'Freak of Nature', 'Crystal Palace Gem', 'Golden Harry Hieover', 'Mrs Parker', Caroline Schmidt', 'Lass o' Gowrie', 'Miss Burdett Coutts', 'Mangle's Variegated' (probably the most famous of them all), and 'Mrs Pollock'. The variegated sorts need more care in over-wintering than their green-leaved counterparts.

Zonals were all single-flowered until 1864, when the first double was produced by Lemoine, in France. Very double sorts, now called 'Rosebuds', were produced from 1880 (though the cultivars available now are all modern). Cactus-flowered sorts appeared in 1889, and dwarf sorts from the 1850s. The first white-flowered zonal came in 1860. In general, among the plain-leaved sorts, there tend to be few older cultivars available, as breeding has continued without a break. Gertrude Jekyll mentions the single-flowered 'Paul Crampel' of 1907, the double-flowered 'King of Denmark' and 'Mrs Lawrence'. She devotes several pages in *Colour Schemes for the Flower Garden* to pelargoniums, and says 'there are no better summer flowers than the single and double zonal pelargoniums ... and none so good for such uses as the filling of tubs and vases' – a surprise for those who only associate her with hardy flowers.

IVY-LEAVED PELARGONIUMS

This very attractive group is based partly on *P. peltatum*. It came to Holland in 1700 and was introduced to Britain in 1701. The group seems to have been popular since the 1820s. Some of the cultivars have been long-lasting; 'L'Elegante', the variegated-leaf sort, was praised in 1887 and is still with us today.

## SCENTED-LEAVED PELARGONIUMS

Many are pure species, a few are hybrids. The first were introduced to Europe in the seventeenth century, but the majority arrived in the eighteenth century. By Edwardian times they were regarded as the sort of plant to be found in old-fashioned gardens. 'Fragrans', a hybrid with pine-scented grey-green leaves, has been known since 1645. The common rose-scented *P. graveolens* was introduced in 1774, as was the even rosier *P. radula*, the proper sort to use in cooking. *P. quercifolium* is spicy and oak-leaved, and *P. crispum* is minty, though better known by its variegated-leaf cultivar, which dates from mid-Victorian times. Other peppermint- and lemon-scented types have been around since the late eighteenth century, the variegated-leaved 'Lady Plymouth' since 1802 and the deliciously orange-peel-scented 'Prince of Orange' since at least 1880.

## 'UNIQUE' PELARGONIUMS

These were developed from *P. fulgidum*, which has brilliant scarlet flowers, and seems to be mentioned first about 1824. A bedding scheme from 1852 suggests using 'Old Purple Unique', edged by 'White Unique'. They were still popular in the 1860s, when an RHS bedding trial was held. Odd, this, for as a group they are unsuitable for bedding and are best under glass. Even then they are not all easy to keep tidy and well shaped. If they sound undesirable, wait until you see the flowers, which are very pretty indeed.

## REGAL PELARGONIUMS

Known as *P. × domesticum*, and called Martha Washingtons in the USA, these are complex hybrids of *P. cucullatum*, *P. fulgidum* and *P. grandiflorum*. They seem to have originated at Sandringham (whence the name), and reached less grand homes around 1877. The original sorts had ruffled petals, though there are now smooth-petalled sorts.

# PENSTEMON

The border penstemons, *P. × gloxinioides*, are the best known. They are unfortunately not always reliably hardy, but with their lovely colours and long-flowering season, they are well worth growing. A few species had arrived in the eighteenth century, but the popular border sorts are based on *P. hartwegii*, which has brilliant tubular scarlet flowers, and came from Mexico around 1825. They were first treated as greenhouse plants, not being grown outside till 1838.

Many other species were introduced in the nineteenth century (David Douglas alone discovering fifteen between 1827 and 1834), and some of these were soon used for breeding and hybridization. In 1839, Paxton's *Magazine of Botany* considered penstemons 'one of the greatest boons conferred upon our gardens by the discovery of the New World'. This was perhaps a little premature. By 1862, their colours were still considered dull, and a great future hung in the balance. By the late nineteenth century, the vogue for herbaceous borders coincided with the appearance of named varieties in a large range of colours, including shades of light blue, mauve, purple, pink and crimson. The penstemon came into its own. Most cultivars available today are more modern, being Edwardian or later. There are, if you do not want to hunt out some of the connoisseurs' varieties (we find most of them difficult to keep), some attractive and reliable seed strains. Cuttings of named cultivars, or of your favourite seedlings, should be taken in August or September and overwintered in a frame.

# PETUNIA

*P. × hybrida*

The flaunting petunias grown today are rather a success story. 'Petun' is a Brazilian word for tobacco, to which the species is closely allied, the first species in fact being described under *Nicotiana*. *P. nyctaginiflora* (the species from which the modern garden plant derives its perfume) arrived in Europe from Brazil in 1823 and *P. integrifolia* from the Argentine in 1831. The plants seem to have become fashionable quite quickly, and by 1840 there were many hybrids. Double bicoloured sorts were introduced from France in the 1840s and became an immediate rage. By the 1880s, petunias were going out of fashion, giving way to the ubiquitous pelargonium. However, the wheel of fashion has turned once more, and they are again wildly popular. In the past, cultivars were propagated vegetatively, and it is still possible to do this if you wish to preserve a particularly good form. Take cuttings in autumn, and overwinter them in a warm greenhouse. The young shoots of these plants can themselves be used for cuttings in February and March.

PHALARIS, see Grasses.

# PHLOX

It is convenient to divide this North American genus into three groups, the annual *P. drummondii*, the tall perennial border plants and the low-growing sorts for the rock garden or the front of the border.

## *P. drummondii*

This was written up in Paxton's *Magazine of Botany* in 1834, as it had just arrived from Texas. The only annual species of *Phlox* in general cultivation, it has always been highly valued since then, and indeed was re-exported to America in the nineteenth century as a garden flower!

### BORDER PHLOXES

*P. paniculata*, introduced in 1730. Most border phloxes are improved forms of this species (a few may be hybrids between this and *P. maculata*). The original flower colour was mauve, a white not being recorded till 1812. The first garden variety was introduced in 1824. In 1839, breeding began in France, and seventy years later, in Britain. Though the pure species is quite tough, and very perennial (but not easily available), the highly selected and improved border cultivars need good, moist, even heavy soil to give of their best. They do, however, have a large colour range and lengthen the season in the garden, being at their peak in August. There is an interesting, though modern, one with a variegated leaf called 'Norah Leigh'.

 *P. maculata* was introduced in 1740. It has cylindrical flower spikes (rather than pyramidal ones, as in *P. paniculata*) and flowers in soft colours of mauve-pink (in the species) to white and rose-pink (in the cultivars). It still just about holds its place in the garden. *P. ovata*, smaller, with purplish flowers, was introduced in 1759.

## LOW-GROWING PHLOXES

On 10 December 1745 the plant collector John Bartram wrote from Pennsylvania to Peter Collinson in England that he was sending 'one sod of the fine creeping lychnis'. This was *P. subulata*, the moss phlox, the first of the low-growing species to reach Britain. Though it continued to be grown throughout the eighteenth century, it did not receive much attention until Victorian times. *P. stolonifera* was introduced in 1800, and *P. amoena* and *P. douglasii* in 1786 and 1827 respectively. All these species require well-drained soil in an open situation.

# PHYSALIS

### *P. alkekengi*
Bladder cherry, Chinese lantern

Caucasus to China. An ancient garden plant, grown in Rome, described by Dioscorides and even illustrated in a copy of his writings made around 512. There are north European references to it in the fifteenth and early sixteenth centuries.

The fruit makes attractive winter decoration, but the plant is invasive; Gerard wrote that it goes 'ramping and creeping within the upper crust of the earth farre abroad'. Parkinson exiled it to the kitchen garden. The larger and finer form *P. franchetii* was introduced from Japan in 1894.

# PLANTAGO

### *P. major*
Plantain

This plant was recommended for use in the garden by Jon the Gardener in the fifteenth century; it was used 'to cure wounds and fosters, belly-flux and costiveness; to thicken the blood, rub into red testicles and warm a cold womb'. His is not an example we are likely to emulate, though the form of the plant called *P.m.* 'Rosularis', the rose plantain, is very much worth growing. In this the normal flower spike has been replaced by a rose-like cluster of green leaves, which makes it amusing and attractive. It is not known when this variant was first collected and grown in gardens. Gerard illustrates it in 1597, and Parkinson says 'The Rose Plantaine hath been long in England.' There is also a form with leaves coloured deep red (*P.m.* 'Rubrifolia'), which has the normal flower spike. This dates from 1878. There is yet another oddity, a variegated-leaved form of *P. lanceolata*, which came from France in 1884.

# POLEMONIUM

### P. caeruleum
Jacob's ladder

Native. Found in the wild with either white or blue flowers, it has certainly been grown in gardens since the early sixteenth century, and probably from long before. Gerard and Parkinson both mention it, but did not know that it is a native. In the eighteenth century, Miller mentions two variants, one with a 'strip'd Flower', and one with variegated leaves, which were both propagated by division. The variegated-leaf plant was still around in the nineteenth century and was 'much used for fine flower gardens'. In 1887, David Thomson calls it 'one of the prettiest and most useful plants for lines and edgings'. He says it was comparatively scarce then. We have not seen it and would be interested to know if it still exists.

Several other species were introduced in the eighteenth and nineteenth centuries. *P. foliosissimum* had arrived from the Rocky Mountains by 1758; *P. humile* (best known for the vigorous light-blue-flowered cultivar 'Sapphire') came from Siberia in 1826.

# POLYGONATUM
Solomon's seal

There are three species native to Britain, and also widespread through-out Europe and Asia. Mentioned by Dioscorides, they are all quite clearly described in Gerard's *Herball* of 1597. All were probably brought into cultivation very early, for medicinal purposes. (Dios-corides used it 'to seale or close up greene wounds'.)

Of the three species, *P. multiflorum* and *P. odoratum* have arching stems with alternate leaves (*P. odoratum* is the smaller, with scented flowers), and *P. verticillatum* has angled stems with leaves in whorls. Miller, in the eighteenth century, mentions a *P. odoratum* variety with double flowers, and later there was a double *P. grandiflorum*, too. Solomon's seals are so long-lived that they must still be in existence.

The now common garden plant is a hybrid between *P. multiflorum* and *P. odoratum*, called *P. × hybridum*. We grow an attractive sort with variegated leaves, of unknown date and origin.

Other species were introduced in the nineteenth century, including *P. biflorum* and the gorgeous *P. commutatum* from North America. All are suitable for shady borders or in light woodland. Gertrude Jekyll planted them with *Trillium grandiflorum* and with the native wood-rush, *Luzula sylvatica*. Nice.

# PRIMULA

Primroses, cowslips, polyanthuses and auriculas have been a passion of gardeners for hundreds of years. So many species from the East have been added since the nineteenth century that the genus still holds its leading place in the garden.

### P. vulgaris

The lovely native primrose, one of the first flowers of spring, has been an inhabitant of gardens since early times. It is mentioned by Jon the Gardener in 1440 and in *The Grete Herball* in 1526; by the time of Gerard and Parkinson dozens of variants are described. The now rare double-flowered form was the most valued, and is recorded in Europe as early as 1500. A double white is also recorded in Europe by the early sixteenth century, but probably did not reach Britain until nearly the mid seventeenth century (Parkinson has only a single white form); it is still grown and is exceptionally pretty. A green-flowered form (still around) was grown by Gerard, and an even more exciting double green one by Parkinson (we have not come across this). The other variants described in the seventeenth century, such as hose-in-hose and jack-in-the-green, we discuss below.

The pink or red form of the primrose belongs to a subspecies, *P. vulgaris* subsp. *sibthorpii*, from Greece, Caucasus and northern Persia. This was grown in Paris before 1635 and seems to have arrived in Britain around 1638. Parkinson described it as 'Tradescants Turkie purple Primrose'.

By 1665, there was a whole sequence of red shades, all choice (as opposed to the double wild primrose, which, Rea notes, is 'so common in every country-woman's garden'). He got all his primroses, incidentally, from a gardener in Lancashire; they must have been already a northern preoccupation. Red doubles were fairly well known by the eighteenth century. The very pretty lilac double, 'Lilacina Plena', or 'Quaker's Bonnet', probably dates from this time. By 1827, Loudon mentions doubles in crimson, purple, lilac, white, yellow and brimstone.

Named varieties of single and double primroses do not in general appear until the late nineteenth century, though the very rare double 'Madame Pompadour' is probably earlier. The double 'Marie Crousse', pink-violet edged with white, received an Award of Merit from the RHS in 1882. The double cultivars prefixed by the name 'Bon Accord' (of which only 'Bon Accord Gem' is readily available now) were raised by the firm Cockers of Aberdeen around 1900.

*P. juliae*, introduced from Georgia in 1911, was used in the breeding of many named single sorts. The 'Garryarde' strain, in which the flowers contrast strikingly with the dark-coloured leaves, was bred from an Irish variety of 1895. Only 'Garryarde Guinevere' is easily available.

The first reference to a blue primrose is in 1648, but it is not reliably documented until the late nineteenth century.

## *P. veris*
Cowslip

Another native, with a history as old as the primrose. There were doubles by the time of Gerard, and they continue to be mentioned throughout the eighteenth and nineteenth centuries. Some are still around, if rare. The lovely common oxlip is a natural hybrid between the cowslip and the primrose, and is the ancestor of the polyanthus, of which more below. *P. elatior* is the true oxlip, an attractive species native to Britain but rare here, though common on the Continent.

## HOSE-IN-HOSE, JACK-IN-THE-GREEN, ETC.

These are amusing 'sports of nature' which occur in most of the species mentioned so far. A hose-in-hose flower is one in which the outer calyx has become petaloid, so there are in effect two single flowers, one slipped inside the other. Such is the 'Cowslips two in a hose' of Gerard, and the 'Double Oxelips Hose in Hose' of Parkinson. There is a hose-in-hose variant of the modern hybrid primula, 'Wanda'.

A jack-in-the-green has a flower in which the calyx has turned leafy, and so the single flower is prettily contained within a ruff of small green leaves. These last much longer than the flower itself, 'abiding', as Parkinson says, 'above two months, almost in as perfect beauty, as in the first weeke'. 'Tipperary' is a modern example.

Still stranger is 'Jacke-an-apes on horsebacke', in which the calyx is partly leafy, partly petaloid, the mixture of leaf and petal giving the impression of 'peeces of flower broken, and standing among greene leaves'. A last oddity is the rare gallegaskin, in which the plant has a swollen and distorted calyx, from which the flower arises, 'which doe somewhat resemble mens hose that they did weare, and tooke the name of Gallegaskins from thence'. Seed strains of moderately authentic-looking 'jacks' are sometimes available.

## P. × variabilis
Polyanthus

This is a hybrid of the primrose, including *P. vulgaris* subsp. *sibthorpii* and *P. veris*. In the twentieth century, blood from *P. juliae* has probably also been involved. The first description of it is in 1665, and the name 'polyanthus' is first used in 1683. John Evelyn also uses the name in his 'Directions for the Gardiner at Says Court' of 1687. A specimen was sent from Oxford to Leiden in that year. On the Continent, the polyanthus became known as the English primula. They were popular in American gardens by the early eighteenth century.

From the mid eighteenth to the mid nineteenth century, the only polyanthuses thought worthy of attention were gold- and silver-laced sorts. Indeed, the word 'polyanthus' became synonymous with these. Its origins can clearly be seen as far back as the seventeenth century in 'A Book of Botanical Drawings' painted by Daniel Frankon for the first Duchess of Beaufort, a famous gardener. The laced sorts were fully developed by the mid eighteenth century, after much work by contemporary florists. The flowers are deep velvety red, even black, and each lobe of the corolla is outlined with a narrow band of yellow or white which loops down into the centre of the flower and divides it into ten neat and perfectly equal portions.

There were soon hundreds upon hundreds of varieties, and by 1780 Abercrombie was writing that they were 'one of the most noted prize flowers among florists'. They reached the height of their popularity around 1840, after which, as usual, there was a rapid decline. A few can still be found, and are delightful though modern.

Once the laced sorts began to slip from favour, gardeners began to pay attention to some of the other types of polyanthus. Doubles, which had been in existence since at least 1770, were taken up once again. Even some of the singles attracted more attention; in 1871, there was a discussion in the gardening press about blue-flowered sorts, which had apparently been known but ignored for some years. Around 1875, Gertrude Jekyll began breeding her own polyanthuses at Munstead Wood. She favoured delicate shades, and so the Munstead strain were all whites and yellows. Several seed firms also became interested in the polyanthus, including Suttons of Reading, Blackmore and Langdon, and Carters. Breeding has continued right up to the present day, and takes place worldwide.

The famous Barnhaven strain was developed by Florence Bellis in Oregon in the 1930s. The range included gold-laced polyanthuses, originally from seed of one of the few remaining plants in this country, jack-in-the-green and hose-in-hose sorts. There was also a marvellous range of fine colours of single polyanthus. However, most modern seed strains have flowers which are much too large, or too bright, to look authentic in any garden earlier than 1950.

## AURICULAS

At least two species are involved in the parentage of the garden auricula: *P. auricula* and *P. hirsuta*. Both grow in the Alps and there is a natural hybrid between them, *P.* × *pubescens*.

*P. auricula* is mentioned by Dioscorides in A D 50 as '*Sanicula Alpina*'; it is described by Matthiolus in 1544, and was grown by Clusius in Vienna around 1573 (as was *P.* × *pubescens*). It is supposed to have been Clusius who introduced *P. auricula* and *P.* × *pubescens* into Belgium, from whence they came to Britain.

By the end of the sixteenth century, Gerard was growing eight different sorts, in colours of white, red, yellow and purple. Parkinson later describes twenty sorts, mostly with mealy leaves, some with 'paste' in the centre of the flowers ('paste' is a frosting of tiny white scales, much admired by enthusiasts, and easily brushed off by bad weather and careless cultivation). One even had the beginnings of stripings in the flower.

All seventeenth-century auriculas were grown in the open ground, and were fairly similar to the ones we grow today as border auriculas (examples include the scented yellow and red 'Dusty Millers'). Parkinson had six kinds with yellow flowers, which were then popular. Comparable yellow sorts are still easily available, many with nice perfumes.

The auriculas with striped flowers soon became very highly valued. Sir Thomas Hanmer in his *Garden Book* (1659) mentions forty sorts, including two with stripes, one purple and white, another purple and yellow. Striped sorts are beautifully illustrated in the work of the seventeenth-century flower painter Alexander Marshall, who also showed one with a double flower. Striped sorts seem to have disappeared, but doubles are still with us in plenty.

An Edwardian garden auricula called 'Zisca',
from *The Garden*, 1908

By the mid seventeenth century, yellow auriculas had become unfashionable, their place taken by reds, purples, crimsons and, oddly, buffs. The type we now call 'alpines', with large white or gold centres to the flowers and leaves without meal, were also beginning to make an appearance. Samuel Gilbert's *Florists' Vade-mecum* of 1693 mentions six doubles, which often fetched £4–5 each. (They still do.)

By the end of the seventeenth century, auriculas began to be grown in pots. By 1731, the pots, when the plants were in flower, began to be displayed on 'stages' (rows of shelves, one upon another, covered with an awning over the top to protect the precious 'meal' on leaves and flowers).

Striped sorts were soon supplanted in popularity, and the new green-edged auricula flowers were first illustrated in some European botanical plates of 1735, and were mentioned in the literature by 1757.

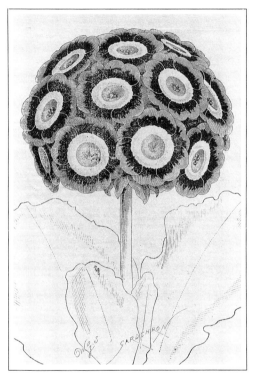

An interesting grey-edged show auricula,
from the *Gardeners' Chronicle* of 1908

The first two named varieties, 'Rule Arbiter', with a green edge, and 'Hortaine', even more exotic, with a white edge, were already in existence by then. Plenty of green-, grey- and white-edged cultivars are still grown, though all are modern. All are, as were the old ones, plants for show, not for the garden; many are remarkably lovely.

Throughout the eighteenth century, auricula shows were held over the country. Much mo.e fun than today, they were always accompanied by a dinner, and were called 'Florists Feasts'. Auriculas were probably at the height of their popularity between 1840 and 1850, the majority of the growers being in Lancashire and Cheshire, and predominantly artisans. Loudon noted that it was 'a poor man's flower, and a fine blow is rarely to be seen in the gardens of the nobility and gentry'.

Today, there are cultivars in all the old show classes: edged; selfs (with a ground colour only and no fancy edge), and alpines. It is also possible to buy seed of double auriculas.

## OTHER SPECIES

Of the alpine species, *P. farinosa*, bird's-eye primrose, is a native. It was grown by Gerard and Parkinson, but, as Parkinson noted, is not reliably long-lived. *P. amoena*, from Europe, was grown by the Victorians. Many of the other species were, in 1887, 'still rather scarce and expensive to be had in quantity'.

None of the moisture-loving Asiatic primulas were introduced before the nineteenth century and none made much initial impression. Of the candelabras, *P. japonica* was successfully introduced in 1870, *P. pulverentula* not until 1905. The drumstick primula, *P. denticulata*, from China and the Himalayas, arrived in 1837.

# PULMONARIA

Lung-wort, Jerusalem cowslip

A genus with early spring flowers and rough, often attractively spotted, leaves. Many make excellent ground cover by summer; remove the spent flower stalks. The leaf markings vary from plant to plant, so good forms have been collected and named. The species also hybridize easily, and there are many natural, as well as garden, hybrids. They are not at all particular as to soil or situation, though the variegations show up in shade.

The commonest, and the earliest grown, is the native *P. officinalis*, mentioned in the fifteenth century. It was used as a pot-herb and was thought to be good for the lungs. The leaves are normally spotted; white-flowered forms, and forms without leaf spots, are mentioned by the seventeenth century. By the early eighteenth century, American gardeners were importing plants from British nurseries.

There is one other native species, *P. longifolia*, grown by Parkinson, with long shapely spotted leaves and flowers of a perfect and vivid blue. Others now grown in gardens are mostly fairly late introductions. *P. mollis* has long, deep green leaves (the largest of all) and flowers of deep blue. It was introduced from eastern Europe and northern Asia by 1816. *P. angustifolia* was introduced from central Europe by 1731. Its leaves are plain green and deciduous, opening with the splendid deep blue flowers. The cultivar 'Mawson's Variety' dates from the end of the nineteenth century, and 'Munstead Blue' is presumably from around the same time.

*P. saccharata*, from Europe, was in gardens by 1863, and has the handsomest leaves of all the species, sometimes spotted so heavily as to make the entire leaf silver-white. There are numerous cultivars. *P. rubra*, from the Middle East, introduced before 1914, is the earliest to flower, often showing its coral-red blooms by December, though the best show comes later. It has large bright green leaves.

# PULSATILLA

### P. vulgaris
Pasque flower

Native to much of Europe and temperate Asia. It is probably an ancient garden plant. As early as the reign of Edward I, it was used to produce a bright green dye to colour Easter eggs. By the end of the sixteenth century, Gerard was growing pulsatillas with red and white flowers; Parkinson added a yellow. These must have been separate but closely allied European species (it is difficult to say which), or perhaps hybrids of these and *P. vulgaris*. The plant was not used medicinally, serving 'onely for the adorning of gardens and garlands, being floures of great beauty' (Gerard). There is a double form, mentioned in the eighteenth century and popular by the early nineteenth century. We have not come across it. Besides the common and single purple, red-flowered forms are easily available; white more rarely. All are lovely.

# RANUNCULUS

There are several buttercups of historical interest, including forms of some native ones which have been grown since the sixteenth century. Nevertheless, the species which fascinated our forebears, from the beginning of the seventeenth century to early in the nineteenth, was the half-hardy *R. asiaticus*. Long cultivated in Turkish gardens, the first plants arrived in Europe in the late sixteenth century. Gerard in

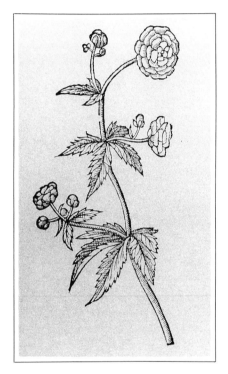

183    *Ranunculus aconitifolius*, a double-flowered
191         form, from Gerard's *Herball* of 1633

1597 has only one sort, which came from Syria, though he also describes a double red. Parkinson in 1629 has several, including single and double reds, and a striped sort. By 1665, there were two types: the older 'Turban' or 'Turkish' sorts, which were coarser and hardier, and the newer 'Persian' ones, more attractive but also more

◁38. *Lychnis chalcedonica,* perhaps a medieval introduction and certainly widely grown by the sixteenth century

▽39. *Lychnis coronaria* 'Occulata'; perhaps seventeenth century

△41. The handsome *Silene dioica* 'Flore Pleno', known since the late sixteenth century

◁40. A pure white form of the ancient rose campion, *Lychnis coronaria*

▷ 43. *Dahlia* 'Red Cross', 1934, but close to early-nineteenth-century types

▽ 42. *Viola* 'Jackanapes', *c.* 1900

△ 45. *Plantago major* 'Rosularis', the medieval rose plant.

◁ 44. *Calceolaria* 'Kentish Hero', similar to nineteenth-century bedding forms tender. As the flower was taken up by the florists, the number of varieties began to proliferate. James Justice, in 1764, lists eighteen sorts of Turkish, and a hundred sorts of Persian. Maddock in 1792 lists around eight hundred sorts altogether, though it is difficult to believe that they were all really distinct.

There were said, by the end of the eighteenth century, to be more varieties of R. *asiaticus* than of any other flower, such was its popularity. But the mighty have further to fall. In the nineteenth century, the ranunculus went from being immensely popular (four hundred varieties listed in a catalogue of 1820) to being called, by 1851, a neglected flower. By 1857, only two nurserymen were still producing it, and by the end of the century, there were few named varieties left, this continuing decline being ascribed to the difficulty of cultivation. In late Victorian gardens, the tougher Turban sorts were recommended for bedding, though the Persian ones were still thought to be superior flowers.

Unnamed R. *asiaticus* tubers can be bought today, in mixed colours. They should be planted, 'claw' downwards, in a sheltered border in the end of February, to flower in June. After flowering, when the leaves begin to yellow, they should be lifted and stored in a dry place. Seventeenth- and eighteenth-century planting schemes were similar to those for tulips and hyacinths (see p. 157).

The prettiest of the hardy buttercups is perhaps the double form of the white-flowered R. *aconitifolius*, called Fair Maids of Kent (or France). From Europe, it was grown here by the late sixteenth century and maintained its popularity until the end of the nineteenth century. It has become uncommon, though we do not understand why. It is easy to grow, needing a fertile moisture-retentive soil in sun or shade. The single form of R. *aconitifolius* was also introduced in the late sixteenth century and can still be found. Another European species in by this date was R. *gramineus*, grown by Gerard in the single form and by Parkinson in both single and double. This has grey-green leaves and shining yellow flowers.

Of the native species, the double form of the meadow buttercup, R. *acris* 'Flore-pleno', is very attractive. Gerard says that this 'hath of late beene brought out of Lancashire unto our London gardens'. R. *acris* also prefers a dampish place, but the bulbous buttercup, R. *bulbosus*, will flourish in drier situations. There is a double form of this which Parkinson, in 1629, says 'is common in every garden through England'. It has lovely and very double flowers of greenish gold. It is sometimes confused with another double buttercup, of uncertain date, called in gardens *R. speciosus* 'Plenus'.

The last old double form is that of the creeping buttercup, *R. repens* 'Flore-pleno'. Though it has a good flower, it is a prolific spreader, best grown in a wild, damp place. It has been in gardens since at least the mid seventeenth century.

We do not imagine that the lesser celandine (*R. ficaria*) was ever grown voluntarily in gardens in early times, though it is mentioned in the herbals. There are garden forms of this; large-flowered, white-flowered, bronze-flowered and doubles, all of uncertain date. A double sort was popular in American gardens by 1725.

# RESEDA

### R. odorata
Mignonette

Libya. An annual plant used in ancient Egypt. Seed was imported to Europe in classical times, and Pliny described the use of the plant for bruises. However, its modern history as a garden flower did not begin until around 1725, when it was grown in France. It seems to have reached England in the 1740s, and was described by Miller in 1752, who thought the scent 'like fresh raspberries'. It was much used as a pot plant to be taken into the house. The shrubby sort, *R. odorata* var. *frutescens*, is mentioned by Loudon. Sweet mignonettes were wildly popular in Regency and Victorian times, and London gardens frequently had whole beds devoted to them.

# ROSMARINUS

### R. officinalis
Rosemary

Southern Europe and Turkey. Grown by the ancient Romans, who used it for garlands and coronets, associated it with fidelity in love and thought it good for the head and heart. Perhaps they introduced it into Britain. It is certainly mentioned in eleventh-century manuscripts, and the Countess of Hainault in the fourteenth century writes of its virtues to her daughter Queen Philippa, wife of Edward III. Sir

Thomas More in the early sixteenth century writes of it beautifully: 'As for Rosemary, I lette it run all over my garden walls, not onlie because my bees love it, but because it is the herbe sacred to remembrance and therefore to friendship, Whence a sprig of it hath a dumb language.' Gerard mistakenly thought there was a native sort, found in Lancashire. Parkinson grew three kinds, including one with broad leaves and one with gold-variegated leaves, the latter called the 'Gilded Rosemary'. He had heard of a double-flowered sort, but not seen it. Rea talked about a double with larkspur flowers, and a double is mentioned again in the eighteenth century. It is difficult to imagine what it can have looked like – it is not around today. Neither is the sort with silver-variegated leaves, which was said by Rea to be the most choice of all. This seems to be first recorded as grown by the Tradescants – it is in the *Musaeum Tradescantium*, compiled in 1654. Miller says the ones with striped leaves 'are somewhat tender'; perhaps the silver-striped one was very much so, for the last mention of it we can find is in a Victorian gardening magazine, *The Cottage Gardener* of 1849. The gold-variegated one, Parkinson's 'Gilded Rosemary', is still with us today, though uncommon.

The ordinary sort of rosemary had reached America by the seventeenth century, and keen gardeners were ordering the gilded sort from London and Amsterdam nurseries by 1728. Winters in the parts of America then settled were generally too harsh for the plants, and they were treated as half-hardy 'greens', and grown in pots and tubs.

Other variants were introduced in modern times. The plant in the wild can have flowers varying from white, pink and pale blue to deep blue. All these are now in gardens, but are of varying degrees of hardiness. There are upright or fastigiate kinds, including 'Miss Jessop's Upright', which was collected by the eponymous lady in northern Africa in the 1890s, and finally the rather tender prostrate sort, *R. officinalis prostratus*, which is first discussed in gardening magazines of the 1920s.

# RUTA

### R. graveolens
Rue

Mediterranean region. This herb does not seem to have been in general use in England until the fifteenth century, which is strange, since it was regarded by ancient and more modern authors as being beneficent and essential. Gerard has a whole page of his *Herball* devoted to its virtues or uses, and Parkinson says, 'The many good properties whereunto Rue serveth, hath I thinke caused the Englishe name of Herbe Grace to be given unto it.' Pliny explains that it was used by engravers, painters and sculptors to preserve the eyesight (they had to eat the leaves) and it is also mentioned by Aristotle and Dioscorides. American gardeners had it by the end of the seventeenth century. Miller in the eighteenth century says the variegated form is 'very common in England'. Plants were supplied to the London markets in the spring, when the variegation is at its best (this is because only the new foliage is variegated). Unusually, this attractive form can be propagated by seed.

# SALVIA

A large genus, encompassing hardy and half-hardy annuals, perennials and sub-shrubs, which has always played an important part in the garden. The earliest species grown were the common sage and clary. One or two others were in gardens by the late sixteenth and early seventeenth centuries. After a long gap, with only a trickle of new introductions, there was a sudden influx of new species in the nine-teenth century, which included all the best-known half-hardy species. Good garden plants have continued to arrive in modern times; *S. haematodes*, for instance, which came from Greece in 1938.

### S. officinalis
Sage

Southern Europe. An ancient garden plant. It was mentioned in 1213 as being an essential plant for all gardens (it still is). By 1629, there were several forms. The one considered the finest was the 'Party-coloured Sage', variegated in white, red and green, presumably similar to the modern *S. officinalis* 'Tricolor'. There was also one which was just variegated white and green, as well the purple-leaved one, now called *S. officinalis* 'Purpurascens'. There are quite a few other forms in existence today; ones with white flowers, or especially broad leaves, or very narrow leaves, or with gold, or green and gold leaves, but it is difficult to set a date to any of these. Several sorts had reached American gardens by the seventeenth century.

## S. sclarea
Clary

A handsome biennial from the Mediterranean region. Again, this was an early introduction, mentioned by Jon the Gardener around 1400. The flowers or the seed, used in wine, were thought by the sixteenth-century herbalists to stir up bodily lust; it is not clear whether the eighteenth-century dessert of clary-leaf fritters was expected to have the same effect. Seventeenth-century American gardeners grew the plant in some quantity. The attractive variant *S. sclarea* var. *turkestanica* is a late-eighteenth-century introduction from Kashmir.

## S. viridis (often still called S. horminium)

From southern Europe. Also called clary. This species has no medicinal properties. Gerard grew a form with purple bracts. John Tradescant, by 1634, had plants with tufts of white or blue bracts. Today, it can also be grown in some interesting dusky pinks.

S. pratensis, meadow clary, a sturdy plant with long spikes of violet-blue flowers, was in gardens by 1597. Gerard also grew *S. glutinosa*, Jupiter's distaff, from Europe and south-west Asia. This is, though, a rather coarse plant, with large leaves and pale yellow flowers, better for a wildish situation than in the flower border.

## OTHER SPECIES

Most of the well-known tender species arrived in the nineteenth century, beginning with the still-popular *S. splendens* from Brazil in 1822, which can vary in flower colour from white, through shades of red, to dark purple. A good form of *S. splendens* was one of the ingredients of the red section of Gertrude Jekyll's September flower borders at Munstead Wood. It, in common with most of the following species, is a tender perennial, now normally grown as a half-hardy annual. In Victorian gardens, plants were lifted in winter, or grown from cuttings.

S. fulgens and *S. microphylla* (still often called *S. grahamii*), both brilliantly scarlet-flowered, arrived from Mexico in 1829. The tender *S. fulgens* is called the cardinal flower, and a variegated-leaf form of this was known by late Victorian times. *S. microphylla* is just about hardy enough to be grown outside in sheltered positions. In Victorian gardens, it was often lifted in the autumn and put in the conservatory, where it would continue to flower all winter. It is lovely.

Another Mexican, the magnificent *S. patens*, arrived in 1838. Called 'transcendentally blue' in a gardening magazine of 1839, it cost half a guinea per plant. Another magazine, of 1842, suggests a truly awful bedding scheme, using *S. patens* with scarlet verbenas! Thomson in 1887 calls *S. patens* 'perhaps the most lively and intense blue-flowering plant we have' and says it can often last in the open ground, if covered in winter. (It doesn't in our Scottish garden.) There is a white form, and a pale blue one called 'Cambridge Blue'. *S. farinacea*, the mealy sage, with blue or white flowers, came from Texas in 1847, and the lovely, though tender, *S. rutilans*, the pineapple sage, with leaves smelling strongly of that plant, from Mexico in 1873. It has spikes of cerise and vermilion flowers all winter.

There are other interesting salvia species. The large woolly silver leaves of *S. argentea* are sometimes seen in gardens; it is a short-lived perennial species which came from the Mediterranean region in the mid eighteenth century (still listed as a rarity in Jackman's catalogue of 1886 at a cost of one shilling). Sometimes seen, too, is *S. uliginosa*, a handsome but not totally hardy species which came from South America in 1912.

# SANGUINARIA

### S. canadensis
Bloodroot, puccoon

This charming small plant with glowing white flowers is from eastern North America. It was growing in Britain by 1680, possibly earlier. 'Puccoon' is its North American Indian name. Miller relates that the Indians used the colourful sap for body paint. He lists a double sort and suggests planting the bloodroot with 'the Dog's tooth Violet, Spring Cyclamen, Persian Iris, Bulbicodium, Sisyrinchium', which sounds nice. Robinson suggests a woodland planting with winter aconite. For such an attractive plant, it is infrequently seen, though not too difficult to find. The lovely double form is rare and expensive.

# SANTOLINA

### S. chamaecyparissus
Cotton lavender

Southern France. First recorded in Britain in Turner's *The Names of Herbes* of 1548, though this attractive and brilliantly white-leaved shrub may have been in use far earlier in the rest of Europe. Gerard wrote 'Lavender Cotton groweth in gardens almost everywhere.' Parkinson countered early in the next century with 'The raritie and novelty of this herb, being for the most part but in the Gardens of great persons, doth cause it to be of greater regard.' However, rare or common, it was valued as a shrub 'to border knots with'. This use as an edging persisted. Miller thought that if santolina plants are 'artfully intermix'd with other Plants of the same Growth, and placed in the front line, they will make an agreeable Variety'; Thomson, in 1887, was still talking of it as 'excellent for edgings in conjunction with dark-foliaged or flowering plants'. Garden traditions are as long-lived as santolinas; hedges of them, even if you don't want a knot, look wonderful.

All the different sorts of santolina grown in gardens (apart from *S. rosmarinifolia*, for which see below) seem to be subspecies or forms of *S. chamaecyparissus*. These include the less formal *S.c.* 'Neapolitana', with much more feathery leaves and lemon-yellow flowers, *S.c.* 'Neapolitana Sulphurea', with paler flowers still, and *S.c.* 'Corsica', a dwarf compact form.

*S. rosmarinifolia* (often seen as *S. viridis*). This plant, also sometimes called in gardens *S. virens*, has green, needle-like leaves and strong yellow flowers. It was introduced by the eighteenth century.

# SAPONARIA

### S. officinalis
Soapwort

Europe, central Russia. There are many common names for this plant in *The Grete Herball* of 1526. According to Parkinson 'Sopeworte is found wilde in many places with us', all of which suggests that it was introduced to our gardens long before. In the days before manu-factured soaps, it was widely used for its cleansing properties (still in use today; delicate tapestries are cleaned with it). Gerard suggests another use; for treating the 'French poxes'. You were, though, only subjected to this treatment if you were poor; it tasted vile. Richer people must have had sweeter, if equally ineffectual, medicines.

Gerard grew the single-flowered sort in three colours; pink, light purple and white, but not the lovely double, which by the time of Parkinson's *Paradisus*, had arrived 'from beyond the Sea'. It quickly ousted the single from gardens. A century later, Miller is quite rude about it, calling it 'a Plant of no great beauty' but admits that 'were it less common, it would be more esteemed'. It is an untidy plant, with invasive roots, but the flowers are immensely pretty. There are three colours in the doubles, white, pink and deep red. The single-flowered one was popular in American gardens by the seventeenth century, and was used to treat the burns delivered by poison ivy. It is now widely naturalized.

*S. vaccaria*, now *Vaccaria segetalis*, was introduced from Europe before 1548. It is a hardy annual, with pretty flowers of white or pink on nodding wiry stems. Good in annual borders and for cutting.

# SAXIFRAGA

A genus which is now popular but is of rather restricted use in period gardens. The two most useful old sorts are both natural hybrids and have one parent in common; both are called London pride.

*S. × urbium*. London pride. Of unknown origin, this is a cross between *S. spathularis* and *S. umbrosa*. *S. × urbium* was much used in nineteenth-century gardens as an edging. There are numerous garden forms, including one with a gold-variegated leaf, and a rarer one with a white-variegated leaf. *S. × urbium* 'Primuloides' is a dwarf form. *S. spathularis*, St Patrick's cabbage, is native to Ireland and the mountains of northern Portugal and north-western Spain. *S. umbrosa* is a native of the western and central Pyrenees. *S. umbrosa* (rather than *S. × urbium*, as has sometimes been suggested) is probably the plant described and illustrated in Parkinson's *Paradisus* (1629) as 'Princes Feather'. It has been recorded as naturalized in Yorkshire since 1792.

The plant described by Miller in the eighteenth century as a geum, with the common names of 'London Pride or None-so-pretty', must be *S. × geum*, a hybrid between *S. umbrosa* and *S. hirsuta*, another native of Ireland, the Pyrenees and northern Spain. He says it 'was formerly in greater Request than at present, it having been in great use for the bordering of Flower-beds'.

Probably these two hybrids have always been confused (there is no great difference between them), and one or other seems to have been used for edging at least since the eighteenth century.

*S. granulata*, meadow saxifrage, is native to much of Europe. Illustrated in Gerard's *Herball* in the single-flowered form, it is better known in gardens in the double-flowered variant. In the eighteenth century, Miller gives the story of its discovery. It was 'found wild by Mr Joseph Blind, Gardener at Barns, who transplanted it into his Garden, and afterwards distributed it to several curious persons; since which time it hath been multiply'd so much, as to become a very common Plant in most Gardens near London; where it is commonly planted in Pots, to adorn Court-yards, etc., in the Spring'.

Gerard also describes *Chrysoplenium oppositifolium*, the opposite-leaved golden Saxifrage, another native, which Phillipps in the early nineteenth century suggests for growing in 'artificial rock-work'.

Alpine sorts which were grown in early gardens include *S. cotyledon* (used in gardens in Europe since the late sixteenth century), and *S. paniculata*, *S. caesia* and *S. geraniodes* (all grown by the eighteenth century). *S. stolonifera* (commonly still called *S. sarmentosa*), mother of thousands, arrived from China and Japan in 1783. The plant is not reliably hardy, except in the extreme south and west, but is often seen as a house plant.

# SCABIOSA

The scabious species grown in early gardens (Jon the Gardener, for instance, mentions scabious in his *Feate of Gardening* of *c.* 1400) would have been native ones, perhaps the field scabious (now correctly called *Knautia arvensis*), or the small scabious, *Scabiosa columbaria*. Gerard in 1597 certainly grew both of these, and *S. columbaria*, at least, is still well worth growing today. Parkinson describes what is probably a white form of *Knautia arvensis*, but also grew the annual *Scabiosa atropurpurea*, the sweet scabious, from southern Europe. In Austria, Clusius received seed of this plant from Italy in 1591, and the first mention of it as being grown in Britain seems to be in 1621. Gardeners had the plant then only with a red flower, though the range had increased by the eighteenth century to include pinks and purples, and is wider still today. In the seventeenth and eighteenth centuries there was a proliferous sort, with one or more small flowers, copies of the large one, hanging around the main flower; this seems to have vanished.

The scabious species most common in gardens today is S. *caucasica*, introduced in 1803 from the Caucasus. The species is normally blue-flowered, but a white form was grown by the end of the century. Breeding work in the twentieth century has produced a range of cultivars, many of which are already rare, or extinct. However 'Clive Greaves', a blue from 1929, and 'Miss Willmott', a creamy white from 1935, are still available.

The attractive low-growing S. *graminifolia*, with silver leaves and lilac flowers, came from Europe in 1683, and the yellow S. *ochroleuca* came from south-eastern Europe soon after.

The popular giant scabious belongs to a different genus, *Cephalaria*. C. *gigantea*, a splendid plant, six feet high with yellow flowers, came from Siberia in 1759. Now it can be found in almost every herbaceous border grand enough to contain it.

# SCILLA

An attractive genus of mostly small bulbous plants. Judging by the number of species and forms described in Parkinson's *Paradisus*, scillas must have been quite highly valued and collected. In the eighteenth century they seem to have gone out of fashion, only to return with even greater popularity in the mid to late nineteenth century, a popularity that has continued to the present day.

Among the species in cultivation by the early seventeenth century were the attractive early-flowering S. *bifolia* (southern Europe to Asia Minor), still common today, in white or blue; the slightly later mid-blue S. *amoena*, from central Europe; the larger early-summer-flowering S. *lilio-hyacinthus*, from western Europe; the August-to-October-flowering S. *autumnalis*, the better of the two native species (S. *verna* is rather boring); and S. *peruviana*, an interesting large-flowered species which, in spite of its name, comes from Portugal, Spain and Italy; it needs a hot, sunny position to flower well. This was grown in America by 1725.

### S. sibirica

Asia Minor, Caucasus and northern Iran. Though perhaps the most popular species today, it does not seem to have arrived in Britain until the late eighteenth century, though it was known in Europe for some time before this.

### S. tubergeniana

It is now correctly called *S. mischtschenkana*, a name unlikely to gain currency among ordinary gardeners; it was introduced from northern Iran and southern Caucasus in 1931.

The bluebell, at one time in the genus *Scilla*, is now called *Hyacinthoides nonscriptus*. It is a native, and is mentioned in Turner's *Libellus* of 1538; it was once used in the parterre, though nowadays it is much better in a wild garden. The Spanish bluebell, *H. hispanica*, has been grown since the seventeenth century. Both of these were grown in several colours.

## SILENE

**S. dioica** (*Lychnis dioica, Melandrium rubrum*)

Red campion

Europe, temperate Asia, northern Africa. The double form of this native, with attractive blowsy rose-coloured flowers, was popular in Elizabethan gardens and is still easily available today. It seems to exist in at least two forms, varying slightly in flower colour, more markedly in leaf shape and texture. All are excellent.

STIPA, see Grasses.

## TAGETES

All the species commonly grown in gardens are half-hardy annuals from Mexico. The African and French marigolds have been grown since the sixteenth century, with other species being introduced later. There is such a large variety of modern seed strains that it is possible to choose sorts that at least resemble those grown in earlier times. The leaves smell disagreeable when handled, and Miller said that for this reason they were 'not so greatly esteemed for planting near Habitations'.

## T. erecta
African marigold

Introduced to Spain in the early sixteenth century, this species became naturalized on the Algerian coast and was collected from there, hence the name. Though the date of introduction to Britain is unknown, Gerard had a single and a double yellow, and Parkinson had doubles in many shades of yellow, as well as single and quilled-petal sorts. By

One of the African marigolds
from Gerard's *Herball* of 1633

the eighteenth century, they had orange and 'brimstone' and, according to Miller, a sort with sweet-scented flowers. Gertrude Jekyll used tagetes in plenty, preferring the orange and the paler yellows ('the full yellow African Marigold has, to my eye, a raw quality that I am glad to avoid').

## *T. patula*
French marigold

Again, this was introduced at some time in the sixteenth century. Turner in *The Names of Herbes* mentions what we presume is *T. patula* ('French Marigolde, Velvet Floure') in 1548. Gerard in 1597 had only a single sort, but Parkinson had a double, the flower in colours of deep yellow shading to orange-crimson. There were quilled sorts by the eighteenth century and orange and brown miniature sorts by 1865.

Other species introduced from Mexico include *T. minuta*, in 1727, the sweet-scented *T. lucida* in 1798, *T. tenuifolia* (syn. *T. signata*) also in 1798 (most strains are from *T. tenuifolia pumila*, the dwarf form) and *T. corymbosa* in 1825.

# TANACETUM

## *T. vulgare*
Tansy

A native plant which has been grown in gardens since the early Middle Ages. In spring, the young leaves were used as a pot-herb or in tansy cakes. The curled-leaved sort, *T. vulgare* 'Crispum', is mentioned by the late sixteenth century, though by the eighteenth century Miller mentions one with a variegated leaf, perhaps now extinct. It may have been the plain sort that was widely grown in seventeenth-century America.

## *T. parthenium*
Feverfew

A plant confusingly ascribed variously to *Matricaria*, *Pyrethrum*, *Chrysanthemum* and, latterly, *Tanacetum*, where we hope it will remain. It is probably a native of south-eastern Europe and is naturalized all over the continent of Europe, as well as in North and South America. There is a double-flowered sort mentioned by the late sixteenth century, and Miller in the eighteenth century describes a kind with quilled central petals surrounded by a row of ray petals, identical to some modern seed strains. He probably had this only in white, whereas it is now available in white or yellow. The golden-leaved feverfew,

*T. parthenium* 'Aureum', is a Victorian plant much used in bedding schemes (though even Gertrude Jekyll used it, if more tastefully). All will do well in sun and ordinary soil. They're short-lived perennials but sow themselves (wildly) true to type.

# THALICTRUM
Meadow-rue

There are two native species worthy of a place in the garden, *T. minus* and *T. flavum*, both described and illustrated by Gerard. He calls them 'bastard Rhubarbs', a name which to our ears lacks charm; by the seventeenth century, they had become 'Tufted [or in the eighteenth century 'Feather'd'] Culumbines', rather nicer. Other handsomer species have been introduced subsequently.

### *T. minus*
Lesser meadow-rue
A plant with forms or subspecies which vary enormously in size, from tiny plants to the three-feet-high *T. minus* var. *maius* (syn. *T. adiantifolium*), grown by Gerard. A splendid background plant but with very invasive roots.

### *T. flavum*
Common meadow-rue
Larger still at four to five feet, this plant has deep green leaves and fluffy yellow flower-heads. The more attractive grey-leaved form, from Spain and north-western Africa (which may or may not be a separate species), *T. flavum* 'Glaucum' (syn. *T. speciosisissimum*), was described, and presumably introduced, in the early eighteenth century.

### *T. aquilegifolium*
Europe, north-western Asia. This, with rich, rosy lilac flowers and light green foliage, was introduced by the early seventeenth century and is described in Parkinson's *Paradisus*. He also grew the magnificent white form, *T.a.* 'Album'.

### *T. delavayi*
Western China. Often described as *T. dipterocarpum*, it is the most elegant of them all; five feet high, with wide branching displays of

mauve flowers. It was discovered by the Abbé Delavay in the late nineteenth century and introduced a few years later. There is a white form, 'Album', dating from 1920, and a very handsome double, called 'Hewitt's Double', in existence by 1937.

# THYMUS

A large and confusing genus, with many species and hybrids. For gardening purposes, thymes divide into creeping sorts, like the native *T. serpyllum*, and the upright ones, like the culinary *T. vulgaris*. Both these species would appear to have been planted early in British gardens. Several had crossed the Atlantic by the seventeenth century.

## CREEPING THYMES

### *T. serpyllum*
Wild thyme

'Serpulum' appears in a tenth-century Anglo-Saxon work and 'wylde tyme' in *The Grete Herball* of 1526. By 1597, Gerard described the type species, with rose-purple flowers, plus a form 'with floures as white as snow', which he had planted in his garden, 'where it becommeth an herbe of great beauty'. This can still be found as *T. s.* 'Album'. He also described a creeping lemon-scented thyme which grows 'upon the mountains of Italy' and Parkinson soon added a creeping thyme with gold-variegated leaves, which he called 'Guilded or embroidered Tyme'. *T. herba-barona*, caraway- or lemon-scented thyme, was introduced from Corsica and Sardinia in 1807.

## UPRIGHT THYMES

### *T. vulgaris*
The highly aromatic culinary thyme is a native of south-eastern Europe. It was used and highly valued in ancient Greece and Rome and it seems likely that the Romans introduced it into Britain. At any rate, since it was of medicinal importance also, it must have been early and widely grown, and Gerard in 1597 thinks it 'so well knowne that it needeth no description'.

## *T. citriodorus*

Upright sorts with gold- and silver-variegated leaves, hybrids of *T. citriodorus*, seem to have been planted since the mid eighteenth century, and were used to edge flower borders. This use survived in cottage gardens well into the 1830s, and was revived as 'new' in 1871 (plants cost 2s. 6d. each).

# TRADESCANTIA
Spiderwort

## *T. virginiana*

Eastern North America. This plant was known on the Continent by 1590 but was introduced into Britain after 1600 and grown by John Tradescant the Elder, after whom it is named. The original sort was blue-flowered but Tradescant also recorded one with white flowers, and one with pink or reddish flowers. Rea, in 1665, had the same colour range, but some sorts had larger flowers and one large red variety sometimes came double. Miller suggested planting them in large borders, where they have room to grow, and recommended them for shade, where the flowers will last longer.

Most modern cultivars are hybrids of several species and go under the name of *T. andersoniana*. Named sorts are not true from seed and must be propagated by division. All are reasonably similar to old types.

# TROLLIUS
Globe flower

There is one native species, *T. europaeus*, which has been grown in gardens since the late sixteenth century, and went under the name of 'Locker Gowlans'. It is an attractive plant with lemon-yellow flowers. Dorothy Wordsworth collected the wild species at Grasmere, and brought it into the garden at Dove Cottage. The local vernacular name was 'lockety'. A modern selection, *T. europaeus* 'Superbus', is often available.

Most of the other sorts of *Trollius* in gardens are recent hybrids – known under the name of *T. cultorum* – between *T. europaeus*, *T.*

◁46. *Lilium chalcedonicum*, first grown by Gerard in the sixteenth century

▽47. The wonderful *Narcissus Eystettensis*, of the late sixteenth century

*Narcissus* 'Van Sion', named by Parkinson after a gardening friend of his

A double form of *Muscari armeniacum*, known since the sixteenth century

▷ 51. *Delphinium* 'Alice Artindale', a now-rare double of 1935

▽ 50. A double buttercup, in our gardens since at least the late sixteenth century

52. The great herbaceous border at Crathes Castle, Aberdeenshire, at its peak in late July, contains many fine o[...] garden plants, some rare, but many easily obtainable

*asiaticus*, which came from north-eastern Asia in 1759, and *T. ledebourii*, also from north-eastern Asia, in 1912. There are no vast differences between the cultivars, which come in yellow or orange.

# TROPAEOLUM

This genus includes the annual nasturtiums, *T. maius* and *T. minus*, as well as several perennial sprawling or climbing species, all from South America.

## T. minus

The earliest of the nasturtiums to arrive was introduced into Spain and soon travelled to Flanders and France, from whence Gerard received seed 'from my loving friend John Robin of Paris'. It was first described by Clusius in 1576. Highly valued and popular for a hundred years or so, it presumably began to lose ground when the stronger-growing and larger-flowered *T. maius* arrived in the late seventeenth century. It was still grown, however, throughout the eighteenth century, and Loudon in the early nineteenth century mentions a double sort, propagated from cuttings. Though pretty, *T. minus* is rarely seen in gardens today.

## T. maius

The date of introduction is usually given as either 1684 or 1686. Miller mentions a double sort in 1754, which he recommends for growing in pots. Gardeners seem to have had, until the nineteenth century, only orange or yellow flowers, but in Victorian times the range expanded to include scarlet and rose. Dwarf or Tom Thumb sorts are also Victorian. Double and semi-double kinds are now available from seed, in the modern Gleam strain. The old double sorts were propagated by cuttings.

Both *T. minus* and *T. maius* were used in the kitchen; the young leaves and the flowers were used in salads, the flowers were used for garnishes (the doubles being preferred for this), and the seeds were pickled when green and used as caper substitutes.

Of the climbing species, *T. peregrinum* (still sometimes sold as *T. canariense*), canary creeper, from Peru, came to Britain in 1755, though

described from European gardens by Dodoens, the herbalist, as early
as 1574. It is a short-lived perennial, usually grown as an annual, with
blue-green leaves and handsome frilly yellow flowers. *T. tuberosum*,
from Bolivia, Peru, arrived in 1827; it has orange-scarlet flowers, and
needs a sheltered position in mild districts. The Scotch flame flower,
*T. speciosum*, came from Chile in 1846. This needs a cool moist soil
and has always done better in the north. It was well known in Scotland
even by 1868. *T. polyphyllum*, a handsome yellow-flowered sprawler,
rather than a climber, came from Chile in 1827.

# TULIPA

There is one tulip that grows wild in Britain, and is also widely
distributed throughout Europe and Asia – *T. sylvestris*. It is not a true
native in the West, perhaps coming originally from Iran, but it has
been naturalized in Europe for centuries, and may have been known
in Italy as early as the twelfth century. It is described in Gerard's
*Herball* of 1597. The flower is yellow, with a greenish tinge, and the
plant is easily grown, though sometimes shy to flower.

The history of the garden tulip begins in Turkey, where it was
cultivated from at least around the beginning of the sixteenth century;
the flower had been vastly admired there since the twelfth century. It
remained immensely popular well into the 1700s, with tulip festivals
and official state tulip growers. The Turks grew flamed or streaked
sorts from the sixteenth century, and preferred lyre-shaped flowers
with dagger-shaped petals, rather similar to the shape of the plant
known today as *T.* 'Acuminata'. This is not a species, but an ancient
garden hybrid, grown in Turkey and Persia since the seventeenth
century.

There are various accounts of the introduction of tulips into the
West. In one, Busbecq, the ambassador from the Holy Roman
Emperor, Ferdinand I, to Suleiman the Magnificent, is supposed to
have sent seeds back to Vienna in 1554. The first tulip from this seed
flowered in a private garden in Augsburg in 1559. A description of
the flower, by Gesner, with an illustration, was published in 1560, the
first known in the West. It was a self- or plain-coloured sort, and was
named *T. turkarum*, though it is not clear whether it was a Turkish
garden variety or a wild tulip taken from the flower-market of
Constantinople (still on the same site).

Another story relates that a cargo of bulbs arrived in Antwerp in 1562. The burghers of Antwerp did not know what they were, and so ate some and, presumably finding them distasteful, threw the remainder on a midden, where a few of them subsequently flowered. These must have been wild species; choice Turkish garden varieties were far too expensive to be bought by the sackful.

The Dutch herbalist Dodoens described the tulip in 1567; according to Hakluyt, bulbs arrived in Britain in 1578. Gerard calls them 'strange and forreine' flowers and describes seven sorts, including an early-flowering red and a late-flowering yellow, and one which sounds as if it had the beginnings of 'breaking'. All the tulips which were valued in Europe, from the beginning of the seventeenth century to the middle of the nineteenth century, were cup-shaped (as opposed to the narrow lyre shape preferred by the Turks). They were 'broken' or striped, and were categorized as bizarres, bybloemens, edgers and roses, according to the ground colour and the type of striping. Self-coloured tulips were only regarded as breeders, providing the base for a new pattern. It was not understood until comparatively recent times that the colour breaks were caused by a virus transmitted by aphids, though it was noticed early on, by Parkinson for example, that the bulbs of flowers that became striped lost vigour. Parkinson also noticed that once a bulb is 'rectified' or infected, it rarely reverts.

The establishment of the striped tulip caused an extraordinary fascination with the flower, which led directly to the tulipomania of Holland (and similar if less extreme manias in other countries), where fortunes were gained or lost over a few (virus-infected) bulbs. One bulb of 'Semper Augustus' (a variety, incidentally, which lasted into the eighteenth century) was sold for nearly 5,000 florins plus a new carriage and pair. The height of this craze was between 1634 and 1637; when the bubble burst, it did so quickly and disastrously. There were, though, revivals, in both Turkey and Holland in the eighteenth century, and even in 1836 a bulb called 'Citadel of Antwerp' fetched £650 sterling.

In Britain by 1823, Thomas Hogg said that a good collection of tulips would cost a thousand pounds and take years of collecting, and by 1846, two popular varieties were listed in a catalogue at twenty guineas each.

Such prices did not last, though there were three sorts of tulip in a catalogue of 1854 at 100 guineas each.

In the nineteenth century, tulip growing became the preserve of the artisan florists of the Midlands and North, though the only remnant of this interest left today is the Wakefield Tulip Society (described as 'old' in a magazine of 1840). It still holds a show every year, the beautifully striped tulips displayed in beer bottles. The varieties that remain, though no doubt as good as the seventeenth- and eighteenth-century ones, are all Victorian. Some, like 'Lord Stanley' and 'Sam Barlow', were being sold until a few decades ago. They are unfortunately no longer available in commerce (the kinds described in catalogues as 'Rembrandts' are broken Darwins, see below, and cannot be compared to the old sorts).

There are several other sorts of tulip which appeared early on. Double tulips are recorded by Clusius in the 1580s, initially in a green colour, but soon followed by red and yellow. Similar flowers were popular in America by 1725. Parrots, varieties with heavily fringed petals, appeared around 1620, but were disregarded by the florists. There are comparable modern versions of both doubles and parrots, though not the old varieties themselves. The so-called cottage tulips were found in cottage gardens in Victorian times and brought back into prominence; some were perhaps antiques, a few can still be found. Good varieties include nice things like 'Mrs Moon' and 'Mother's Day'. The group called the Darwins date from 1889. Mendels were derived from Darwins around 1920.

Tulips can be quite long-lived, so no doubt many forgotten varieties await rediscovery. Interesting old sorts still in commerce include 'Keizerskroon', with a red flower broadly edged with yellow, a genuine old cultivar dating back to around 1750, and 'Couleur Cardinal', scarlet tinged purple, grown since 1840.

Most of the species tulips were introduced no earlier than the last quarter of the nineteenth century, apart from *T. sylvestris*, already mentioned, and *T. clusiana*, the lovely lady tulip, probably introduced in the early seventeenth century.

VACCARIA, see *Saponaria*.

# VERATRUM

Handsome plants with tall strong flower spikes and large pleated leaves appearing early in spring; they are slow to increase, so they are not as frequently grown as they deserve. They thrive in moist rich soil, and do well in partial shade, making striking border plants. Miller, in the eighteenth century, pointed out that slugs and snails adore veratrums; diets have not changed.

*V. album*, from Europe, was the first to be grown in this country; it is mentioned in *The Grete Herball* of 1526 and is illustrated in Gerard. It has greenish-white flowers, rather larger than the blackish-purple ones of *V. nigrum*, from southern Europe, which was grown here by 1596. *V. nigrum* is, however, a splendid plant, used by Gertrude Jekyll to provide strong foliage in her Spring Garden, along with *Myrrhis odorata*, *Euphorbia characias* subsp. *wulfenii* and *Bergenia cordifolia*. As she points out, there are not many herbaceous plants with strong foliage early in the year. *V. viride*, with a green rather less striking flower spike, was introduced from North America in 1763.

The old moth mullien, from Parkinson's *Paradisus*, 1629

# VERBASCUM

Mullein

There are several native mulleins, also found throughout Europe and Asia. The long stems of *V. thapsus*, Aaron's rod, were dipped in tallow and used as torches, a long-established practice that was first recorded in Roman times and is commemorated in the English name 'hygtaper', first used in *The Grete Herball* of 1526. Gerard describes this species, as well as the dark mullein, *V. nigrum*, and the yellow-flowered moth mullein, *V. blattaria* (the lovely white-flowered variant was grown by the early seventeenth century). All these species are still in gardens today, though uncommon. Much more likely to be seen are the yellow and mauve flowers of *V. chaixii*, introduced from Europe in 1821 (there is a white form of this too), and the yellow flowers of *V. olympicum*, introduced in 1883. There are also many twentieth-century hybrids, in good colours, derived partly from *V. phoenicium*, the purple mullein from southern Europe and northern Asia, grown in Britain by 1597. All these plants are biennials or short-lived perennials.

*Verbena* 'Tweedieana', named after its discoverer,
from *Paxton's Magazine of Botany*, 1830

# VERBENA

The half-hardy perennial bedding verbena, *V. × hybrida*, is the result of crosses between *V. peruviana*, *V. incisa* and *V. tweedii*, all introduced from South America between 1826 and 1837. The hybrids were becoming very popular by 1844, and were soon taken up by the florists. In 1861, one nurseryman had eighty thousand plants for sale and even at this date many of the varieties were described as 'old'. The verbena became almost synonymous with bedding, until overtaken by the pelargonium. In 1887, Thomson describes a large range of colours, including shades of scarlet, crimson, rose and pink, lavender and lilac, purple and white. Some varieties had a white eye to the flower and others were scented. They were all grown from cuttings struck in autumn or spring. The named cultivars available today are mostly of uncertain provenance, but many at least resemble the old sorts. Lovely things include the scented and soft pink 'Silver Anne', the deep purple 'Hidcote', the very loud scarlet 'Huntsman'. The shrubby and unscented 'Sissinghurst' is probably a species. Verbenas are most often

*Verbena chamaedrifolia*, one of the parents
of all bedding verbenas, from *The British Flower Garden*, 1829

grown now as half-hardy annuals in a variety of seed strains in mixed colours. Anything you like can usually be propagated by cuttings and overwintered under glass.

Two other species, also from South America, are frequently grown and can be overwintered in mild districts. *V. bonariensis*, introduced in 1726, has rose-lavender flowers, and *V. venosa*, late eighteenth century, has small purple flowers.

# VERONICA

Easily grown plants, often making useful contributions to the border, with *V. incana* and *V. gentianoides* providing effective ground cover. The spikes of pretty flowers, generally blue or white, do not last long.

*V. spicata*, the spiked speedwell, is native and is described in Gerard's *Herball*, as is *V. teucrium*, from Europe and northern Asia. Both these species have numbers of modern cultivars.

Several species were introduced in the eighteenth century. *V. virginica*, one of the largest and most effective, came from eastern North America in 1714. Miller describes only the one with blue flowers, though there are now equally pretty white and pink forms. Its late summer flowers are most welcome in tired flowerbeds. *V. longifolia*, only a little less attractive, came from Europe and northern Asia in 1731, and the silver-leaved, mat-forming *V. incana* from Russia in 1759. *V. gentianoides*, another mat-former, with narrow spikes of silvery blue flowers, came from the Caucasus in 1784. The white-flowered form is equally pretty, as is the variegated-leaf sort, good in shade. The handsome *V. exaltata*, with plumes of tiny clear blue flowers, came from Siberia in 1816.

# VINCA

The greater and lesser periwinkles are evergreen mat-forming sub-shrubs, pretty, if sometimes over-vigorous, ground cover. The greater periwinkle needs to be restricted to a wildish situation, perhaps under trees, or on banks, as it is territorially ambitious. The lesser periwinkle, which makes a close weed-excluding mat, can be used almost anywhere. Shears will keep it in check.

### *V. minor*
Lesser periwinkle

Its probable origin is south-western and central Europe, but it is now widely naturalized. It was used by the ancient Romans, who wove the flowering trails into wreaths for ceremonial occasions, and it may even have been they who introduced it into Britain. It was certainly here early; it was used in the Middle Ages to garland criminals on the way to execution; in the fourteenth century, it was called 'joy of the ground'. Chaucer calls it 'pervinke' and *The Grete Herball* of 1526, 'perwynke'. It is recorded as naturalized by the early seventeenth century.

Gerard grew blue-flowered and white-flowered kinds, as well as a double purple. By the eighteenth century, there were blue, white, red, double purple and double blue flower colours, and varieties with gold- and silver-variegated leaves. All are still fairly easily available. There are various modern cultivars. The one associated with Miss Jekyll has white flowers and a very neat habit.

### V. major
Greater periwinkle

Probably native to the western and central Mediterranean region, but again widely naturalized, in Britain as well as elsewhere. Though we do not know when it was introduced, it seems to have been later than *V. minor*. The basic species, with glossy green leaves and blue flowers, is recorded in Gerard's *Herball*. There are now various cultivars. The sort with silver-variegated leaves and pale blue flowers, called *V. major* 'Variegata' or 'Elegantissima', was used in late Victorian gardens but may well be earlier.

# VIOLA

An important genus, and one which contains many lovely species. One of these, the sweet violet, *V. odorata*, has been of importance in the garden since early times. Later, a complex hybrid group which appeared in the early nineteenth century, the pansy or viola, *V. × wittrockiana*, swept the world.

### V. odorata

A native flower, widespread throughout Europe, Asia Minor and northern Africa. It has always been popular and, as early as *c.* 320 BC, according to Theophrastus, violets were being grown in specialist nurseries and sold in the market at Athens. The name occurs frequently in classical literature; for instance, in a tenth-century Persian manuscript on the cultivation of flowers, and in a sixth-century covering note that Bishop Fortunatus sent with some plants to Queen Radegond, who was supervising the layout of a nunnery garden at Poitiers. In medieval times, they were one of the most common garden flowers, frequently painted and written about. The violet is the third in the trinity of symbolic flowers, as in this medieval carol:

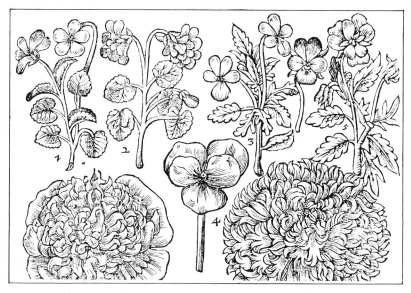

Sixteenth-century viola species, from Parkinson's *Paradisus*, 1629

O fragrant rose, lily chaste
O violet of purity
Thine eye of grace upon us cast
*Noster misericorde.*

They are mentioned by all the early English writers on gardens: by Jon the Gardener in the fifteenth century; in the sixteenth century by Thomas Tullis, Sir Francis Bacon (who says in 'Of Gardens', 'That which above all yields the sweetest smell in the air is the Violet'), and Gerard (who, even more enthusiastic, writes 'yea Gardens themselves receive by these the greatest ornament of all, chiefest beautie and most gallant grace').

Gerard grew *V. odorata* in purple and white, and had also double flowers in the same colours. Parkinson added a single red. He also noticed, sharp-eyed gardener that he was, that *V. odorata*, late in the season, produces cleistogamous seed (seed set without the flower having opened). By the eighteenth century the range of doubles had increased; Miller lists six doubles in different colours, including purple, white, red, ash-coloured and spotted white and purple, as well as a violet with variegated leaves (there were several such around in the nineteenth century, but we are not sure whether they still exist).

Double violets used to be trained as 'tree violets', a skill first noted in France by 1730 and which reached its height in Britain in the mid nineteenth century.

By the late eighteenth century, violets began to be grown as a commercial crop on quite a large scale, especially in France, and later became the symbol of the House of Bonaparte (they were a favourite flower of the Empress Josephine). From the beginning of the nineteenth century, they were set on a rising curve of popularity which reached its apogee in Europe, Britain and America in the early years of the twentieth century. Thereafter, there was a slow decline, until, by the Second World War, violet growing had almost ceased.

Violets were grown commercially almost entirely for cut flowers, and so enormous numbers of varieties were bred to produce an exciting colour range, flowers which were long-stemmed and long-lasting, and resistant to disease. Other species of *Viola* were probably involved in the breeding, which produced such magnificent cultivars as 'The Czar' in 1863. This lovely flower has large rich purple flowers on long stems, and was itself much used in the breeding of later cultivars.

The colour range of the many that survive stretches from purples ('Luxonne', 1888, and 'Lianne', 1906), to reds and pinks ('Amiral Avellan', 1893, 'Perle Rose', 1902, and 'Rosine', 1920), to blues ('St Helena', 1897, a pale lavender-blue favoured by Gertrude Jekyll, and 'John Raddenbury', 1895, mid-blue), and whites ('Rawson's White', 1888, and 'Mrs R. Barton', 1930). We especially like the unusual lilac-mauve of 'Norah Church', a seedling collected from the wild in 1930, and the rosy-salmon of 'Cœur d'Alsace', from 1916.

The old hardy double violets were also considerably improved and the colour range widened further in the nineteenth century. Very few of them have survived, and those that do are very rare. Rarer still, or extinct, are some very beautiful hardy semi-double ones bred in the early years of the twentieth century. ('Mrs David Lloyd George' was one of these.)

Doubles which are still obtainable today are Parma violets. They are quite unlike *V. odorata*, being rather tender, with glossy green leaves and even more strongly scented double flowers. Though they were traditionally grown under glass (partly to provide early flowers), they will in fact survive reasonably well outside in sheltered places or under a cloche. Their origin is obscure. They may have come originally from Asia Minor, but it was from Italy that they were distributed through Europe at the end of the eighteenth century. The first sort grown in Britain was called the 'Neapolitan violet'. By the 1860s there were four different colours, and by 1914 there were over forty different cultivars. They were a favourite flower of Queen Alexandra and enormous numbers of plants were grown at Windsor. Cultivars still available today include 'Marie Louise' (deep lavender-mauve, and introduced in 1865), 'Duchesse de Parme' (soft lavender, first recorded around 1870) and 'Comte Brazza', or 'Swanley White' (introduced in 1883).

## *V.* × *wittrockiana*

The garden pansy or viola has a complicated history involving several species. When it began, in the early nineteenth century, hybridization was probably based on just two, *V. tricolor* and *V. lutea*.

*V. tricolor* is the native wild pansy, or heartsease, which has been in gardens since at least medieval times, and appears in many medieval illuminations. Gerard and Parkinson both grew it (Parkinson had a double sort), and John Evelyn planted it in his parterre at Sayes Court in 1687. *V. lutea* is also native to Britain, and is mentioned by both Gerard and Parkinson. However, it seems to have been the more exotic central European subspecies, *V. lutea* var. *sudetica*, which was initially used in hybridization.

Two aristocrats and their gardeners are recorded as being instrumental in this, both quite independently of each other, and both in the second decade of the nineteenth century. Lady Mary Bennet and her gardener, Mr Richardson, grew all sorts of *Viola* species, including *V. tricolor* and *V. lutea*, in a heart-shaped bed. Amongst the resultant seedlings were found plants that went on to produce the first pansies. The second story is more prosaic; Lord Gambier and his gardener, Mr Thompson, simply selected interesting seedlings from *V. lutea*.

James Lee, a nurseryman from Hammersmith, became interested, and before long had produced many exciting new sorts. These were then taken up by the florists, who made strict rules regarding the development of the flower. Progress was extraordinarily fast; there were four hundred named varieties of what were by then called 'show pansies' described in a monograph issued between 1835 and 1838.

The florists' rules restricted the potential of the flower so much that the next innovation had to come from the Continent, where there were no such self-imposed restrictions. Show pansies, exported to France and Belgium, developed other characteristics, and the results were flowers with handsome and strongly blotched petals. These were re-imported into Britain around 1850, and called 'fancy pansies'. They gradually superseded the ossified show pansies in popularity. Few old named cultivars of show and fancy pansies are available today. Modern seed strains have to substitute. Chosen with care, they can approximate to the size and colouring of the old flowers.

The next development in the story lay with James Grieve, of the Scottish firm Dickson's of Edinburgh, in the 1860s. He wanted to make the pansy a more suitable plant for bedding, and so crossed show pansies with both *V. lutea* and *V. cornuta*. The very successful results were first known as tufted pansies and then as 'violas' (sometimes described now as *V. × williamsii*).

'Violas', in their turn, became exhibition flowers, reaching the height of their popularity around 1892. Many named cultivars are still available. Lovely ones include: 'Lady Tennyson' (a splendid white), 'Pickering Blue' (a large sky-blue exhibition variety), 'Bullion' (a very perennial golden-yellow, from around 1867), 'Maggie Mott' (an exquisite silvery-mauve, popular by 1910), 'Jackanapes' (with upper petals red-brown and lower petals yellow), and 'Irish Molly' (a fascinating greenish bronzy-yellow that we have found difficult to keep).

In 1872 a Dr Stuart of Chirnside, Berwickshire, began to breed for a 'rayless' viola (the rays are the blackish lines that radiate from the centre of the flower in many *Viola* species). He crossed violas back with *V. cornuta*. The attractive results became known as 'violettas'. These retained some of the delicacy of shape of the *V. cornuta* flower, as well as the matted habit of growth of the species, but combined these with an ability to flower more freely and for longer periods. The first violettas were white or light-coloured, but the range soon expanded. William Robinson was keen on them and grew many at Gravetye. Further exciting sorts were raised in the twentieth century by E. B. Crane, and new ones continue to appear. There are some marvellous colours, from the faded mauve-pink of 'Lady Saville', to the dusky lilac of 'Lorna' and the milky 'Moonraker'.

There are vast numbers of *Viola* species, many of interest to the specialist. For the general gardener, one of the most useful is *V. cornuta*, a good mat-forming species introduced from the Pyrenees in 1776. The pure species has pale lavender flowers, but there are variants in white and deeper blues. It is extremely useful under shrub roses, where it has the attractive habit of clambering into the bush.

# VISCARIA

### *V. vulgaris*
Catchfly, sticky Nellie

Europe, including Britain, Siberia, Japan. The simple native flower was planted in gardens by Elizabethan times. Double-flowered sorts were popular by the mid eighteenth century, often planted in pots. By the late nineteenth century, there were, and still may be, two double-flowered cultivars available: 'Plena' and 'Splendens Plena' (which had flowers of a brighter colour). We have only found one. There still is an easily acquired white-flowered sort.

# Biographies

**E. A. Bowles**, 1865–1954. The son of a minor landowner, he was prevented from entering the Church by family matters. These, together with the garden he developed at Myddleton House, and various charitable enterprises, occupied the rest of his life. He published many fascinating and successful garden books, often illustrated with his own drawings (splendid), and water-colours (less so). The *My Garden* . . . sequence of 1914–18 are especially useful. He is commemorated in many plant names.

**Clusius**, or Charles de l'Escluse, was born in Arras in 1526 and died at Leiden in 1609. Son of a country gentleman, he first studied medicine, but soon became fascinated by all aspects of natural history and the antique works of man. He translated one of the most important Renaissance herbals into French in 1557, travelled through much of western Europe, and published letters of men who travelled more widely still. He wrote the first European flora, and died a revered botanist.

**Dioscorides**. A Greek writer living in the first century B C. He's known for his only extant work, the *De Materia Medica*, which formed, along with the works of Hippocrates and Galen, the basis of medical practice for the next fourteen hundred years. The oldest surviving version is a manuscript dated from around A D 512.

**John Gerard**, 1545–1612. Herbalist and gardener to Lord Burghley, treasurer to Elizabeth I. A passionate collector of new plants, many via merchant friends who travelled abroad. Vast numbers of plants find their first description either in his *Catalogue* of 1596, or in the far more famous *Herball* of 1597. Based on earlier European books, both for facts and woodcuts, the *Herball* has been popular ever since, not least because of Gerard's marvellous way with the language. Many of its shortcomings were removed by Thomas Johnson, who edited the 1633 volume, adding many new plants and illustrations. In the text, we distinguish between these two editions, both major landmarks in the history of gardening.

**Sir John Hill**, *c*. 1716–75. Something of a rapscallion, Scots, and an apothecary. His difficult temperament shows in the pages of his attractive books. We have made substantial use of his *Eden: or a Complete Body of Gardening* of 1755.

**Gertrude Jekyll**, 1843–1932. Of independent means, she was at first passionately interested in painting and the decorative crafts. Later, because of failing eyesight, her interest turned to gardens and gardening. To these she brought all her painterly skills, inspiring, through her numerous articles and books, a widespread interest in the design possibilities of herbaceous plants. She herself designed gardens, produced plants for sale and published many important books, which are still, if you don't find the personality that pervades them too irritating, immensely worth reading.

**John Claudius Loudon**, 1783–1843. A Scottish farmer's son who moved to London from a Scottish nursery, and was soon attracted into publishing and an entrepreneurial life. He produced extraordinary quantities of books, magazines and partworks. None made him financially secure. The most useful, in this context, is the *Encyclopaedia of Gardening* of 1822, with many subsequent editions (we used the one of 1824).

**Philip Miller**, 1691–1771. Curator of the Apothecaries' Garden at Chelsea, where he was responsible for the introduction of many new plants. His attitude to both botany and gardening in general was, to say the least, conservative; however, his *Gardeners Dictionary* was immensely successful, appearing in edition after edition, often revamped for different sectors of the gardening public. We have mostly used the edition of 1754.

**John Parkinson**, 1567–1650. Apothecary to James I, but also a passionate collector of flowers. His *Paradisi in Sole Paradisus Terrestris* of 1629 offers a delightful picture of early-seventeenth-century gardens. He was not a natural writer, though his enthusiasm is infectious, and the woodcuts are rather poor.

**Henry Phillipps**, 1779–1840. A popular Regency garden journalist, producing somewhat slight garden books, perhaps to be read by idle ladies on hot summer afternoons. He is most interesting when writing of contemporary gardens and flowers, though we have made use of his *Flora Historica* of 1824.

**John Rea**, writing between 1665 and 1677. A shadowy but intriguing man, a nurseryman whose *Flora* of 1665 furnishes a fascinating list of the posh plants of the late seventeenth century. He is the first gardener that we have come across who so clearly believed, as many now do, that you are what you grow.

**William Robinson**, 1838–1935. An Irish gardener who, moving to London, turned rather from plants to the page. In book after book, and article after article, he attacked the bedding mania he hated so much, and tried to show the gardening public the delights of the wild garden and of the old flowers, then almost forgotten. He found it impossible to write a dull sentence, though the syntax sometimes quarrels with the sense. However, he became a prosperous publisher, and bought an estate called Gravetye. We have used his *The English Flower Garden* of 1883, and various other works.

**David Thomson**, 1823–1909. Gardener to various Scots grandees, he found time to edit magazines and write books. None of the last are at all original, though they do show what average gardeners were doing in average gardens in the late 1800s. His books give numerous lists of popular plant varieties, as well as numbers of rather alarming planting schemes.

**John Tradescant the Elder**, *c*. 1570–1638. Gardener to various aristocrats, including the Cecils at Hatfield House. He was responsible for the introduction of numerous fruit tree varieties, roses and other flowers into Britain.

**John Tradescant the Younger**, 1608–62. Followed his father as gardener to the king, at Oatlands. He travelled widely in North America, and many new garden plants were listed in his *Musaeum Tradescantianum*, compiled in 1654.

**William Turner** (Revd), *c*. 1508–68. A turbulent divine, frequently having to live abroad, where he gained a considerable reputation. As well as religion, he was also passionate about medicine and botany. He published two major works, the first an inventory of names of herbs in 1548, the other a herbal that appeared in 1551. Both contain the first references to many garden plants.

# Further Reading

*The list below suggests a few books which might help if you want to explore some of the design ideas more fully. Most are easily available and well illustrated, and most give full bibliographies that will help if you want or need to take your researches even further. The early sources are all in facsimile editions; you will find that important old garden books are being reprinted in increasing numbers.*

Berrall, Julia S., *The Garden, an Illustrated History*, Penguin Books, 1978.

Boniface, Priscilla, *The Garden Room*, Royal Commission on Historical Monuments (RCHM), 1983.

Brown, Jane, *Gardens of a Golden Afternoon*, Allen Lane, 1982.

Carter, Tom, *The Victorian Garden*, Bell & Hyman, 1984.

Coats, Alice M., *Flowers and Their Histories*, A. & C. Black, 1956.

Coats, Alice M., *Garden Shrubs and their Histories*, Studio Vista, 1963.

Fleming, Lawrence, and Gore, Alan, *The English Garden*, Mermaid Books, 1979; paperback, Michael Joseph, 1982.

Forsyth, Alastair, *Yesterday's Gardens*, RCHM, 1983.

Gerard, John, *The Herball or General History of Plants* (revised and enlarged by Thomas Johnson), 1633; facsimile edition, Dover Publications, 1975.

Huxley, Anthony, *An Illustrated History of Gardening*, Paddington Press, 1978; paperback, Macmillan (Papermac), 1983.

Jekyll, Gertrude, *Wood and Garden*, 1899; facsimile edition, Macmillan (Papermac), 1983.

Jekyll, Gertrude, *Colour Schemes for the Flower Garden*, 1908; facsimile edition, Antique Collectors Club, 1982; facsimile edition with foreword, glossary and colour photographs by Graham Stuart Thomas, Penguin Books, 1983.

McLean, Teresa, *Mediaeval English Gardens*, Collins, 1981.

Miller, Philip, *The Gardeners Dictionary*, 1754; facsimile edition, Wheldon and Wesley, 1969.

Parkinson, John, *Paradisi in Sole Paradisus Terrestris*, 1629; facsimile edition, Dover Publications, 1976.

Robinson, William, *The Wild Garden*, 1870; facsimile edition, Century Publishing, 1983.

Robinson, William, *The English Flower Garden*, 1883.

Scott-James, Anne, *The Cottage Garden*, Penguin Books, 1981.

Sitwell, Sacheverell, *Old Fashioned Flowers*, 1939.

Strong, Sir Roy, *The Renaissance Garden in England*, Thames & Hudson, 1979.

Stuart, David, *Georgian Gardens*, Robert Hale, 1979.

Stuart, David, *The Kitchen Garden*, Robert Hale, 1984.

Thacker, Christopher, *The History of Gardens*, Croom Helm, 1979.

Thomas, Graham Stuart, *The Old Shrub Roses*, Dent, 1979.

Thomas, Graham Stuart, *Climbing Roses Old and New*, Dent, 1983.

# List of Nurseries

*Almost every nursery in the country will have, if you look hard, some old plant of interest. However, those we list below are good places to start looking. Not everyone will send plants through the post, but all issue some kind of catalogue. Most of the businesses are quite small, so it is helpful if you enclose a large stamped and addressed envelope with your first inquiry.*

### United Kingdom

Helen Ballard
Old Country
Mathon
Malvern
Hereford WR 13 5PS

Blackmore & Langdon
Pensford
Bristol
Avon BS 18 4JL

Walter Blom & Son
Coombelands
Leavesden
Watford
Herts WD2 7BH

R. Bowlby
PO Box 156
Kingston-upon-Thames
Surrey KT2 6AN

Bressingham Gardens
Diss
Norfolk IP22 2AB

Candlesby Herbs
Cross Keys Cottage
Candlesby
Spilsby
Lincs PE23 5SF

Careby Manor Gardens
Careby
Stamford
Lincs PE9 4EA

R. G. M. Cawthorne
28 Trigon Road
London SW8 1NJ

Beth Chatto
White Barn House
Elmstead Market
Colchester
Essex CO7 7DB

Chiltern Seeds
Bortree Stile
Ulverston
Cumbria LA 12 7PB

Great Dixter Nurseries
Great Dixter
Northiam
Rye
East Sussex TN31 6PH

Green Farm Plants
Bentley
Farnham
Surrey GU 10 5JX

Herterton House Garden
  Nursery
Hartington
Cambo
Morpeth
Northumberland N E 61 4 B N

Hollington Nurseries
Woolton Hill
Newbury
Berks R G 15 9 X T

Hopleys Plants
Much Hadham
Herts S G 10 6 B U

W. E. Th. Ingwersen
Birch Farm Nursery
Gravetye
East Grinstead
W. Sussex R H 19 4 L E

Kingstone Cottage Plants
West under Penyar
Ross on Wye
Hereford H R 9 7 N X

Old Inn Cottage Nursery
Piddington
Bicester
Oxon O X 6 O P Y

J. and E. Parker-Jervis
Marten's Hall Farm
Longworth
nr Abingdon
Oxon O X 13 5 E P

Plants from the Past
The Old House
Belhaven
Dunbar
East Lothian E H 42 1 N U

Ramparts Nursery
Bakers Lane
Colchester
Essex C O 4 5 B D

Stone House Cottage
  Nursery
Stone
nr Kidderminster
Hereford D Y 10 4 B G

E. Strangman
Washfield Nursery
Horns Road
Hawkhurst
Kent T N 18 4 Q U

West Blackbutts Nursery
West Blackbutts
Stonehaven
Grampian A B 3 2 R T

### United States

Appalachian Gardens
P O Box 82
Waynesboro
P A 17268

Country Gardens
74 South Road
Pepperell
Mass 01463

Crownsville Nursery
1241 Generalsway Hwy
Crownsville
M D 21032

Duo Herbs
2015 Potshop Road
Norristown
P A 19403

Golden Meadow Herb Farm
431 South St Augustine
Dallas
Texas 75217

McClure and Zimmerman
  Bulbs
1422 W. Thorndale
Chicago
Ill 60660

Meadowbrook Farm
  Nursery
1633 Washington Lane
Meadowbrook
P A 19046

Merry Gardens
Camden
Maine 04843

Midwest Wildflowers
P O Box 644
Rockton
Ill 61072

Moreau Landscape Nursery
89 County Road East
Colts Neck
N J 07722

Topiary Art Works
P O Box 574
Clearwater
K S 67026

J. Th. de Vroomen Bulbs Co
P O Box A 66140
Chicago
Ill 60666

Waterloo Gardens
136 Lancaster Avenue
Devon
P A 19333

White Flower Farm
Litchfield
Conn 06759

# Index